Apartheid in Palestine

GHADA AGEEL   *Hard Laws*

Editor   *and Harder Experiences*

Apartheid in Palestine

 THE UNIVERSITY OF ALBERTA PRESS

Published by

The University of Alberta Press
Ring House 2
Edmonton, Alberta, Canada T6G 2E1
www.uap.ualberta.ca

Copyright © 2016 Ghada Ageel

LIBRARY AND ARCHIVES CANADA
CATALOGUING IN PUBLICATION

Apartheid in Palestine : hard laws and harder
experiences / Ghada Ageel, editor.

Includes bibliographical references
and index.
Issued in print and electronic formats.
ISBN 978-1-77212-082-0 (paperback).—
ISBN 978-1-77212-101-8 (EPUB).—
ISBN 978-1-77212-102-5 (kindle). —
ISBN 978-1-77212-103-2 (PDF)

1. Israelis —Colonization —Palestine.
2. Palestinian Arabs —Israel—Relocation.
3. Palestinian Arabs—Legal status, laws, etc.—
Israel. 4. Segregation—Israel. 5. Arab-Israeli
conflict—1993-. 6. Israel—Ethnic relations. I.
Ageel, Ghada, 1970-, editor

DS113.7.A63 2015
956.94'0049274   C2015-907148-8
C2015-907149-6

First edition, first printing, 2016.
Printed and bound in Canada by Houghton
Boston Printers, Saskatoon, Saskatchewan.
Copyediting and proofreading by
Joanne Muzak.
Maps by Wendy Johnson.
Indexing by Adrian Mather.

The University of Alberta Press is committed to
protecting our natural environment. As part of
our efforts, this book is printed on Enviro Paper:
it contains 100% post-consumer recycled fibres
and is acid- and chlorine-free.

The University of Alberta Press gratefully
acknowledges the support received for its
publishing program from the Government of
Canada, the Canada Council for the Arts, and
the Government of Alberta through the Alberta
Media Fund.

This book has been published with the help of
a grant from the Canadian Federation for the
Humanities and Social Sciences, through the
Awards to Scholarly Publications Program,
using funds provided by the Social Sciences and
Humanities Research Council of Canada.

*This book is dedicated to every woman, man, and child in Gaza,
in recognition of the steadfast resilience with which they have shaped an
unprecedented chapter of human history. Through the people of Gaza,
it honours all Palestinians in historic Palestine and in exile.
My heart is full of love for Gaza.*

Contents

RICHARD FALK   **Foreword**

May 2015

FROM MANY POINTS OF VIEW, the

FROM MANY POINTS OF VIEW, the struggle between Jews and Arabs over historic Palestine, which has gone on for almost a century, is at a critical juncture. Since the early 1990s, most hopes for a peaceful resolution of the conflict depended on a diplomatic framework agreed upon in Oslo and solemnized by the infamous 1993 White House handshake between Yitzhak Rabin and Yasser Arafat, with a smiling Bill Clinton standing tall between these embattled leaders. As of now, there is a widespread realization that diplomacy cannot under present conditions produce a sustainable peace for the parties. This became clear when negotiations collapsed in April 2014, ending what Secretary of State John Kerry insisted was "the last chance" to realize a two-state solution. Although the United States may again try to push the parties to engage in direct negotiations, it would seem more for the sake of public relations than to find an end to the conflict.

This Oslo framework was so one-sided from the outset as to seem structurally incapable of ever producing a fair outcome, given the bisecting of Occupied Palestine, splitting the West Bank from Gaza, entrusting partisan United States with the honest broker role, failing even to affirm a Palestinian right of self-determination, and the

IX

exclusion of international law from the negotiations. Excluding international law may have been most damaging bias of all, allowing the Israelis to continue their unlawful land grabbing encroachment on post-1967 Palestine (expanding settlements; building the separation barrier, and constructing a network of settler only roads), with the United States using its geopolitical muscle to insulate Israel from any adverse consequences through the years.

So, with Oslo in shambles, new tendencies on both sides are becoming evident.

Israeli internal politics have been drifting further and further to the right and seem on the verge of producing a consensus that will favour a unilaterally imposed solution that will leave the Palestinians squeezed either into barren Bantustans on the West Bank or incorporated into an Israeli one-state solution, in which the best that they can hope for is to be treated decently as second-class citizens in a self-proclaimed Israeli ethnocracy. Beyond this, even these diminished democratic elements in the Israeli reality would be threatened by the prospects of a Palestinian majority, leading many prominent Israelis to throw their democratic pretensions under the bus of ethnic privilege. The Knesset signalled the adoption of such an approach when it elected Reuven Rivlin, a fierce advocate of a single Israeli state encompassing the entirety of Palestine, as president of Israel. To be sure, liberal-minded Israeli Zionists, among them distinguished novelist Amos Oz, are worried by these developments, warning that, however belatedly, Israel's only hope for real peace is to accept a viable Palestinian sovereign state on its borders, but it seems as if such concerns are politically irrelevant voices in the wilderness.

On the Palestinian side, the relevant discussions are more in the realm of aspirations, pinning hopes on a renewed cycle of intensifying resistance by an array of non-violent tactics and bolstered by a growing global solidarity movement that follows the tactics and guidance of Palestinian civil society leaders. If such an assessment is correct, it represents something quite new, shifting the locus of expectations from the level of governments to that of people and popular mobilization. In these respects, the formal governmental actors have become marginalized, with the Palestinian Authority compromised due to its partially collaborative and dependent relationship with Israel and the United States, and Hamas limited in its capacity to provide international leadership, although its leaders have repeatedly expressed their readiness for long-term peaceful coexistence with Israel. The question is whether such a globally based and populist Palestinian national movement can exert sufficient pressure on the Israeli established order to force a recalculation of interests in Tel Aviv, a process comparable to what occurred so dramatically in South Africa two decades ago, a drastic change by the governing white elite that was signalled there by the utterly surprising release from prison of Nelson Mandela, who was up until then alleged to be South Africa's number one terrorist.

There are other post-Oslo developments of relevance as well. The European governments have been breaking ranks by announcing in different ways their recognition of Palestinian statehood and the desirability of admitting Palestine to full membership in the United Nations. Such steps, although entirely symbolic and likely unable to alter policies, are challenges to the notion that only the United States can speak to the conflict. These European initiatives contain some ambiguities, as well, because they still seem yoked to some variant of the Oslo two-state mantra, and even seem to call for resumed direct negotiations. I can only ask, "to what end?" given past futility and Israel's undisguised moves toward imposing a unilaterally satisfying outcome without worrying as to whether the Palestinians like it or not. The Palestinian Authority has taken these steps in a different direction by urging the UN Security Council to adopt a resolution requiring Israeli withdrawal to 1967 borders by November 2016.

It is with these various considerations in mind that Ghada Ageel's edited volume should be positively received as a timely and welcome addition to the vast literature that addresses various

facets of the Israel/Palestine unfolding reality. This volume's most
striking feature is how well calibrated the various chapters are to
this latest phase of struggle as depicted above. The book is built
around the central organizing principle that there are three vital
perspectives that enable an understanding and appreciation of both
the suffering endured in the past by the Palestinian people and
their moral, political, and legal entitlements when contemplating
the future.

By distinguishing between those Palestinians whose life story is
dominated by the traumatizing experience of a lost homeland,
those whose engagement with the Palestinian struggle for justice is
a matter of core political identity, and those who are scholars and
activists that seek to interpret the conflict from the academic
perspectives of international law and international relations, Ageel
has woven for readers a rich fabric of understanding. This understanding focuses on dispossession and displacement as the essential
outcome of the Nakba of 1948, the catastrophe that drove as many as
eight hundred thousand Palestinians from their cherished homeland,
a story long at the core of the Palestinian experience but only recently
told to non-Palestinians in a persuasive manner as the Israeli
Holocaust narrative of victimization had dominated public spheres
of perception. The activists and scholars represented in this book
are not neutral purveyors of knowledge but individuals of diverse
backgrounds who believe that peace will come to these two people
if and only if justice is rendered by reference to Palestinian rights,
which have been denied and encroached upon for so long.

What is worth noticing about this way of framing inquiry is that
it gives scant attention to the conventional empowerment strategies
of either armed struggle or diplomacy. The section reporting the
lived memories of Palestinians are moving narratives about the
past that give existential credibility to what it meant to uproot the
Palestinian people, especially those from villages, from their homes
and communities.

The section devoted to the tactics, strategies, and engagement of
activists seeks to discern effective tactics to challenge an untenable

status quo that the organized international community lacks the will and capability to overcome, even though the whole tragedy of Palestine can be traced to colonialist policies (the Balfour Declaration and the League of Nations Mandate) after the First World War and the attempted imposed UN partition plan after the Second World War.

The final section on morality, politics, and law reinforces the cries of anguish of the Palestinian witnesses and validates the work of the activists by providing well-documented and reasoned support for the main Palestinian grievances. Together, then, this volume, without saying so directly, speaks perceptively to the new realities of the Palestinian national struggle.

There is no attempt made by editor or contributors to assess the current stage of Zionist thinking and that of the Israeli leadership. In one respect Ari Shavit's 2013 book, *My Promised Land: The Triumph and Tragedy of Israel*, makes the best case for Israeli behaviour, acknowledging the cruelty and violence of Palestinian dispossession, and its ugly sequels, but strains to justify everything done to the Palestinian people as "necessary," part of an "us" or "them," either/or reality. This kind of Israeli thinking is prevalent in several forms, being especially split on whether an Israeli-imposed solution should seek to be humane in its treatment of the subjugated Palestinians or will need to continue to rely on an iron fist approach. If one puts aside propaganda disseminated for external consumption, Israel's present conception of peace is preoccupied with fears, security requirements, and territorial ambitions, leaving no room for any serious attention to Palestinian rights or what might make peace sustainable and just for both peoples.

In the end, I commend Ghada Ageel for so bravely sharing her own story while guiding us on a comprehensive journey that takes us up to the present historical moment. We cannot read these various contributions, each excellent on its own, without being both moved and instructed. What we come away with is a sense of both the victimization and empowering agency of the Palestinians as a *people*, with less interest and expectations associated with either

the formal leadership representing Palestine in diplomatic venues
or the relevance of governmental diplomacy and the UN to move
the conflict toward an acceptable outcome at this time.

Of course, if we are moved to affirm the vision encapsulated in
this volume, then we need to get beyond the conventional thinking
of political realism. This kind of thinking is bound to be defeatist at
this time, given the disparity in military capabilities and the degree
to which Israel's hard power seems to be calling the shots. Yet, since
1945, this kind of realism has consistently produced failed policies
and surprising outcomes. From the great victory of Gandhi's India
over the British Empire to the unlikely defeat of the United States
in the Vietnam War, almost all struggles involving political destiny
of a country have been eventually won by the side that perseveres
and gains control of world public opinion by winning the legitimacy struggle involving justice, law, and morality. There is little
doubt that, since the Lebanon War of 2006, the Palestinians have
been winning this legitimacy struggle as a result of the intensely
negative perceptions throughout the world in reaction to the merci-
less military operations carried out by Israel in Gaza in 2008–2009,
2012, and 2014, as well as the 2010 attack on the flotilla of humanitarian ships seeking to break the blockade of Gaza that has been
punishing the entrapped civilian population for years.

In effect, quietly yet powerfully, Ghada Ageel and her band of
collaborators are telling us to reimagine the Palestinian national
struggle, and even to relate to it in an effective and knowledgeable
manner. This book gives us the pedagogic and activist tools we need
to participate meaningfully and responsibly in the greatest of all
unresolved colonial era struggles. It should be of interest to anyone
concerned with overcoming oppression, seeking justice, and
exploring the outer limits of non-violent struggle by a brave people
who have endured generations of collective suffering.

GHADA AGEEL   **Preface**

I WAS BORN IN PALESTINE, where
the weather is relatively warm. My first winter in Canada was one
of the harshest I had ever experienced. I had lived in cold weather
before but not the cold of Edmonton in the winter of 2010-2011. The
huge piles of snow, temperatures as low as -40°C, a windchill that
froze my eyelashes while I waited for a bus—I was not familiar with
or prepared for this kind of cold. In early March 2011, despite the
cold, I was one of about a hundred people to attend the Israeli
Apartheid Week (IAW) in Edmonton—an annual international
event that was first held in Toronto in 2003.

We came to IAW events because we were committed to justice
and equality and because we were eager to know more about
the past and present conflict in Israel/Palestine and how to find
a way forward. IAW participants came from academia and the
wider community: faculty members and students from various
departments, people from church and grassroots organizations,
young and old—different faces, colours, and accents representing
the wonderful mosaic of my new home, Canada. The week-long
series of presentations, workshops, film screenings, and cultural
events aimed to educate people about the realties of Israel/

Palestine and to raise awareness around the boycott, divestment, and sanctions (BDS) movement and its goal—respect for basic Palestinian rights under international law.

IAW was organized by the Palestine Solidarity Network (PSN) at the University of Alberta. The PSN is a non-profit, grassroots collective that advocates and upholds the human rights of Palestinians in the face of ongoing oppression, occupation, and discrimination. The week was endorsed by many local groups, including the Alberta Public Interest Research Group, Independent Jewish Voices, Canadians for Justice and Peace in the Middle East (University of Alberta branch), Cinema Political Edmonton, and the Edmonton Coalition Against War and Racism.

Having recently arrived in Edmonton from Exeter University in the UK, my engagement with the nascent Edmonton IAW was minimal, although I had attended IAW events at Oxford University in 2009 and 2010. But, because I had lived in Palestine for most of my life, my engagement with the reality of apartheid was maximal. I was inspired by the 2011 gathering, and, after further discussions with friends, I began to realize that there was an urgent need for a publication that would explore the analogy of apartheid in relation to Israeli practices, policies, and laws towards Palestinians so that public discussion could be well-informed, thoughtful, and respectful. It seemed to me that such a publication should involve many different voices and that it could enrich debate, enhance understanding, and help to overcome misunderstandings among groups and people. I worked out a proposal for a book that aimed to speak to, and engage with, a broad readership, and I sent the proposal to the University of Alberta Press. To my surprise, a few weeks later, the press responded positively. Unfortunately, I was too overwhelmed just then by my disaster management work in the Great Slave Lake area to develop the book proposal.

In March 2012, IAW was held again in Edmonton, and the success of the week was obvious. There were even more sponsors of the event, including the Faculty for Palestine (Alberta), the Global

Exchange, Feminist Edmonton, the Canada Palestine Cultural Association, and the Breath In Poetry Collective. The turnout was larger, and the debate in the local media between those in favour of widening the public discussion about Palestine and those against using the framework of apartheid was hot. I regretted my earlier inability to be concerned about the issue in a practical way. In June 2012, I contacted the University of Alberta Press again to see if they were still interested in my proposal. They replied positively and suggested that I gather materials for a manuscript. I wasted no time sending out invitations to authors so that the important task of writing could begin.

Since the early 2000s, many books, reports, and articles have been published on the Israel/Palestine problem. This work has sought to document and challenge Israeli apartheid and to disseminate information about the Palestinian struggle for dignity, equality, and self-determination. It has also described similarities between this struggle and that of certain indigenous peoples struggling for their rights in North America as well as under apartheid in South Africa. A wise Israeli sociologist, Eva Illouz, even recently compared the present circumstances of the Palestinians to conditions of slavery. She argues that these conditions present one of the great moral questions of our time and that they are similar, in certain respects, to the slavery that divided the United States in the nineteenth century. Her argument is simultaneously simple and shocking. Illouz writes, "if a person or a group creates mechanisms to alienate the freedom and life of another, that person is not technically speaking a slave but s/he is subject to conditions of slavery." She further suggests that when 70 per cent of the Palestinian population "live in conditions in which their freedom, honor, physical integrity, [and their] capacity to work, acquire property, marry and, more generally, plan for the future are alienated to the will and power of their Israeli masters, these conditions can only be named by their proper name: conditions of slavery." Illouz asserts that the "the occupation started as a military conflict and, unbeknown to itself, became a generalized condition of domination, dehumanizing Palestinians, and ultimately dehumanizing Israelis themselves."[1]

I attended almost all of the 2012 IAW events. After seeing the eagerness of people—ordinary people who cared for both Palestinians and Israelis and who wanted to know more than what was available in the short week of presentations—and after witnessing the debate that emerged after the meeting in corridors, in the media, and among colleagues and friends, I started thinking more about the structure and nature of this collection. I wanted it to be something that could communicate effectively with each person in the IAW audience, academic and non-academic alike. I wanted it to answer their questions and tell the story of the Palestinians—a full version of the story.

As editor, it seemed to me that book should bring together contributions that are normally kept separate, or, if they are combined, are brought together without drawing attention to their distinctive character as forms of knowledge production. My proposal explicitly combined personal experience, activist argument, and academic analysis. It also cut across the disciplines of sociology, history, and political science so that a detailed account of what has happened since 1948 could be told and so that certain significant writings on Israeli/Palestinian realties could be understood within a broader context. The book would discuss, describe, and analyze in a new way the roots of a great problem—one that has now been making news for over sixty-seven years.

In the summer of 2014, Israel launched a new assault on Palestine (mostly Gaza)—its third major military offensive in five years. The deaths of a high number of Palestinians (2,310), the majority of whom were civilians, and the immense destruction of Gaza have been the focus of media attention and protest movements around the world, including Canada. Millions of people are now seeking to understand this very public war, and my dearest hope is that many of these people will welcome the essays in this book.

Within this single publication, three different kinds of authors—indigenous, activist, and academic—write bold and compassionate essays to introduce readers to the issues underlying the Israeli/Palestinian conflict and to explain the present situation. A unique addition to the Israeli/Palestinian debate, the book flows from personal memoirs to political and historical analyses to activist yet scholarly essays to draw readers into the issues. The relations between the chapters and their overall connection with today's reality of apartheid emerge gradually. The essays in the first section describe a collective historical and generational experience and thus define the book's main issues: the experience of dispossession, discrimination, and living under a settler colonial regime that practices apartheid. The essays in the second section analyze the political, militarized infrastructure developed by Israel to establish this apartheid. This section also focuses on relevant political activism. The third and final section is characterized by the academic approaches it takes to many of the same issues raised in the first two sections. Because these issues will be familiar to the reader by this point in the book, even readers who are not accustomed to scholarly style will find this section accessible and useful. My hope is that the book's unique combination of personal and historical information, activists' calls for action, and political analysis will encourage the reader to understand the complexities and the urgency of the problem and draw appropriate links between the issues of Nakba, apartheid, and settler colonialism.

An anthology is by definition collaborative work, and collaboration is exactly what this work about. This collection consists of related responses to the many observations, questions, and remarks made by those who attend IAW and express themselves elsewhere on campus and in the media. It demonstrates a richness and vitality of debate on this urgent issue. It invites both individuals and groups to leave their state of mute inaction, fear, and anxiety and to proceed to a confident ability to talk, understand, and act. It confirms the principle of academic freedom, opening spaces for more opinions, engaging more voices, and widening perspectives.

The essays presented here attempt to expose facts behind events that have shaped and are still shaping the world our children will inherit. They point to an inevitable conclusion: to change for the better, we must first understand well.

NOTE

1. Eva Illouz, "47 Years a Slave: A New Perspective on Occupation," *Haaretz*, February 7, 2014, http://www.haaretz.com/news/features/.premium-1.572880.

Acknowledgements

THIS BOOK would not have been possible without the extraordinary support of a number of people who were extremely generous with their time, comments, and encouragement. For all of them I am sincerely grateful and eternally indebted.

I will begin by expressing my appreciation for my husband, Nasser, who helped me all the way through the writing process. A simple thank you could not possibly suffice. He was always there for me, cheering me up whenever my spirits or energy flagged. Without his personal and emotional support, it would have been impossible to complete this book. With each passing day, I come to realize more fully and deeply just how lucky I am to have him in my life. All my love.

I am indeed grateful to my friend Nisha Nath, who first suggested this project and introduced me to the University of Alberta Press. I am also thankful to Palestine Solidarity Network, which invited me to take part in the University of Alberta Israeli Apartheid Week, an event that motivated me to undertake this book. This work is a direct result of the experiences and debate that took place during and after IAW sessions of 2011 and 2012.

I'd like to communicate my appreciation to all the contributors of this book. They accepted my invitation to write on this very
important topic and did so splendidly. They have been patient with
me when the project lengthened. Special thanks to Peter Midgley,
amazing editor at the University of Alberta Press, who helped
me throughout the process of writing by answering queries and
providing support. Also, a special thank you to all of the talented
editors on the team at the University of Alberta Press.

Several people have generously expended time and effort to
read sections of my work and offered valuable advice. Professor
James Steele at Carleton University deserves special thanks for his
extraordinary generosity in providing me with speedy and useful
comments, advice, and editing, even during the Christmas season.
I wish him and his family serenity and much happiness. Special
thanks go to Michael Brown, the director of opinion and analysis
at the Institute for Middle East Understanding, for reading and
commenting on my Introduction and parts of my work. He has been
extremely generous with his time when help or advice was needed.
I also would like to thank to Kristin Leppington for helping me in
the initial stage of the proposal.

Sincere thanks to Rela Mazali for her comments, editing skills,
and friendship over the past nine years. Whether I was stuck in
Gaza, stranded on borders or in airports, or in the UK and Canada,
whether it was calm in Gaza or whether Gaza was under attack,
Rela's telephone calls, email messages, and very real help continued
to reach me, offering unending support. She has made a world of
difference. I am also grateful to Professor Yasmeen Abu-Laban for
her guidance and constructive advice. Her comments have offered
me valuable insights and directed my attention to different aspects
and issues directly related to this project. She has been remarkable
and generous in her support throughout this process.

From the bottom of my heart, I thank my friend Donna Coombs-
Montrose, the chair's executive assistant in the Department of
Political Science at the University of Alberta. She offered me

moral support; with her big heart, warm smile, and friendship, she makes the campus a better place. Words cannot express how deeply grateful I am to my cherished friend Andrew Karney. He has been a steady, crucial source of support through countless difficult moments when no one else was there to offer practical help. It is his caring generosity that has sustained me and enabled me to reach this point. Many thanks to Jane Frere for so generously making the images of her exhibition available to me.

I am indebted to my family in Canada, who have patiently endured my long working hours and my exhausting work schedule. A big hug to my children Ghaida, Tarek, and Aziz, who were patient with me all the way in waiting for mum to finish her work. Special thanks and unending gratitude to two caring and wonderful women who made me who I am today and planted in my heart seeds of love for life and land: my mother, Alia, and my grandmother, Khadija. Their wisdom, sacrifices, experiences, commitment, and stories helped shape my identity, and their continuous prayers provided me with strength and hope. My thanks to my wonderful sisters, Samia in Gaza and Taghreed in Turkey, who ensured continuity of the spirit throughout the time spent in working on this book. With their consistent encouragement, they always managed to put a smile on my face. Thanks also to my sister Dr. Sana and her husband Nedal in Edmonton and my sister Dr. Lubna in Gaza. I am lucky to have all of you in my life.

Finally, warm thanks to my camp folks in Khan Younis, all the relatives, friends, and neighbours who have believed in me and supported me so enthusiastically, and to all Gazans who made history with their legendary steadfastness. It is no wonder that Gaza's symbol is the phoenix—the ancient firebird that rises from its own ashes. Finally, to all Palestinians, wherever they are, despite the odds, we still hold tight to our inalienable rights. To all of you, I say thank you, and I salute you.

GHADA AGEEL **Introduction**

IT WAS TUESDAY, AUGUST 19, 2014 when the temporary, nine-day ceasefire—announced hours before I crossed into Gaza—fell apart. Immediately, fearful uncertainty returned to the faces of everyone around me, and remained the primary expression throughout an entire week of horror and trauma. This week was a continuation of fifty-one consecutive days of a death-raining sky that left deep scars on all Gazan souls and minds. As we sat through a bombardment in darkness, with only a tiny makeshift light, we planned our evacuation. We might hear a warning "knock" on the roof of our house from a lightweight missile, or we might survive an explosion and have to flee—who would do what and how? I will never forget the terrible stress of those moments.

Expecting the unexpectable, I stowed my documents, passport, and money in a small bag that I hung around my neck. For most of that week, I sat next to my Mom's bed, fully dressed and with my shoes on. My brothers were to carry my mother out on a mattress, as they had carried out my eighty-nine-year-old grandmother, Khadija, after our neighbour's home had been flattened to the ground by an F-16 missile that also caused major damage to my uncle's home. In an instant, decades of hard labour my family had invested in the house was trashed. According to the escape plan, my sisters-in-law, Wafa and Arwa, would carry out their children, the little money they had, and a few valuable belongings. I was to lead out my two children, Tarek and Aziz, and take my Mom's medications along.

Exactly one week later, on Tuesday, August 26, around sunset, the scene in besieged Gaza was totally transformed with the announcement of an open-ended ceasefire halting the onslaught that had taken the lives of over 2,300 Palestinians. The vast majority of the dead were civilians, including 540 children. The assault had also left over 12,000 people wounded, most whom now faced a permanent disability. Following the announcement, people from all walks of life burst into the streets to celebrate. Everyone was there—old and young, women and men, Muslims and Christians, town dwellers and refugees from the camps, left-wingers and right-wingers. Virtually all inhabitants of this impoverished tiny enclave rejoiced for the end of the nightmare, for the survival of those who lived—despite the aggression and the odds against them—and for, as the Gazans put it, the victory of their resistance.

Unable to join the crowd, my Mom started singing happily and my six-year-old son, Aziz, stormed into the living room with a breathless announcement: "Mom, it's like Eid in Gaza. You never told me that Eid could start at night." Excited and frenetic, Aziz described the celebrations in the streets of the refugee camp that I come from. He said the people there were shaking hands, hugging each other, and distributing sweets. He proudly showed us the money one of my relatives had given him for being a brave boy who crossed the ocean from Canada to be here with them in Khan Younis. "The Gaza team won!" Aziz ruled. My mother quickly snatched her wallet, searched for some change, and added a few Israeli shekels to his treasure.

Happiness, alas, doesn't last long in besieged and occupied Gaza. The joy was gone the following day. The very people who had celebrated just hours earlier were grief-stricken once again when morning light began to reveal the horrific scenes of devastation. The grief was every bit as shattering as the rain of death they had endured during the seven-week assault. For many decades now — and especially since 2006 — Gazans have lived through old, ongoing tragedies in combination with new unfolding ones. Grief and tragedy are the norm in Gaza.

On Monday, September 15, I crossed the Egyptian border at Rafah, leaving Gaza to head back to Canada via Egypt. Getting out of the Gaza ghetto was a miracle. In Gaza, Palestinians need multiple miracles just to practise normal life. The Rafah crossing into the outside world — Gazans' only escape hatch not controlled by Israel — has very restricted criteria for those permitted to leave. Since the beginning of 2014, it has been mainly closed, except for a few sporadic days when it was partly open. The Egyptian officer handed us our stamped passports. I was now officially free to go. I looked at the faces around me — mostly young ones just about to be returned to Gaza — and I walked away battling tears. It was excruciating to watch them forced back to endure the inhumane blockade that they were trying to escape — a condition imposed by Israel and its allies on this strip of land. In Gaza, all life continues to be held hostage, partly because of the silence and inaction of the international community.

Upon arriving in Cairo, I heard the shocking news. Two distant members of my family, along with hundreds of emigrants, many of whom were refugees from Gaza, were missing after a fishing boat had sunk. They survived the barbarism of Israel's war of aggression and succeeded in making their way out of the impoverished, sealed enclave, only to be swallowed up by the Mediterranean. My heart was broken.

Leaving the troubles of my Gazan home and reaching Canada — a safe place that I now also call home — provided a moment of relief. But this respite was brief because I kept remembering the devastation I had seen and because I had to leave behind almost two million people to an unknown fate — half of them under eighteen years of age. While I was trying to understand how I had felt and acted when

I was living those critical life and death moments, I realized I had been faced with some extremely difficult situations and responsibilities. I was there with my disabled mother, my grandmother, my brothers, their wives and children, and my own children. I was also with the rest of the Gazans in our home, Khan Younis camp. Outside my family home near a familiar sandy street was a palm tree planted by my Dad before he passed away. (He died after a short but very painful battle with cancer in 2006—the year the blockade was first imposed. His medical conditions might have been treatable, even curable, beyond the borders of Gaza but, with the blockade, he didn't even have access to proper painkillers.) Down this street a little way was As'ad's small grocery shop where Aziz loved to buy his candies. But over the summer of 2014, accompanying all this, there was the harsh reality of living in darkness with only few hours of power a day, the unbearable lack of water for performing daily routines, the failure of communication systems, and the deafening sound of drones and explosions. Everywhere frightened faces reflected the horrible reality of being under attack. There was no safe place to run. Yet I felt a duty to protect children and disabled persons, and I experienced the horror of imagining the loss of a son, a mother, or a brother. I was also aware of my inability to escape death or to provide assistance to those in need. Every Palestinian in Gaza endured these conditions and emotions. Everyone was waiting his or her turn. It was horrible. I felt devastated. I reached Canada and wanted time and space to feel sad and to grieve. I wanted to breathe.

In the midst of my desperation—my vivid memories of barbarism and scarring fears—the reviewers' reports to my publisher concerning this book were forwarded to me. The positive reviews were a fantastic and timely ray of sunlight. I was drowning and they held out a lifesaver, offered me hope. The responses meant that this volume—this composite analysis—could be offered to people seeking to understand the most recent aggression on Gaza, the third in the past five years.

Although Israel has stated that it attacked Gaza to defend itself against Hamas missiles, this claim ignores a sequence of events, reported by the *Times of Israel*. The paper has acknowledged that Hamas fired missiles on June 30, 2014 for the first time since the November 2012 ceasefire "in revenge for an Israeli airstrike several hours earlier." The attack was against my town of Khan Younis, and it "killed one person and injured three more," including a child.[1] While acknowledging this incident, the paper failed to mention another critical fact that is crucial to understanding the sequence of events leading to the recent aggression: Israel did not fulfill the terms of the 2012 agreement signed in Cairo between Hamas and Israel. The agreement calls for an ending of all hostilities between the two sides. The parties also agreed to the following: "Opening the crossings and facilitating the movement of people and transfer of goods and refraining from restricting residents' free movements and targeting residents in border areas. Procedures of implementation shall be dealt with after 24 hours from the start of the cease-fire."[2] But after the ceasefire, Israel did not deal with "procedures of implementation." Israel has reneged upon its promise to facilitate freedom of movement and the transfer of goods within Gaza ever since the signing of the truce. Between November 2012 and June 2014, Israel enjoyed safety and freedom. But the blockade continued and Palestinians in Gaza remained isolated from the world, besieged, and denied many of the basic daily rights and freedoms that people living in most other countries take for granted.[3] In 2013 alone, eight Palestinian civilians were killed and sixty-six were wounded by Israeli army in the Gaza Strip. One of these civilians was extrajudicially executed by an Israeli warplane in the centre of Gaza.[4] In the same year, not a single Israeli was killed or injured as a result of Palestinian rockets, which were the "lowest in a decade," according to Prime Minister Netanyahu, and mostly launched in response to Israeli strikes and incursions.[5] To ensure continued peace for the Israelis, and to bring back dignity and hope for the Palestinians in Gaza, many reports—by the United

Nations, UN humanitarian officials, and other international organizations—have urged a lifting of this inhumane blockade that strangles the livelihood of Gazans and is still the main reason for the impeded development of Gaza.[6] This action has been recommended partly because 70 per cent of Gazans are women and children, 50 per cent are under the age of eighteen, and 80 per cent live below the poverty line.[7] The massive damage done in July and August 2014 to the already fragile infrastructure of Gaza—the destruction or damage of over 100,000 homes, 62 hospitals, 278 mosques, and 220 schools—has made ending the blockade even more imperative.[8]

The reviewers' evaluations of this volume were timed perfectly, making possible an urgent and critical analysis of the causes of the immense destruction in Gaza over the summer of 2014—an aggression that was also characterized by the displacement of a quarter of Gaza's population. Three-quarters of this displaced population were refugees who had been originally driven from their homes in 1948 and have lived under direct Israeli occupation since 1967 and under blockade for almost a decade. The reviewers recommendations have now made it possible to see, through multiple lenses, the broad historical context of recent events in Israel/Palestine and the current relations and connections of colonial and settler colonial states support for Israel.

Soon after the summer's aggression, on October 13, 2014, the British House of Commons, speaking with a single voice, passed a historic decision to recognize the state of Palestine. Coming from the Parliament of the UK, this modest, symbolic gesture provided Palestinians at large with a brief respite from despair. It was much appreciated, especially by the people of Gaza, who were mentioned frequently in the parliamentary debate. Ireland soon followed the UK with a decision to formally recognize Palestine as well. On October 22, Ireland's upper house passed a motion calling on the Irish parliament to recognize the State of Palestine. The snowball effect also reached Sweden. On October 30, Sweden recognized the occupied state of Palestine officially, becoming the first

Western European state to do so. "Our decision comes at a critical time," the Swedish Foreign Minister Margot Wallstrom told reporters, "because over the last year we have seen how the peace talks have stalled, how decisions over new settlements on occupied Palestinian land have complicated a two-state solution and how violence has returned to Gaza."[9] The snowball then included Spain and France. On November 18, Spain's parliament overwhelmingly passed a motion calling for the government to "recognize Palestine as a state."[10] A similar resolution was approved by France's lower house of the parliament on December 2, 2014. Before 2014 came to a close, a string of other European parliaments (Portugal, December 12; Belgium, December 11; and Luxembourg, December 17) held similar parliamentary votes and symbolically backed statehood for Palestine. The rise up of support continued in 2015. On February 27, 2015, Italian lawmakers voted by 300 to 45 to pass a non-binding resolution that encouraged the government to recognize Palestine as a state. And, on May 13, 2015, two days before the sixty-seventh anniversary of Palestinian Nakba, the Vatican, in a symbolic but very significant treaty officially recognized the state of Palestine. That formal recognition by the Vatican, which has profound religious interests in the Occupied Palestinian Territory (OPT), is a powerful signal of legitimacy of the Palestinian demands for rights, justice, and independence.

Huge shifts are taking place today in the struggle for Palestinian rights and self-determination. Commitment to and compassion for Palestinian's rights are growing. Solidarity groups, networks, and campaigns that support Palestinians have accomplished a lot. According to the Palestine Solidarity Campaign in the UK, for example, 61,023 person contacted 645 members of Parliament (MPs) in July and August of 2014, urging them to pressure Israel to stop its collective punishment of Palestinians. That's almost every MP in Parliament. It is within this context that we ought to read October's landmark victory vote for recognition of Palestine—with 274 to 12 voting in favour of the motion.

The support for Palestinians' rights is steadily growing across university campuses in Europe and North America. Similarly, boycott, divestment, and sanctions (BDS) movement has grown significantly since 2005. Dozens of international actions, endorsements, statements, and letters are calling on international civil society to support BDS against Israel until the rights of the Palestinians are respected. On July 14, 2014, some sixty-four influential public figures, including seven Nobel laureates, called for an international arms embargo on Israel because of "war crimes and possible crimes against humanity" in Gaza.[11] They also urged the UN as well as governments across the world to take immediate steps towards implementing a comprehensive and legally binding military embargo on Israel, similar to the one imposed in the past on apartheid South Africa. A few weeks earlier in June, the 1.8-million strong Presbyterian Church in the United States voted in favour of divesting $21 million from three corporations linked with Israel's military and facilitating Israel's occupation of Palestine (Caterpillar, Hewlett Packard, and Motorola). Also, in February 2014, the American Studies Association overwhelmingly endorsed participation in a boycott of Israeli academic institutions, and the American Anthropological Association followed suit in September with a statement also endorsing an academic boycott of Israel. These developments have constituted a dramatic increase in international solidarity with Palestinians and their rights in the wake of the political earthquake of July 2013. Then, for the first time ever, the international community took a tough practical stance against Israeli policies of colonization. I am referring to the European Union directive explicitly excluding Jewish colonies in the West Bank (including East Jerusalem) from all future agreements between the EU and Israel. The directive covers all areas of co-operation with Israel, including economics, science, culture, sports, and academia. One or two decades from now, I believe that histories of Israel/Palestine will dwell on these events in detail and emphasize the civil campaigns that counteracted the passive policies of numerous world governments, finally supporting Palestinians' demands for justice, equality, and freedom.

Meanwhile, international organizations such as the United Nations Relief and Works Agency (UNRWA), the World Bank, Oxfam, the European Union, the United Nations Office for Coordination of Humanitarian Affairs (OCHA), and the Euro-Mid Observer for Human Rights all issued reports on the extremely bleak situation in the OPT and especially in Gaza. Numerous institutions and high-profile individuals echoed the same basic message. UNRWA warned that conditions in the OPT were reaching a critical point. The Euro-Mid Observer estimated that Palestinians were on the brink of a catastrophe. The UN said that Gaza was submerged in despair and would become uninhabitable by 2020. US Secretary of State John Kerry stated that Israel's settlements in the OPT were illegitimate and constituted an obstacle on the road to peace. Oxfam described the situation in the OPT as urgently requiring both political and practical help. The head of the Gaza office of the United Nations OCHA determined that the siege and the conflict had to end if the lives of Palestinians were to improve at all. The World Bank reported that exclusive Israeli military control over the OPT was undermining the Palestinian economy and contributing to rampant unemployment, estimated at 45 per cent by the UN.[12]

Despite this major shift in international attitudes, Israel announced construction of yet more illegal settlements on Palestinian land. Just days after the ceasefire agreement, when all eyes were focused on the devastation of the tiny Gaza Strip, Israel declared the expropriation of four thousand dunams of Palestinian-owned land in the Bethlehem area, representing the largest single land seizure in the past thirty years. (A dunam is about a quarter of an acre or about one thousand square metres.) Several days later, in early September 2014, Israel announced confiscation of another two thousand dunams in the South Hebron Hills. In Jerusalem, this land theft is happening quietly each day as a result of orders issued by the Israeli authorities in November to confiscate 12,852 dunams of

Palestinian land that belongs to the village of Beit Iksa, north of Jerusalem. These tracts of land will be used both for establishing new illegal colonies and expanding existing ones. Earlier, in the summer of 2013, the so-called Prawer Plan mapped out the demolition of forty Palestinian Bedouin villages in the Naqab (Negev) desert and called for the expulsion (dubbed "relocation") of up to forty thousand Palestinian citizens of Israel and for the confiscation of over eight hundred thousand dunams of their land. If carried out, this intensification of the ongoing ethnic cleansing of Bedouins would amount to a third Nakba (catastrophe).

The 1996 assessment of the Israeli/Palestinian impasse summed up by former Secretary of State and National Security Adviser Henry Kissinger remains relevant today. In an interview with the *Washington Post*, Kissinger concluded that Israel's inability to crush the Palestinian will to end the occupation and colonization left Israel with four options: "ethnic cleansing, an apartheid state, incorporating the Arab population into the Jewish state or some form of separation of the two communities: a Palestinian entity."[13]

Given the failure of the peace process and its proposed two-state formula, and given Israel's full rejection of a one-state solution, the remaining options are either an apartheid state or ethnic cleansing, that is to say, another Palestinian Nakba.

Comparisons of Israel's policies to those of apartheid South Africa are met, almost invariably, with expressions of indignation. Equally heated controversy ensues when the Palestinian exodus, widely known in Palestinian narrative as the Nakba, is linked directly to the establishment of the state of Israel. This book takes on these two controversies—apartheid and Nakba—from the points of view of both Palestinians and Israelis, scholars as well as activists. In doing so, it addresses and illuminates some of the most entrenched taboos that simultaneously frame and suppress Israeli/Palestinian discourse.

This volume brings together first-person Palestinian narratives since the 1948 exodus, activist work, and academic research to analyze the Israeli/Palestinian situation. From their stories of 1948 through to today, Palestinian writers connect with present-day activists (who now form part of various global anti-war movements) and engage with modern scholars who are also discussing questions about Israel/Palestine: What actually happened in 1948? What is really happening today, and what are the links between the two? What kind of connecting threads link the 1948 Nakba and the contemporary apartheid regime? How does all this connect and play out in academia and solidarity groups and among the exiled people and those living on the frontlines of currently occupied Palestinian territory?

In this book, indigenous voices, activists, and scholars present their views from their very different vantage points. Drawing on personal stories and meticulous research, their common accomplishment is a better understanding of the situation and what needs to be done to achieve equality and a just peace. The book is a historical documentation of the dispossession of 1948 and a detailed account of why many Palestinians and some Israelis see themselves today as part of a system of apartheid that continues and extends this dispossession. It clarifies why an increasing number of scholars and activists over the world support this view and, with it, the Palestinian call for justice, including the current call for BDS as a means to achieve this goal.

The book comprises three thematic sections: the first from indigenous Palestinians, a second offered by activists, and a third contributed by academics, experts, and scholars. When these different perspectives—all based on varied research, unique personal experiences, and discrete analyses—are considered together, they form a rich body of knowledge. The careful rigour of the scholarly chapters and the clear, personal testimonies about lived experiences make this collection an exceptional resource for educating readers about the Palestinian story and history since the Nakba of 1948. The book is also an accurate record of the apartheid reality of Israel/Palestine today. While its authors share many principles and beliefs and oppose the same injustices and practices, each writes from different standpoint and deals with a particular aspect of the Israel/Palestine matrix. The separate chapters all address the related issues of displacement, complicity, denial of freedom, and apartheid while creating a multi-focused yet cohesive fabric. As it discusses dispossession, resistance, exile, activism, colonialism, and occupation, the book recounts the history of both a people and a land.

The volume's analytical framework is provided through its unique organizational structure that speaks from three broad sites of knowledge—personal, activist, and academic—and cuts through three disciplines—history, political science, and sociology. The structure of the book is designed draw the reader into the multilayered issues of this conflict, issues that mainstream media often ignores. It brings together writings that are typically kept separate or are combined in anthologies without drawing attention to their distinctive character as forms of knowledge production. This format reflects how the conceptual framework of Israeli apartheid has evolved, grounded in a Palestinian experience and global activist movement and taken up by activists and academics alike.

It is my fervent hope that this book will be of significant value to the academic and research communities in North America, Europe, and beyond. It should also be of interest to students of the Middle East in general and of Palestine in particular. I likewise believe that it will help Palestinians face the challenges of today. These problems are entangled in multiple layers of an extraordinary conflict that includes occupation, segregation, colonization, and siege. Every chapter is meant to help untangle some of these knotted threads and to contribute to a better understanding of Palestinians' conditions, narratives, and aspirations. This collection, therefore, is a contribution to Palestinian studies that is devoted to the documentation, research, and analysis of Palestinian affairs in relation to the Arab–Israeli conflict.

It is also consistent with rights-based research, which holds indigenous voices to be a constituency vital to both peacemaking and research. The extent to which indigenous knowledge and voices are integrated into academic inquiries bearing regional, global, and human significance directly affects the very credibility of the study. Therefore, giving indigenous people, in this case Palestinians (Ageel, Skeik, Bekai, and Baroud) a say within a collection forming part of Palestinian studies is a prerequisite. Palestine has already become a hot and contentious subject (particularly among academics, pro-Israel advocates, and politicians), and it requires a growing, up-to-date knowledge base generated by research, teaching, reporting, and academic inquiry. The fact that these chapters were collected under exceedingly difficult conditions underlines this importance of turning increased attention to the Palestinian struggle for freedom and dignity. By shedding light on the injustices of exile and dispossession and on the harsh situation in the OPT, the authors make clear to various audiences the absence of a future of dignity and prosperity for Palestinians. Moreover, the publication of this book occurs against a backdrop of the recently shattered peace process and of the despair that Palestinians are living in today, particularly those in Gaza.

This book is likewise situated in the context of critical race theory and studies of colonization as a global, historical process. Leading scholars in the field (Razack, Bakan and Abu-Laban, and Hammond) have contributed chapters, bringing to bear critical writings on colonial (British) and settler colonial (Canada) support for Israel. As most studies focus on either Israel/Palestine or single national contexts and then survey broad contexts such as global Palestine, the important contributions of these scholars are a key feature of this book.

Documenting the Palestinian story and taking the Nakba as a start point usually evoke a flurry of emotions. While the book contains a few personal narratives, these are really only a small sample of stories retained in aging memories, in danger of being lost forever. Such stories preserve an important part of the Palestinian narrative and provide a vivid and complex representation of past and current conditions of Israeli apartheid. The Palestinian narrative also includes examining the hegemonic site of struggle for Palestinians, exposing the longstanding patterns of misrepresentation that are deeply linked to the Israeli state's historical attempts to erase Palestine from the map and historical memory since 1948, and returning the Palestinian cause to the world agenda. Clarifying this narrative is a prerequisite for achieving justice, given the inhumane image of Palestinians so frequently featured in the mainstream media. The human Palestinian narrative presented in this book works to support the universal and inalienable right of a people, in this case the Palestinians, to live in freedom and peace and, in the process, to encourage more research on Palestine.

In the first four chapters of this volume, Part I: Indigenous Voices, distinct Palestinian voices are heard. Ghada Ageel, Reem Skeik, and Samar El-Bakai narrate the history of their families' villages and towns up to the present—Beit Daras, Jaffa, and Birya—most of which were demolished in 1948. The authors shed light on the history of Israeli policy of a systematic ethnic cleansing of Palestinians through the experiential narratives of its victims/survivors/resistors. These chapters focus on narrating a collective historical and generational experience from different Palestinian standpoints. The stories are typical of the three broad narratives of Palestinian lives following the moment of the Nakba in 1948. Their personal stories reflect the history, reality, and aspirations of ordinary people. As Bertolt Brecht discerningly wrote, in the homeland, even the voice sounds clearer.[14] These authors attempt to explore just how much clearer that voice can be made to ring and, perhaps more importantly, how that voice approaches and supports or departs from and contradicts world academia and current activism. The Palestinian accounts in this book are, in addition, a confirmation of an innate love and yearning for one's homeland. The spirit of

Palestinian poet Salem Jubran's line prevails: "As the mother loves her disabled son...I will love you my homeland."[15]

The fourth and final chapter in Part I, Ramzy Baroud's contribution, offers a thorough analysis of the means by which Palestinians can understand their individual narratives as part of a larger story positioned within an accurate Palestinian history and a body of articulated Palestinian thinking. This chapter also discusses theoretically the power of the personal narratives of ordinary people and their capacity to create a concrete understanding of the dynamics actually driving the conflict.

Chapters in Part II: Activist Views are written by partisans, both Palestinian and Israeli. They build on the personal and collective narratives of the first section, using experiential accounts of activism as a legitimate site of knowledge production. Two of the chapters in this section are written by Jewish Israeli women—Rela Mazali and Tali Shaprio—who detail their activist histories against Israeli apartheid. The other two are written by Palestinian, North American women: Huwaida Arraf, who was born in the United States and later became a co-founder of the International Solidarity Movement (ISM), and Rafeef Ziadah, a Palestinian Canadian who became the spokesperson for the BDS. Part II includes firsthand accounts from the frontlines, and perspectives on the growing number of campaigns, networks, and BDS efforts against Israel's occupation.

In each of these activist accounts, there is a focus on identifying and analyzing the colonial, militarized, apartheid infrastructure of Israel, including, significantly, a discussion of Palestinian prisoners and the whole system of imprisonment that is so fundamental to the Israeli apartheid system (Mazali) and the emergence of certain solidarity movements with Palestinians, and cultural boycott of Israel, which includes a discussion of the political nature of Israeli culture, especially the entertainment industry (Shapiro). Central to this section is the narration and analysis of the history of popular Palestinian struggle from the first intifada in 1987 through the post-1993 Oslo era into the second intifada of 2000 and then to the rapid development of the international solidarity movement (Arraf). Ziadah traces the conditions leading up to the emergence of the call for BDS during and after the period of the Oslo Accords and gives an overview of the overall trajectory of the movement in its first ten years.

The views expressed in Part II reflect the growing popularity and number of pro-Palestinian groups and campaigns currently active across university campuses in Europe and North American—groups that are now becoming bolder, more visible, and more successful. These activist accounts also dig deeper into how this once local cause is going global and increasingly attracting participants such as churches, labour unions, and students. Through activists' stories of popular resistance and BDS, and through their co-operation with each other and with advocates around the world, the reader will better understand the motion, emotions, and rationale behind this worldwide trend towards strong solidarity.

In Part III: Academic and Expert Insights, there are five additional chapters, written by seven Canadian and British experts. They investigate some of the issues raised by the first two groups of chapters using a distinctly academic lens. They provide evaluations of the production of politicized knowledge, focusing on competing discourses in the ongoing battle over the political truths that define the history of Palestinian struggle. Each draws on scholarly knowledge production to examine and provide an analytical vocabulary for understanding the broader historical contexts in which the structures of Israeli apartheid and resistance movements have emerged.

This section also draws attention to the conceptual tools currently used in analyzing the long history of Israeli colonization and apartheid in Palestine. Keith Hammond provides a historic account of the role of British colonialism in Palestine both pre- and post-1948. He discusses the relationship between the British Labour Party and the Zionist groups in Britain and the influence the latter had on Palestine. He also emphasizes the role of new technology and youth in producing a new epistemology for the Palestinians and advocates for the need for a moratorium on European support for Israeli research as a necessary condition to stop its discriminatory policies against Palestinians. Abigail Bakan and Yasmeen Abu-Laban explore the growing economic and security ties between Canada and Israel. They also examine the growing forms of resistance to and contestation of Israeli apartheid as expressed by Palestine solidarity activists and account for the complex ways in which attempts to ban the word *apartheid* have found their way in Canadian educational institutions. The chapter also discusses Canada's strong alliance and support of Israel and its negative role in the UN and other international forums. In their account of silencing of academic freedom of speech, James Cairns and Susan Ferguson provide examples of attacks on students, faculty, and academic institutions involved in criticizing the Israeli policies of colonialism and occupation of Palestinian land. The authors provide a theoretical framework to contextualize notions of "truth," "subjective knowledge of the subaltern," and the hegemonic ideology of the state, including the Israeli liberal story. The chapter advocates academic and activist forms of knowledge and declares them necessary in telling the actual history of Israel's violations of Palestinian human rights. Sherene Razack traces the gender and race arrangements of settler spatiality, arguing that settler violence is bodily and spatial. With a background in Canadian colonial violence against Aboriginal people, Razack compares Canadian colonial power and its targeting of human bodies with that of Israel's policies and practices in the OPT. The chapter is partly based on the author's observations of the separation wall and checkpoints in the OPT, but very much grounded in conceptual and empirical examples drawn from other settler colonial spaces, including Canada and South Africa. Finally, Edward Corrigan, an expert immigration lawyer, examines the validity of using apartheid as an analogy as he reviews Israel's policies toward the Palestinians. He explores the question of whether the analogy applies to Israel's occupation of the Palestinian Territories and treatment of the Palestinian population through an extensive review of international law on discrimination, the prohibition of crimes against humanity, including apartheid, the International Court of Justice, and other international legal instruments. These chapters also focus on the idea that discourses and public space are very much contested even while the terrain of contestation is highly unequal. This argument is consistent with a main theme of the book—Palestinians are not simply victims of Israeli violence but active agents in building anti-colonial/anti-racist/anti-apartheid movements that begin with a struggle for the self-determination of Palestinians. Among other things, research presented in this section examines governmental and institutional stances concerning Israel/Palestine and the policies of Israel and world governments towards the Palestinian people.

The purpose of this book is to contribute to a richer and more constructive discussion regarding Israel/Palestine. Its chapters have been collected and published in a spirit of stubborn hope and on the understanding that a serious scholarly conversation is vital for providing the next generation with a better future. This discussion—whether conducted from an Israeli, Palestinian, or international point of view—is not only an effort to build awareness from within but also simultaneously to move the two peoples towards a reconciliation based on a better understanding of what could amount to full equality in terms of fundamental rights. Refraining from such a discussion can only pour fuel onto the fires of confrontation and hate. Indeed, the surest way to feed the ongoing conflict is to ignore its roots. What is necessary if a pathway is to be blazed towards a just peace between Israelis and Palestinians is not merely negotiations, and certainly not walls of separation, but rather a comprehensive reckoning within the entire framework of displacement and apartheid. A first step in this direction is moving beyond a superficial map of the conflict to an understanding its underlying reality, that is, of the Nakba and the dual regime of law and daily life that currently distinguishes Palestinians from Israelis.

Notes

1. Avi Issacharoff, "Hamas Fires Rockets First Time since 2012, Israeli Officials Say," *Times of Israel*, June 30, 2014, http://www.timesofisrael.com/hamas-fired-rockets-for-first-time-since-2012-israeli-officials-say/.

2. "Text of Israeli Hamas Cease Fire Agreement," *Jerusalem Post*, November 21, 2012, http://www.jpost.com/Defense/Text-of-Israel-Hamas-cease-fire-agreement.

3. Daniel Levy, "Israeli Self-Defense Doesn't Include Killing Civilians," *New York Times*, August 22, 2014, http://www.nytimes.com/roomfordebate/2014/07/22/self-defense-or-atrocties-in-gaza/israeli-self-defense-does-not-permit-killing-civilians.

4. Palestinian Centre for Human Rights (PCHR), *Annual Report 2013* (Gaza City: Palestinian Centre for Human Rights, 2014), 28, http://www.pchrgaza.org/files/2014/annual%20English%202013.pdf.

5. Nathan Thrall, "Hamas's Chances," *London Review of Books* 36, no. 16 (August 21, 2014): 10–12.

6. United Nations Relief and Works Agency for Palestine Refugees in the Near East (UNRWA), "Statement of the Deputy Commissioner General of UNRWA on the Occasion of the Launch of the OPT Emergency Appeal," December 9, 2014, http://www.unrwa.org/newsroom/official-statements/statement-deputy-commissioner-general-unrwa-occasion-launch-opt; Oxfam, "Lifting Blockade Crucial to Gaza Economy," press release, August 14, 2014, http://www.oxfam.org.uk/media-centre/press-releases/2014/08/gaza-lifting-embargo.

7. Keith Ellison, "End the Gaza Blockade to Achieve Peace," *Washington Post*, July 29, 2014, http://www.washingtonpost.com/opinions/keith-ellison-end-the-gaza-blockade-to-achieve-peace/2014/07/29/e5e707c4-16a1-11e4-85b6-c1451e622637_story.html.

8. UNOCHA, "Occupied Palestinians Territories: Gaza Emergency Humanitarian Snapshot (as of August 29, 2014, 8:00 hrs)," September 1, 2014, http://www.unochaopt.org/documents/humanitarian_snapshot_31_august_2014_opt_v4.pdf; "One-Third of Gaza Mosques Destroyed by Israeli Strikes," Middle East Monitor, August 29, 2014, https://www.middleeastmonitor.com/news/middleeast/13813-one-third-of-gazas-mosques-destroyed-by-israeli-strikes; "UN Agency Ramps up for Gaza Reconstruction Push," UN News Centre, October 19, 2014, http://www.un.org/apps/news/story.asp?NewsID=49118#.VJerOF4APA.

XLIII

Introduction

9. Simon Johnson, "Sweden Recognizes Palestinian State, Hopes Will Revive Peace Process," *Reuters*, October 30, 2014, http://www.reuters.com/article/2014/10/30/us-sweden-palestinians-recognition-idUSKBN0IJ1DU20141030.

10. Herb Keinon and Eitan Arom, "Jerusalem Slams Spain's Parliament for 'Palestine' Recognition Vote," *Jerusalem Post*, November 19, 2014, http://www.jpost.com/Arab-Israeli-Conflict/Jerusalem-slams-Spanish-parliament-for-calling-on-Madrid-to-recognize-Palestine-382245.

11. "The Arms Trade and Israel's Attack on Gaza," *Guardian*, July 18, 2014, http://www.theguardian.com/world/2014/jul/18/arms-trade-israel-attack-gaza.

12. Euro-Mid Observer, *Slow Death: The Collective Punishment of Gaza Has Reached a Critical Stage*, September 2013, http://www.euromid.org/report/SlowDeath.pdf; "Israel Must Abide by Gaza Ceasefire Agreement, Says UN Rights Expert," *UN News Centre*, December 5, 2012, http://www.un.org/apps/news/story.asp?NewsID=43681&#.VTbfaCHBzGc; "Kerry: Israeli Settlements are Illegitimate," *Al Jazeera*, November 6, 2013, http://www.aljazeera.com/news/middleeast/2013/11/kerry-israeli-settlements-are-illegitimate-20131161359490940.html; House of Commons International Development Committee, "The Humanitarian and Development Situation in the Occupied Palestinian Territories," *House of Commons*, UK, vol. I, July 24, 2008, http://www.publications.parliament.uk/pa/cm200708/cmselect/cmintdev/memo/humanitarian/ucm1002.htm; also see Oxfam, "Memorandum Submitted by Oxfam," *Oxfam*, April 17, 2008, http://www.publications.parliament.uk/pa/cm200708/cmselect/cmintdev/522/522i.pdf; UN General Assembly, "United Nations Seminar on Assistance to Palestinian People Opens in Vienna with Focus on Relief, Recovery, Reconstruction in Post-War Gaza," press release, March 31, 2015, http://www.un.org/press/en/2015/gapal1328.doc.htm; Alex Shams, "World Bank: Israel Control of Area C Costs Palestine $3.4 Bln Annually," *Ma'an News Agency*, October 8, 2013, http://www.maannews.com/Content.aspx?id=636933; Ban Ki-moon, "Secretary-General's Remarks on the International Day of Solidarity with the Palestinian People," *UN*, November 24, 2014, http://www.un.org/sg/statements/index.asp?nid=8223.

13. Henry Kissinger, "Rooting the Peace Process," *Washington Post*, July 1, 1996, A17, qtd. in Mary King, *Mahatma Gandhi and Martin Luther King Jr: The Power of Nonviolent Action* (Paris: UNESCO Publishing, 1999), 473.

14. Brecht cited in Oudeh Basharat, "The Palestinian Narrative Has Won," *Haaretz*, March 24, 2011, http://www.haaretz.com/print-edition/opinion/the-palestinian-narrative-has-won-1.351497.

15. Salem Jubran qtd. in ibid.

PART I   **Indigenous Voices**

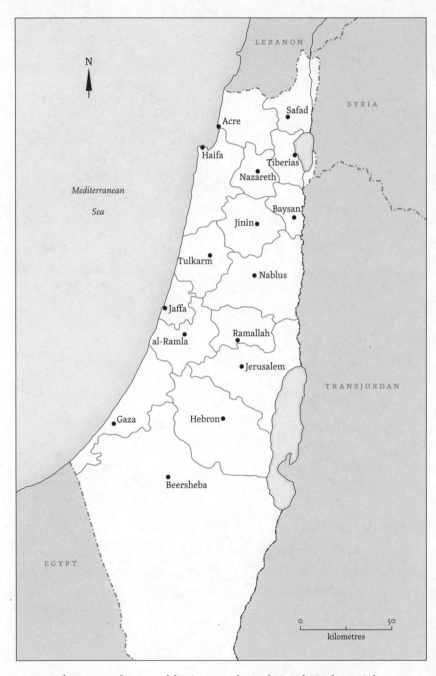

Palestine, 1947: districts and district centres during the British Mandate period.

1 Beit Daras

Once upon a Land

SIXTY-SEVEN YEARS AGO, Khadija,   3
a young, pretty woman from the village of Beit Daras woke up to a
tragedy that ravaged her heart and altered her life forever. She and
her two young children were evicted from their home. Abdelaziz
was three and Jawad just one. The horror was etched on all of her
neighbours' tearful faces, a language and reality they shared for
decades—some to this day. When her husband, Mohammed, rejoined
his family in June 1948, Khadija didn't need to ask about the fate of
their home. His eyes answered her question. Beit Daras was no more.

Today, over six decades after the expulsion, Khadija still remembers the horror of the 1948 dispossession and those unhappy days.
She bears witness to an ongoing present that is not much different
from a tragic past—a past that has cast a dark shadow not only
over her life but also over the lives of the generations that followed.
All of her dreams, hopes, and good work were blown away by the
savage winds of war and time. Unable to return to her home in Beit
Daras, one of the villages of Gaza District under the British Mandate,
Khadija was obliged to live in the greatest uncertainty about her
future in one of Gaza's eight refugee camps established by the United
Nations when hundreds of thousands of Palestinian refugees were

prevented by Israel from returning home. Across the border of Gaza—
to the south in Egypt, to the north in Lebanon and Syria, and to the
east in Jordan—there are currently over five million Palestinian
refugees who still, like Khadija, live a life of perpetual waiting,
enduring multiple hardships in their long exile (UNRWA 2013).

Khadija, eighty-nine, a mother of ten and grandmother of sixty-
eight, now lives in tragic circumstances in the Khan Younis refugee
camp. Once she owned a house, farms, and land, and she enjoyed
honour, dignity, and hope. She was part of the Beit Daras community, a village that no longer exists on world maps. It has been
demolished, together with over five hundred other Palestinian
villages. Khadija's tale is a story of a land that has been emptied of
its people and of a people who have been separated from their land
and segregated from each other—some never to be reunited. Over
70 per cent of the current population of Gaza are refugees whose
stories closely approximate Khadija's. Either they themselves or
their parents or grandparents were driven from their homes in
1948. Israeli military forces systematically destroyed hundreds of
Palestinian villages during and after the 1948 war, as one of six
measures included in a "Retroactive Transfer" plan approved in
June 1948 by the Israeli finance minister and prime minister to
prevent Palestinian refugees from returning home (Badil 2009, 10).
Since 1967, the population has lived under direct Israeli occupation
and, for almost a decade now, in a prison effected by Israel's blockade.
This population is ghettoized in a tiny 1.5 per cent of the original
territory of historic Palestine. Meanwhile, Palestinians in the West
Bank are ghettoized in less than 10 per cent of the original territory
of Palestine. But they, in addition, have been fragmented and forced
into dozens of isolated cantons, only moving between or in and out
of these with Israeli permission. Reminiscent of apartheid South
Africa,[1] a humiliating and arbitrary system of checkpoints, separation walls, ID cards, and permits issued by Israel circumscribe and
control Palestinians' lives and their freedom of movement, whether
to or from work or school.

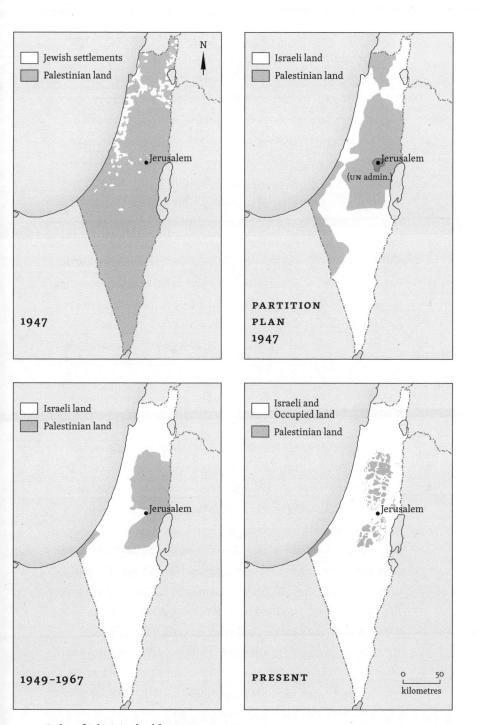

The loss of Palestinian land from 1947 to present.

This chapter describes similarities in Palestinian experiences from 1948 until the time of writing, in 2014. As the story of two generations reveals, comparisons can be drawn between the present and past. History seems to repeat itself over and over; denial, however, remains the main feature of the Palestinian experience. While generational analogies can never be full, the comparison strives to shed some light on parallels whose implications should be considered when analyzing the broad historical context of the ongoing impasse in Israel/Palestine. I argue that the present situation is an extension of policies and actions carried out almost seven decades ago. Just as the forces of expulsion, destruction, segregation, and domination that initiated in 1948 have continued to intensify, so too has the steadfastness of the Palestinians. Repeated wars have destroyed the foundations of their homes, but these have failed to destroy the foundations of their nation and their identity. Despite the savage winds of war and time, the new generations still hold on tight to their long-postponed rights and dreams to return home.

Beit Daras

Situated forty-six kilometres northeast of Gaza and approximately one hour by car from Khan Younis, Beit Daras was completely destroyed by Zionist troops prior to and after the establishment of the state of Israel. The villagers, mostly peasants,[2] defended their homeland with the means they had at the time. They fought several fierce battles between March and June 1948 to save their native land. Hundreds of men and women sacrificed their lives or were massacred during these months and afterwards. Incapable of withstanding the well-equipped, trained, and more numerous Zionist military troops based in nearby Jewish settlement of Tabiyya, Beit Daras succumbed after more than four battles.

Before the village was ethnically cleansed in 1948, approximately three thousand people lived in Beit Daras; some four hundred houses, one elementary school, and two mosques stood there (Baroud 2010, 6). Virtually nothing is left today. According to historian Walid

Khalidi, "the only remains of village buildings are the foundation of one house and some scattered rubble. At least one of the old streets is clearly recognizable" (Khalidi 1992, 522).

Khadija's family was well known, respected, and wealthy. They owned hundreds of *dunums*.[3] In fact, they owned one-quarter of the land of Beit Daras. They grew all sorts of crops, including wheat, corn, sesame, barley, and lentils as well as cucumbers, tomatoes, and sunflowers. There were also fields for grapes and trees—apple, fig, and citrus—which provided fruit throughout the year.

In early March 1948, a few months after the passage of the UN partition resolution relating to Palestine, the Zionist leadership devised a blueprint known as Plan Dalet "to achieve the military fait accompli upon which the state of Israel was to be based" (Khalidi 1988, 8). According to Plan Dalet, "operations can be carried out in the following manner: either by destroying villages (setting fire to them, by blowing them up, and by planting mines in their rubble), and especially those population centres that are difficult to control permanently; or by mounting combing and control operations according to the following guidelines: encirclement of the villages, conducting a search inside them. In case of resistance, the armed forces must be wiped out & the population expelled outside the borders of the state" (Badil 2010). The Zionist leadership instructed the Haganah, the main Jewish underground military in Palestine, to prepare to take over the Palestinian parts assigned by the Jewish Agency. The Haganah had several units and each one received a list of villages it had to occupy or destroy and inhabitants to expel (Morris 2009, 38). Most of the villages were listed to be destroyed. Beit Daras was among them. The Givati unit drew the assignment.

According to Plan Dalet, Jewish forces were ordered to cleanse the Palestinian areas that fell under their control. Israeli historian Ilan Pappe describes this cleansing: "Villages were surrounded from three flanks and the fourth one was left open for flight and evacuation. In some cases it did not work, and many villagers remained in the houses—here is where massacres took place" (2008).

This was precisely what happened in Beit Daras during the last battle.

Fearing for the life of her young children after several fierce battles that claimed many lives, Khadija decided to spend a few nights in nearby Isdud. She intended to return in the mornings to her home and fields to work. On a sunny day in May, she felt tired and opted to take Jawad with her to Beit Daras and to leave Abdelaziz in Isdud with other family members. At sunset, she was still tired and decided to spend the night in her home. That night Zionist troops attacked the village once again. Their usual tactic was to surround Beit Daras from three sides and leave the fourth one, leading to Isdud, open. But this time they had mined the road leads to Isdud. Hearing heavy planes bombing and shooting, Khadija, carrying Jawad, searched for safety.

Bombs fell from everywhere and gunfire surrounded her. One step forward, she recalls, a bomb blast back. She was very frightened. Women and children screamed as they searched for a way out. Khadija didn't scream, but Jawad did. Tears streamed down her face. Everyone was terrified. Some people took their animals so they wouldn't be killed. Then the mines started to explode. Horses, cows, sheep, and people ran in different directions. Still the bombs fell. Worse was to come. Planes attacked from the sky. Bullets felt close to her head and legs. But she continued to run. She has often remarked that a gate to hell opened that day and never closed. When she reached Isdud, she knocked at the first door. When it was opened, she heard someone crying. It was Jawad. She had dropped him behind in her panic.

Late the next afternoon, after the battle had finished, Khadija returned to her village. The road to her home was littered with bullet shells and covered in blood. Many homes were blown up. More dead bodies than she could count were on the roads. Men were burying them. One of her relatives was among them. She felt her heart stop; this man was the only son in his family and was recently married with two children. The Haganah carried out a massacre in Beit Daras and then returned to their settlement.

From the early days of Nakba—the "catastrophe"—in direct violation of UN resolutions, every effort was made to prevent the return of those expelled (Flapan 1987). When Khadija's uncle and cousin returned to Beit Daras after the last battle to fetch some food and clothes from their home, they were arrested by Haganah and imprisoned for several years. They were relatively lucky as other people from Beit Daras had been killed in the preceding weeks. The Zionist troops didn't want anyone to return to their home, and they shot anyone they found returning. A female relative of Khadija went with a man from the village to get food from their homes and fields. While they were harvesting corn to fill their sacks, Zionist militia forces started shooting at them and the man was killed.[4]

Third Generation of Refugees
I am the eldest granddaughter of Khadija. I inherited the genes of a refugee from my father, Abdelaziz, Khadija's eldest son. Growing up in a refugee camp in the Gaza Strip, decades after the destruction of Beit Daras, my grandmother told me the story of our village. At the time, during the 1970s, it was too dangerous even to mention the word *Palestine*. We were denied the right to study, read, or possess anything related to our homeland. My grandmother stepped in to close that gap of historical denial. She didn't forget our land, contrary to the prediction of David Ben-Gurion that the old generations would die and young generations would forget (Al Awda 2012). The story of our lost village was, in the accurate words of Ramzy Baroud, "a daily narrative that simply defined our internal relationship as a community" (2008). Telling the story of her village, Khadija knew, would not bring back the dead from the grave, nor would it return Beit Daras. But telling the story would help to prevent Beit Daras from being exiled from human memory and history. It would also help us—the new generations born in the camps—to learn our history. That was her mission.

My real introduction to the horrors of life and the meaning of life, death, and home was back in 2003, during one of the many

Israeli military invasions of the Khan Younis camp. The dark realities of those bleak moments struck me hard in both heart and mind as I ran in the middle of the night, carrying my son, then aged three, in search of safety. But, in Gaza, there is no place that can be called safe. Despite this reality, people under attack run because they naturally feel that staying still, while the Israeli tanks are advancing and destroying their neighbours' homes, is to risk their lives. What intensifies that feeling is the death coming from sky— from the American-made Apaches that hover above their heads. Death, at these moments, is palpable. The barrier between life and death vanishes as a bullet streaks past my head or a shell shakes my body. It is one bullet or shell of the many menacingly zooming around me. As the tenuous nature of life is exacerbated, the will to a safe life gets stronger.

That night, fifty-five years after the destruction of Beit Daras, and the military occupation of what remains of historic Palestine, I, the third generation of Palestinian refugees, found myself carrying my son, fleeing to nowhere, and leaving the place that I regarded as home. That night, I repeated the same scenario that occurred in 1948 when my grandmother carried my dad, Abdelaziz, and my uncle, Jawad, and made her way to nearby Isdud looking for temporary safety and waiting for things settle down so that she could return to her home. That night, the Israeli military forces carried out the same old practices and the same old polices to maintain their domination over our space and souls. They surrounded the camp from three sides, destroyed the houses that they planned to destroy, and then they withdrew to their Gush Katif bloc of colonies. With each attack, more homes were demolished, more people displaced, and more atrocities committed. Furthermore, the separation fence inside Gaza also expanded, as the Israeli military swallowed more and more of what little land remained to us. More aggressive policies of massive land grab are currently taking place in West Bank, expanding Jewish-only colonies at the expense of Palestinians' land and destroying any connectivity of people or feasibility and possibility of a viable Palestinian state.

Amid all of that horror, the memories of heated debates between my grandmother and me about my home, my village, and my home-land began to feed one another. I asked my grandmother many questions during our conversations. These were followed by more questions—questions that many of my generation also asked. Why didn't you stay in Beit Daras and die there? Why do I have to be a refugee and live this misery? Why was I brought to this poor life in which I need to queue for food rations and second-hand clothes at UN distribution centres?[5]

During those bleak moments, I saw how woven together these disparate fragments of past and present are. They shift back and forth again and again. I've come also to feel how selfish I was when I was concerned only about myself—my image, my pain, my life, and my future—and never about her. How naive I was to think that her saving the lives of her children was a cowardly act. How short-sighted I was when I thought that land is more important than human life. And how dare anyone say that Palestinian mothers don't love their children and leave them to die.

My grandmother has been separated from her land and home for many years now. Despite the passage of time, she has neither found a safe place to live nor been able to return to her home. Unlike her, on the morning following the attack on that horrible night, I could return to my family home in the Khan Younis camp. Other neigh-bours were also able to return to their tents that morning—shelters that could serve as their homes until they rebuilt new ones.

Pictures coming from Gaza in winter 2012 after the Israeli attack on the tiny besieged strip, as well as winter 2014 after the summer attack, showed newly homeless families sitting in their tents in the cold. The photos reminded me of my neighbours' tents in 2003 and the tents of 1948 that were pitched before my time. That year, my grandmother spent the harsh winter in tent camps provided by voluntary organizations. The only hope for her then was the one offered by UN Resolution 194 of 1948. Article 11 of the resolu-tion reads, "Resolves that the refugees wishing to return to their homes and live at peace with their neighbors should be permitted to do so at the earliest practicable date." The UN Relief and Works Agency (UNRWA) visited the refugees' tents to count the number of persons in each family so the agency could provide blankets. My grandmother's extended family received fifteen blankets. It was very cold then, and the donation was very much appreciated. This past winter the Palestinians of Gaza were likewise given blankets— but without the UN resolutions.

Similarly, in 2008, Fawziya Kurd and her paralyzed husband were given a tent after their home in Jerusalem was demolished. After living ten days in this tent, her husband's strength ran out and he passed away. The questions Fawziya put to the renowned Israeli journalist Gideon Levy summarize the meaning of the loss: "Had you been in my husband's place, all his life in house and suddenly in the street, what would you have said? What would you have felt? If you lost a cell phone—how angry you would be, and he lost his home. All his money and his entire life and suddenly he is thrown out into the street" (Levy 2008).

In summer 2014, similar to 2012 and 2008 aggressions on Gaza, Israel repeatedly systematically targeted the Palestinian infrastructure. The goal was to make the loss and the punishment a collective one. If a Palestinian did not lose a family member or a house or a business, then he or she would have to pay on the collective level. The Israeli forces shelled clinics, schools, homes, offices, factories, mosques, hospitals, shelters, bridges, orphanages, power stations, water wells, and stadiums. The president of the Fédération Internationale de Football Association (FIFA), Joseph "Sepp" Blatter, wasn't alone when he said he was "very much touched" after the targeting of the Gaza football stadium. Football is "connecting people and giving hope"; the destruction of the stadium, Blatter said, hurt him personally (BBC 2012). In this aggression, I wept for the ninety-six thousand homes that were bombed—for the homes that I knew and for other homes that I did not know. I wept for bridges. Yes, I wept especially for the bridge that used to connect Gaza City and the Nusairat camp. I travelled over that bridge hundreds of times. Blatter was right when he referred to the impact of this punishment on hope and on connecting people. My tears were seemingly endless. I wondered whether my weeping would ever cease. My grandmother said her tears were the same when Beit Daras was destroyed in 1948.

In the 1970s, a few years after Israel occupied the Gaza Strip and the West Bank, refugees were allowed to visit their villages. When my great-grandfather was asked why he had not done so, he told my grandmother that he would prefer to die rather than walk on the ruins of his home and village. My house, he said in a choked voice, "is my flesh, my sweat, my blood and my bone. It's me, the broken human being you see now. How do you expect to walk on your body?" He then turned his back on my grandmother to hide the tears that she could still feel.

Nothing in this life is harder than walking on the rubble of one's own home. It is one of the harshest and most painful things that can happen in life. Home is a sense of belonging, safety, and comfort, and a place of life's memories, whether sweet or bitter. When the Israeli occupiers began to carry out their policy of house demolition, they knew this operation was going to be one of the most painful punishments for the Palestinians. They knew it would hit them in the heart. Levy's conversation with Fawziya Kurd ends with her quietly telling him to close his eyes. Then she asks, "What do you see? Darkness. That's what I see." Her words convey all the pain and turmoil that Palestinians endure. Darkness was exactly what I saw, walking on the rubble of my uncle's home destroyed in the August 2014 Israeli attack on Gaza.

This form of collective punishment also denies Palestinians a concept of possession, a sense of belonging, and an idea of home. It is as if the occupation were designed to strip the Palestinians of their last dreams and possessions. Psychologically, the Israelis appear intent on depriving Palestinians of even the hope that one day they will own their homes or return to their original dwellings. The Palestinians are therefore left confined within an enormous open-air prison that is called Gaza and within the Bantustans on the West Bank. The message is clear: get out of this land.[6]

In the 1980s, my grandmother visited Beit Daras. In great shock at the level of destruction and unable to locate her home, Khadija asked her son Abdlehakeem to leave her alone for some time. She started to walk around the beautiful village that had completely vanished. She first found the old quarry, overrun with sand and overgrown with grasses. Then she recognized a small part of the mosque's foundation. Finally, she located her home. A part of the wall from her house remained. She hugged the wall and rubble and sobbed over her sweet home with all its memories, which had become a pile of small stones. She also wept where the sycamore tree no longer grew—a place where she used to rest every day. After returning to Khan Younis from Beit Daras, she was sick for a month, and she then understood the reason why her father did not visit his village after the expulsion.

When my grandmother speaks about her home and village, there is always a magic flash in her eyes—something that I didn't understand for years. In 2004, I began to comprehend the connection. That year, the home of my closest friend, Sahar, was demolished. To stand in the rubble of this home—a place that had witnessed the best days of my childhood—was devastating. In her home, which was just a few streets from my own, I had learned the meaning of love, care, and true friendship. It vanished in an instant under a Caterpillar bulldozer. As her family moved out of the camp in search of a new home, we were separated from each other. All that remains are memories—some good, some bad. Among the latter, is my memory of Sahar's home vanishing in an instant.

How many Palestinians have died in defence of their homes? And how many non-Palestinians have sacrificed their lives to defend the homes of others? The legend of Rachel Corrie, the American peace activist who opposed her government's support for Israel's militarism and occupation, is only one example. In March 2003, Rachel was killed in the Rafah refugee camp by an armoured bulldozer while defending a Palestinian home against demolition (Rishmawi 2005). Rachel's courage sent a strong, profound, and abiding message against Israeli policies that deny Palestinians the right to a home. Her message was similar to that of Martin Luther King Jr.'s. From his jail cell, King wrote, "We who engage in nonviolent direct action are not the creators of tension. We merely bring to the surface the hidden tension that is already alive" (1963). Rachel's heroic, non-violent, and firm commitment to justice and human dignity brought to the surface one of the critical issues that Palestinians face in their daily lives. Rachel exposed the hidden brutality of the occupation and the denial of basic human rights to Palestinians. With such humanity Rachel became a significant reminder to Palestinians of the justness of our cause and that we are not forgotten.

In summer 2014, I looked from the roof of my family home in Khan Younis. For as far as the eye can see, grey concrete boxes crowd next to each other and on top of one another. Due to the lack of space, the camp expands every year towards the sky to accommodate the many children born in limbo there. The sky above Khan Younis camp would be magnificent if Israeli drones were not there, buzzing and watching us 24/7. The spectacular view of the Mediterranean beach, which is less than a kilometre from the camp, would be very beautiful if the Israeli guard ships were not there. The image of the children in my camp climbing the tree next to our home to have a look at the beach is still vivid in my mind, and it's heartbreaking. For almost four years in a row, the people of Khan Younis were denied the right to go to the beach. For the sake of the seven thousand Jewish settlers occupying the best areas in Gaza, Israel imposed on the Palestinians racial and territorial separation based on nationality, in addition to its repressive military occupation. That de facto separation imposed in Gaza then, as well as the ones in West Bank now, and the isolation nowadays is more akin to political apartheid than an occupation regime. As a 2007 *Haaretz* editorial explains, "One side—determined by national, not geographic association—includes people who have the right to choose and the freedom to move, and a growing economy. On the other side are people closed behind the walls surrounding their community, who have no right to vote, lack freedom of movement, and have no chance to plan their future."

The Khan Younis refugee camp is the place my grandmother and my parents called home while waiting to return to their real home in Beit Daras. Khan Younis is the place where I was born, raised, and educated. It is also the place where my grandmother, my father, and I, like every other Palestinian in the camps, were imprisoned in our house every night when the Israeli military imposed a shoot-on-sight curfew from 8 P.M. until 6 A.M. through most of the years of the first intifada. And this is the place where I feel I am pushed and squeezed and where I feel that I am exiled in my own land. This is also the place where I often think about Beit Daras and Palestine, about my grandmother and my people. It is where I think of those who lay down their lives defending our right to live in freedom— and of those who destroyed that freedom. Faces and names from all generations—women, men, and children—come together to complete the picture. They include the many faces of people who are currently trying to somehow make an impossible life bearable for their families and children in an extraordinary situation.

Looking just beyond the camp towards the eastern, northern, and southern borders of Gaza intensifies the feeling of being strangled. Barbed wire encircles the space. Concrete bunkers, metal boxes, and military towers with snipers strike the eye and encircle one's vision, one's soul, one's dreams, and one's space. People feel as if death lurks in each corner of the minimal space left to them. Everything around them is a reminder of the restrictions and threats they live with as a result of the occupation and the inhumane blockade. The occupation is also a reminder of the denial of our rights. It is both a physical and a psychological denial, and it makes one's soul constrict.

Soon after occupying the West Bank and Gaza in 1967, Israel put in place policies and practices to reinforce its domination and impose segregation. Most of the Palestinians who happened to be outside Palestine before June 1967 automatically lost their right to return and became displaced persons. Israel denied them the right to return to their refugee camps and towns. Nor were they allowed to return to their original homes of 1948 as stipulated in UN Resolution 194. An estimated four hundred thousand Palestinians were displaced after the 1967 war. Half of those affected were refugees who had already experienced expulsion in 1948. They thus became refugees for a second time and were again left with nothing.

Immediately after the 1967 war, the Israeli reason for expelling the Palestinians from Gaza was revealed in the internal discussions of the Israeli cabinet. Golda Meir, later prime minister, suggested that Israel should keep the Gaza Strip while "getting rid of its Arabs." The cabinet agreed. Prime Minister Levi Eshkol explained that those expelled during the 1967 war would not be allowed to return because "We cannot increase the Arab population in Israel" (Eshkol qtd. in Chomsky 2012).

My grandmother's brother, my great uncle, was one of those Palestinians denied the right to return home. He was working in Saudi Arabia when the 1967 war was started by Israel. In 1999, after living thirty-two years in exile, my grandmother's brother and another relative were allowed to visit her. When they reunited, my grandmother asked the two of them to have seats. To her surprise the stranger shook her hands and kissed her head. It took her half a minute of close scrutiny to recognize the stranger as her brother. At that moment, he wept, realizing that he was a stranger to his own sister. He had expected that he would receive a warm welcome and that she would take him into her arms. He was not prepared for her cold hands and voice. When Khadija recognized him, she started crying too saying, "He's my brother, he's my brother." They hugged each other and cried for a long time. Soon the more distant relative and everyone else in the room were also crying.

Palestinians have been seared in the flames of the unjust policies of displacement, segregation, occupation, and imprisonment.
Although these events are strong in the collective memory of
Palestinians, very few people seem aware of the link between
the ongoing conflict and the enormous tragedy of the Nakba that
befell the indigenous Palestinian population in 1948 as a result of
the creation of Israel. The claim by Israel's Prime Minister Golda
Meir in 1970 that "There are no Palestinians" enhanced that misunderstanding of Palestinian peoplehood. The world seems not to
understand that when Israelis and others speak of the "Jewish state
of Israel" they are talking about the ethnic cleansing of my grandmother. Likewise, the world seems not to understand that when the
Israelis speak of "the War of Independence" they are talking about
the Nakba.

Approaching seventy years after the 1948 Nakba, Palestinian
life is still crippled by the constraints of segregation, the chains
of occupation, and many discriminatory measures, including
permits,[7] checkpoints,[8] and the apartheid wall[9] that are primarily
employed to dispossess Palestinians (Jamjoum 2009). The 1948 and
1967 policies of separation and denial are still in force. My great
uncle's situation in 1999 was not different from that of Andalib
Odwan's, a Palestinian student from Gaza, who was denied the
right to attend her university in Beir Zeit in 2012. The Israeli court
ruled that granting Odwan travel permit would "undermine the
'separation' policy, which is based on both security and political
considerations" (Rudoren 2012).

The denial of Palestinian families' right to visit their sons and
daughters in the Israeli jails for years on end, a breach of the
Geneva Conventions, is another example of these ongoing policies.
When Gilad Shalit, perhaps the most famous prisoner in history,
was held in Gaza, Israel cancelled the visitation rights for thousands of Gazan prisoners in Israel. This was called "proportionate
pressure." After Shalit's release in 2011, the policy of isolation
nevertheless continued. Aside from a denial of rights, "the name of
the game here is submission" (Hass 2012).

Conclusion

The Palestinian Nakba was—and continues to be—a deliberate disaster that has altered the life of millions of Palestinians. In 1948 and over the many years that have followed, Israeli colonial occupation destroyed—and continues to destroy—Palestinian homes and homeland. The cruel hardships currently endured by Palestinians are essentially no different than the harms experienced by their grandparents and great-grandparents back in 1948. In reaction to continuing Israeli-made crimes, new generations of Palestinians relate to the Nakba and become more acutely aware of it. Despite devastation after devastation, and in the face of aggression after aggression, the native population of Palestine has managed to stand firm. In the ruins of their homes and their shattered hopes, Palestinians remain standing. It's no wonder that Gaza's symbol is the phoenix—the ancient firebird that rises from its own ashes. This spirit is the Palestine that I know. This is the nation to which I proudly belong.

When I saw my grandmother following last summer's Israeli attacks on Gaza, she was unusually happy. She looked at me and my children—Tarek, who was fourteen, and Aziz, six—and, to my surprise, she repeated what she told me in 2012. She said that she was no longer worried about Beit Daras. Neither was she worried about the water well, the land, the farms, and the sycamore trees, nor about the passage of time and the future that she's wanted for so long. Then she said, "For many years, I felt as if I were walking alone. And as you know walking alone is not a pleasant way to make a journey. Now, because of my age, I cannot walk, but I'm not alone anymore. I can now rest in peace even if I am not yet in Beit Daras. I now know that Beit Daras is in your heart, and I also know that you are not alone in your journey. Don't be discouraged. We are getting there."

1. Apartheid (apartness or separateness in Afrikaans) was a system of legal, racial, economic, and social segregation enforced by the governments of South Africa between 1948 and 1994. It set aside 13 per cent of the land as "Bantustan," homelands for black South Africans in which they were dominated and oppressed, meanwhile maintaining the privilege of white South Africans. The International Convention on the Suppression and Punishment of the Crime of Apartheid, adopted in UN General Assembly, Resolution 3068 (XXVIII), November 30, 1973, states that "the crime of apartheid," which includes similar policies and practices of racial segregation and discrimination as practiced in South Africa, "shall apply to certain inhuman acts committed for the purpose of establishing and maintaining domination by one racial group of persons over any other racial group of persons and systematically oppressing them." This includes, "the deliberate creation of conditions preventing the full development of such a group or groups, in particular by denying to members of a racial group or groups basic human rights and freedoms, including the right to work, the right to form recognized trade unions, the right to education, the right to leave and to return to their country, the right to a nationality, the right to freedom of movement and residence, the right to freedom of opinion and expression."

2. One Haganah intelligence service agent reported in 1947, "The *fellah* (peasant) is afraid of the Jewish terrorists…His strength is insufficient to fight the Jewish force…(the) majority are confused, frightened….all they want is peace and quiet" (qtd. in Morris 2009, 32).

3. A dunum is one thousand square metres.

4. In late 1948, an official cable was issued to all Israeli division and district commanders in the north: "Do all you can to immediately and quickly purge the conquered territory of all hostile elements in accordance with the orders issued. The residents should be helped to leave the areas that have been conquered" (qtd. in Badil 2009, 10).

5. I have to admit that when I was young the package of second-hand clothes, which was distributed annually, was a moment of happiness and joy to each child in the camp, including me.

6. Since the beginning of the Israeli occupation of the West Bank and Gaza Strip, and according to Israeli government statistics, which were compiled by the Israeli Committee Against House Demolition, Israel has demolished approximately twenty-seven thousand Palestinian homes and other structures crucial to a family's livelihood (Woodward 2012).

7. The Israeli army limits the movement of West Bank Palestinians on 430 kilometres of roads, upon which Israelis are allowed free movement. On 137 kilometres of these roads, the army completely prohibits Palestinian travel; on the other 293

kilometres, only Palestinians who have permits are allowed to travel (B'Tselem 2009, 13).

8. Israel maintained an elaborate checkpoint system along the network of road-ways throughout the West Bank functioning as controlling valves, opening or closing regions at the occupation's discretion. As of July 2011, there were 520 checkpoints and movement obstacles in the West Bank (Human Rights Watch 2012).

9. Israel continued construction of the wall or separation barrier around East Jerusalem. Some 85 per cent of the barrier's route falls within the West Bank, placing many settlements on the—so-called Israeli side—of the barrier. The barrier led to the confiscation of private land and separated many Palestinian farmers and Bedouin from their lands (Human Rights Watch 2012).

21

REFERENCES

Al Awda. 2012. "Famous Quotes." Al Awad: The Palestine Right of Return Coalition. Accessed November 15. http://www.al-awda.org/quotes.html.

Badil Resource Center for Palestinian Refugee and Residency Rights. 2009. *Survey of Palestinian Refugees and Internally Displaced Persons, 2008–2009*. Edited by Ingrid Jaradat Gassner. Bethlehem: Badil Resource Center for Palestinian Refugee and Residency Rights. http://www.badil.org/phocadownload/Badil_docs/publications/survey08-09/survey08-09-executive-summary.pdf.

———. 2010. "*The Nakba (1947–1949)*." May 28. http://www.badil.org/es/monitoreo-continuo-de-los-desplazamientos/item/1373-the-nakba-1947-1949.

Baroud, Ramzy. 2008. "Revealing a Massacre, or Stating the Obvious." *Global Research*, July 21. http://www.globalresearch.ca/revealing-a-massacre-or-stating-the-obvious/9629.

———. 2010. *My Father Was a Freedom Fighter: Gaza's Untold Story*. London: Pluto Press.

BBC. 2012. Interview with Sepp Blatter. BBC World Service, December 21. http://www.bbc.co.uk/podcasts/series/wswf.

B'Tselem. 2009. *Human Rights in the Occupied Territories, 2008 Annual Report*. Jerusalem: B'Tselem. http://www.btselem.org/download/200812_annual_report_eng.pdf.

Chomsky, Noam. 2012. "Palestine 2012—Gaza and the UN Resolution." *Chomsky.Info*, December 1. http://chomsky.info/articles/20121201.htm.

Flappan, Simha. 1987. *The Birth of Israel: Myths and Realities*. New York: Pantheon Books.

Haaretz Editorial. 2007. "Where Is the Occupation?" *Haaretz*, October 3. http://www.haaretz.com/print-edition/opinion/where-is-the-occupation-1.230452.

Hass, Amira. 2012. "For Israel, Punishing Palestinians is Not
    Enough." *Haaretz*, May 2. http://www.haaretz.com/opinion/
    for-israel-punishing-palestinians-is-not-enough-1.427649.

Human Rights Watch. 2012. "World Report 2012: Israel/Occupied Palestinian
    Territories." *Human Rights Watch*, January. http://www.hrw.org/
    world-report-2012/world-report-2012-israeloccupied-palestinian-territories.

Jamjoum, Hazem. 2009. "Not an Analogy: Israel and the Crime of Apartheid."
    Electronic Intifada, April 3. http://electronicintifada.net/v2/article10440.shtml.

Khalidi, Walid. 1988. "Plan Dalet: Master Plan for the Conquest of Palestine." *Journal of
    Palestine Studies* 18 (1): 4–33.

Khalidi, Walid, ed. 1992. *All That Remains: The Palestinian Villages Occupied and
    Depopulated by Israel in 1948*. Washington, DC: Institute for Palestine Studies.

King, Martin Luther Jr. 1963. "Letter from a Birmingham Jail [King, Jr.]." April 16.
    African Studies Center, University of Pennsylvania. http://www.africa.upenn.
    edu/Articles_Gen/Letter_Birmingham.html.

Levy, Gideon. 2008. "Eleven Days after Fawziya and Mohammed al-Kurd Were
    Evicted from Their East Jerusalem Home, Mohammed Died. Fawziya
    Now Lives in a Tent." *Haaretz*, December 18. http://www.haaretz.com/
    twilight-zone-non-jews-need-not-apply-1.259774.

Morris, Benny. 2009. "Lashing back 1947–1948." *Quarter Journal of Military History* 21
    (3): 30–41.

Pappe, Ilan. 2008. "State of Denial: Israel, 1948–2008." *The Link* 41 (2). *Americans for
    Middle East Understanding*. http://www.ameu.org/The-Link/Archives/State-of-
    Denial-Israel,-1948-2008.aspx.

Rishmawi, George. 2005. "Rafah House, Which American Activist Corrie Was Killed
    Defending, to Be Rebuilt." International Middle East Media Centre, November 17.
    http://www.imemc.org/article/15074.

Rudoren, Jodi. 2012. "Fighting for Women in the 'Dark Heaven' of Gaza." *New
    York Times*, October 20. http://www.nytimes.com/2012/10/13/world/
    middleeast/andalib-adwan-shehada-a-bold-voice-for-gaza-women.
    html?pagewanted=all&_r=0.

United Nations, General Assembly. 1948. Resolution 194 (III). December 11.
    http://unispal.un.org/UNISPAL.NSF/0/C758572B78D1CD0085256BCF0077E51A.

United Nations Relief and Work Agency for Palestine Refugees (UNRWA). 2013. "About
    UNRWA." Accessed January 14. http://www.unrwa.org/etemplate.php?id=47.

Woodward, Michelle. 2012. "Demolishing Palestine." *Jadaliyya*, September 19. http://
    photography.jadaliyya.com/pages/index/7431/demolishing-palestine.

Beit Daras

REEM SKEIK

2 I am from there, I am from here

I am from there, I am from here,   23
but I am neither there nor here.
I have two names, which meet and part,
I have two languages, but I have
      long forgotten
which is the language of my dreams.
—MAHMOUD DARWISH, "Exile"

THIS EPIGRAPH belongs to the much-celebrated Palestinian poet, Mahmoud Darwish, whose poetry succeeded in delineating the strife of Palestinians living in exile and under occupation. His words educated the ignorant and encouraged those struggling with injustice. This excerpt not only defines my contending Canadian and Palestinian identities, but it also helps to convey the conflicting status of both my grandfathers, a refugee from Jaffa and a prisoner in Gaza.

I am from there: A Tale of Jaffa

Growing up around my maternal grandparents meant a plethora of guilty pleasures: having easy access to candy at all times, receiving the toys I desired without question, and, my favourite, obtaining a sizeable dose of intriguing bedtime stories. The stories that resonated with me the most were my grandfather's stories. They never ended with "and they lived happily ever after" like other children's bedtime stories usually did. In fact, his stories never ended at all! I soon realized that my grandfather's intentions were not to put me to sleep, but rather to open my eyes to reality—our reality. His stories introduced me to my homeland and tracked his forceful exile out of it.

My maternal grandfather is called Abu Kamal (literally, father of Kamal); in Arabic convention, men are usually named in reference to their firstborn son. I called him *Sedo*, which is an Arabic term of endearment that Palestinians often use when addressing their grandfathers. Just like all his bedtime stories, Sedo Abu Kamal's journey also begins with "once upon a time in Jaffa" (pronounced "ya-fa"). He was born in the city of Jaffa, Palestine, in 1929, to a blue-collar worker and a mother who raised seven children. His family lived an ordinary peaceful life in a two-storey house in a neighbourhood called Hay el Manshia, which was about one hundred metres away from the Mediterranean Sea. His childhood was pleasant, abundant with memories of playing with friends, weekend picnics with the family by the sea, and the occasional unexcused absence from class to take a dip in the Mediterranean. Jaffa was known in Arabic as *aros al bahr el abyad al mutawaset*, which translates into the beautiful bride of the Mediterranean Sea. It was one of the only thriving modern metropolises in the region during the early twentieth century, and became the hub of Palestinian economy, industry, and culture.

Agriculture and trade strengthened Jaffa's economy through the export of oranges (see UNISPAL 1921). In fact, Jaffa was predominantly known for its opulent orange groves, which is why my grandfather remembers spring being his favourite season. For four consecutive months, the air was filled with the scent of orange blossoms. He gleefully recalls stories of quarrelling with his mother regarding the state of his hygiene during spring; for he would find it amusing to test how long the perfume of orange blossoms would mask his unbathed body.

Jaffa was also the cultural centre for Palestine, accommodating the major newspapers and publication centres. After graduating from high school at the age of seventeen, my grandfather began working at a printing press for *Al-Difa'* (the defence), one of the major newspapers in Jaffa (see Abu Shehadeh and Shbaytah 2008/2009). Unfortunately, he was only able to work there for about a year before being expelled from Jaffa at the start of the Nakba (catastrophe) in 1948.

Hay el Manshia was in northern Jaffa and led into southern Tel Aviv, which was inhabited by Palestinian Jews living next door. Sedo Abu Kamal described the relationship between the Palestinian Jews and Arabs living there as one of peaceful coexistence. He recalled the many interreligious friendships he developed during his childhood. During the 1930s and 1940s, the interreligious disputes only emerged with the gradual arrival of illegal Jewish and Zionist immigrants; aided by the British who supplied them with weaponry, these immigrants were being smuggled into Jaffa by sea under the cover of night (see UNISPAL 1935 and Quigley 1990). However, the violence between the Arabs and the Zionist militia began to escalate in early 1948. For several consecutive months, gunshots were heard almost every night. Sedo Abu Kamal believes this was used as a scare tactic to agitate the residents of Jaffa so that they would voluntarily choose to leave their properties. However, the Zionist militia quickly realized that the Jaffa residents were not going to abandon their homes that easily, so the militia began to bomb unoccupied and government buildings in midday.

Around mid-1948, the once sparkling city of Jaffa descended slowly into oblivion. It hit home for my grandfather on April 28, when tanks began to move in on Hay el Manshia and the Zionist militia attacked with grenades and small arms, firing at the houses so the residents would evacuate, but also at the residents as they evacuated. His neighbourhood and several surrounding neighbourhoods were being continually shelled. The streets were in a panic, and people where running everywhere seeking refuge. The lucky families were carrying a few items with them as they fled. However, most families, including my grandfather's, could only hold on to their children, as well as the keys to their homes, which they hung on chains around their necks. For my grandfather and his family, the road to refuge led them about twenty-five kilometres east of Hay el Manshia, into another neighbourhood called Hay Ennuzha, where his uncle lived. Sedo Abu Kamal vividly recalls the sinister atmosphere as he rode to his uncle's house. He told me it felt like the longest ride of his life. The city was grey with smoke and dust, and everything was being shelled around them. They were driving carefully to avoid being hit by the bombs that were raining down on Jaffa and to avoid hitting any of the people who were running panicked through the streets. He remembers they were running barefoot.

Eventually, my grandfather and his family managed to make it to his uncle's house. They planned on staying there until the situation settled down and they could return home. Hay Ennuzha was not under attack as of yet. Unfortunately, after five days, most of the neighbourhoods in Jaffa had already been targeted, and the chaos followed them east into Hay Ennuzha. But, unlike earlier that week, Sedo Abu Kamal remembers the masses drifting in unison. They were all heading towards a place he used to cherish, but, on that specific day, he didn't want to go there because he knew it meant only one thing: that they would be parting with Jaffa.

Against their will, the people of Jaffa arrived at Al Minaa (the Jaffa harbour). The once beautiful blue waters were now orange. The boats that used to be filled with oranges for export were being emptied into the Mediterranean Sea to allow people to board them.

There were thousands of people at the Jaffa harbour. It took my grandfather and his family hours to get onto one of the boats. The boats were heading in three different directions: some to Egypt, others to neighbouring Gaza, and others still to Beirut, Lebanon, which is where my grandfather and his family headed. This was his last memory of Jaffa.

My grandfather's family was considered one of the lucky few because they had relatives that they could stay with in Lebanon, unlike so many other Palestinians who had no choice but to take shelter in refugee camps in Gaza, Lebanon, and Egypt. After about ten days there, they heard news that their house, along with all other houses in Hay el Manshia and the neighbouring Hay Rshaid, was completely demolished (see Rempel 2003; Badil 2009, 10–11). Nevertheless, they still saw this as a temporary situation, anticipating that it was only a matter of time before they could return to rebuild their home. Unfortunately, temporary turned into permanent on May 14, 1948, when the state of Israel was declared.

Now that the majority of Jaffa's Palestinian Arab inhabitants were expelled, the Israeli army occupied the city and started enforcing its own laws. All the families that were expelled, including my grandfather's, were not compensated for their land and property (see Shehadeh 1985, 43–46). Israel essentially legalized the theft of Palestinian land, as all the residents who fled their homes and properties during the aggression were denied any rights to those premises. The property they previously owned now belonged to the Israeli government, and this government could do with it as it pleased, since the original occupants had technically "abandoned" it. Their stolen land had become home to someone else, and the expelled residents were no longer referred to as Palestinian citizens but as Palestinian refugees (see Abu Shehadeh and Shbaytah 2008/2009).

Palestinian refugee came to represent a new identity category on its own, one distinct from any other refugee case in the world. If you make a choice to leave your homeland and to live somewhere else, maybe due to economic or political instability, then you choose to immigrate, perhaps with the hope that you'll make it back home someday—but also if you choose to. On the other hand, if you are forced to leave your homeland, generally due to war, then you seek refuge somewhere else until the situation allows for you to return to your home. But if you are forced to leave your homeland, your property is stolen and handed over to someone else, and you are stripped of your citizenship and are not permitted to return home, then you are most certainly a Palestinian refugee. Regardless of UN Resolution 194, which calls for Palestinian refugees' right to return to their homeland, my grandfather and his family—as well as many other Palestinian refugees—are still not permitted to return (see Rempel 2008/2009). To this day, members of some of these families still wear their keys on a chain around their neck. According to Sedo Abu Kamal, since these Palestinians cannot live in their homes, their homes must live within them.

My grandfather's journey after exile continued for a few years in Lebanon. He attended college part-time in the city of Beirut, but eventually was granted a working visa to Kuwait to work as a layout artist for a Kuwaiti newspaper. Shortly after moving Kuwait, he got married and thereafter raised four children as well as three grandchildren, including me. He spent thirty-five years of his life in Kuwait; however, Palestinians, along with other foreigners, faced many obstacles in Kuwait. Non-Kuwaitis were not eligible for citizenship, which meant that families were obliged to renew their visa every year if they were not granted a visa for a few years at a time, and the visa could only be obtained through a Kuwaiti guarantor or employer. They also had no rights to ownership, meaning they could only rent property in Kuwait no matter the duration of their stay. Public education was not free for non-Kuwaiti residents and although post-secondary education was accessible, they required relatively higher averages and tuition than Kuwaiti citizens to enter any field of study.

Although these issues affected all foreigners in Kuwait, they presented a more serious struggle for the Palestinians due to their refugee status; unlike other foreigners, Palestinians did not have a homeland to return to. Therefore, they could never have a sense of security and stability. Thus, my grandfather could not retire in Kuwait after living and working there for thirty-five years. His sons could not stay there if his visa was terminated, unless they were each granted a work visa through a Kuwaiti guarantor. Additionally, Palestinians such as my grandparents were often refused pilgrimage to the Islamic holy city Mecca (in Saudi Arabia) due to their refugee status. And eventually, all Palestinian refugees in Kuwait, including my grandfather's family, had to endure yet another expulsion following the end of the Gulf War in the early 1990s.

Prior to the Gulf War, one of my uncles, who had become a Canadian citizen, applied to sponsor my grandparents so they could live in Canada with him. Fortunately, the application was accepted, thus providing my grandparents with a place of refuge and stability after they were expelled from Kuwait following the Gulf War. However, my parents, two siblings, and I were destined to head in another direction.

I am from here: A Tale from Gaza

My father was originally from Gaza City, and he met my mother while working in Kuwait. As soon as they were wed, he decided to take a precautionary measure; he initiated a family reunification application in order to grant my mother residency in Gaza, which had been under Israeli occupation since 1967. The process was usually difficult and time-consuming, and not all applications were accepted. My parents' application process lasted five years, during which my parents were forced to travel frequently back to Gaza, but my mother was finally granted residency. Despite the long, grueling process, my mother's residency in Gaza eventually proved indispensable; as was the case with other Palestinians, my parents were expelled from Kuwait after the Gulf War and had nowhere to turn but Gaza.

I was very sad to be separated from my maternal grandparents as they headed to Canada, and I accompanied my parents and two siblings to Gaza. It seems, however, that I was destined to embark on a new journey, through which I tracked my paternal grandfather's footsteps in another corner of Palestine. Gaza may not have appeared as majestic as the pre-Nakba Jaffa that Sedo Abu Kamal had always described to me, but that did not matter to my wide-eyed six-year-old self; I had finally set foot in my homeland, my Palestine—once the substance of bedtime stories, now the substance of reality.

Of course, Gaza remained occupied by the Israeli forces until 2005, which is why my family considered our stay there temporary. In retrospect, however, the five years I spent there not only opened my eyes to the harsh reality of living under occupation, but it also gave me the opportunity to meet the rest of my family and live with my paternal grandparents. Thus, I was finally able to consolidate the two sides of my family history and start making sense of my individual identity.

In particular, I tried to immerse myself in my paternal grandfather's life story within Gaza. In contrast to Sedo Abu Kamal's aptitude for storytelling, my paternal grandfather, Sedo Abu Majed, preferred not to communicate his life story orally. Perhaps his share of trials and tribulations had left him unwilling to discuss the past with his grandchildren. Fortunately for me, however, he had documented his entire life in a large stack of journals dating back to the 1920s. These journals hold the key to my late grandfather's life story.

Sedo Abu Majed was born in Gaza in 1912, the eldest of eight children. He was raised to stand up for his rights and never felt forced to do anything he did not believe in. This became apparent early on. At his elementary school, children were required to wear shorts as part of the school uniform. But my grandfather viewed this requirement as a basic violation of his "freedom of choice," so he decided to drop out of school at the age of nine. After that incident, he spent most of his time surrounded by ticking clocks in his father's watch repair shop. Soon, he began to learn the trade and was eventually able to run his own watch repair shop after turning eighteen in 1930.

Around this time, Gaza was in the midst of a mass illegal Jewish migration into the city. Although deemed unpatriotic and downright treacherous by most Palestinians, a very small number of Gaza residents had started selling their land to illegal Jewish immigrants after being blackmailed or offered ludicrous amounts of money. As the presence of illegal Jewish immigrants became more conspicuous, protests began to break out all over Palestine, as local British forces, illegal Jewish immigrants, as well as "treacherous" landowners were targeted. These protests eventually culminated in the so-called Arab revolt in 1936. The British forces retaliated by arresting many of these Palestinian protesters, including my grandfather, and unfortunately sentenced him to death along with a group of other protesters in their twenties. Sedo Abu Majed's name appeared in the daily newspaper, along with all other prisoners on death row. A clipping of that newspaper article remains in one of my grandfather's journals to this day.

Evidently, my grandfather's death sentence did not go through, and neither did the other prisoners' sentences. A renowned and highly esteemed lawyer got involved and was able to pull some strings to get the prisoners' released and their sentences annulled; he had connections with the British forces as well as most of the families in Gaza. Of course, this came as a most pleasant surprise to my grandfather, who was expecting imminent death! In his journals, he writes in great detail about how nerve-wracking it is to know the exact day you will die. He writes about waiting for the day to come, if only to end his misery.

Although Sedo Abu Majed was released after roughly two months in prison, the emotional stress of that whole ordeal contributed to his falling ill with jaundice soon after. Based on his doctor's diagnosis, the jaundice was so severe that for the second time in a short period, my grandfather was awaiting certain death. But God truly works in mysterious ways. After forty days of illness, Sedo Abu Majed slowly began to recover and was finally able to return to his beloved profession of watch repair. This time, however, he vowed to stay out of political affairs because, as his bitter experiences had clearly shown him, time was too precious to be wasted on politics. Yes, Gaza was falling apart in front of his eyes, but he chose to adapt to life under occupation. Having cheated death twice in one year, the twenty-four-year-old was now determined to live as "normal" a life as possible in occupied Gaza.

The years that followed were thankfully less eventful for my grandfather. However, Gaza was gradually becoming more populated with the arrival of illegal Jewish immigrants as well as Palestinian refugees from neighbouring cities and villages during the Nakba in 1948. But all throughout, my grandfather worked at his shop and kept to himself, never again getting involved in politics. He married in 1946 and was blessed with six children; unfortunately, it seems that he was destined for more political drama, despite his best efforts. The Palestinian/Israeli conflict was growing more vehement with each coming year. Additionally, in 1967, Gaza became occupied by Israeli forces, which began to extensively raid Gaza so as to expand its control over the newly seized land. In response, a group of Palestinians referred to as *Feda'yeen* (resistance groups), would bomb the Israeli-built bridges connecting neighbouring Palestinian towns to Gaza to stop the Israeli forces from entering Gaza. These bombs were built using alarm clocks.

One day in 1968, one of these bombs did not explode, and the Israeli forces were able to trace the serial number on the back of the alarm clock all the way to a local watch shop—my grandfather's watch shop. That same day they arrested Sedo Abu Majed along with his sixteen-year-old son who worked with him at the shop. In reality, my grandfather and uncle were not involved in the bombings; Sedo Abu Majed tried to explain that they sold a large number of clocks every day, so it was highly probable that the *Feda'yeen* were buying his clocks and turning them into bombs without his knowledge. But the Israeli forces did not believe him. Still, my grandfather expected they would remain in custody only for a while, as the Israeli forces would still be looking for the *Feda'yeen* who planted the bomb. Unfortunately, they stayed fixated on him and his son, utilizing a number of cruelly "innovative" torture methods in the hopes that they would confess to being involved in the bombings.

The most common torture method was solitary confinement, which was agonizing particularly because my grandfather knew his son was somewhere in that prison but could not be certain what kind of torture he was being subjected to. Another method involved binding my grandfather's arms and legs while suspending him from the ceiling and beating him for long periods of time—sometimes for a whole days at a time. Meanwhile, my uncle was being subjected to the same brutal methods of torture. At other times, the Israeli forces would place both of them in adjacent cells and beat one of them while the other listened.

However, my grandfather admits that the most tormenting method was mental torture. One day, five members of the Israeli forces took my grandfather and uncle for a drive to a secluded, deserted area, gave my grandfather a shovel and ordered him to dig a grave for his son. They shoved my uncle into the hole and slowly began to shovel dirt over him—they were burying him alive! They forced my grandfather to watch this horrific scene for a few minutes, then three of the men drove off with him, while the rest stayed on to bury my uncle. The men drove around with my grandfather for hours, giving him one more chance to confess to the bombings because, as they claimed, they could still save his son from being buried alive.

They did not end up burying my uncle alive, but the Israeli forces repeated the whole process once more, this time switching the roles so that my uncle was forced to dig a grave for his own father.

After six months, the Israeli forces realized my uncle would never confess to being involved in the bombings and presumed that, at his age, he probably never had a big role in the process. My grandfather, on the other hand, spent an entire year in prison, only being released after one of the *Feda'yeen* responsible for the bombing cleared his name. After his release, it took my grandfather five years to pay off the large debt that had accumulated during the year he was imprisoned. As before, he returned to the supposedly quiet business of watch repair. However, he now knew that no matter how hard you try, you could never totally disengage yourself from your social and political climate.

Over the next few years, Sedo Abu Majed watched as each of his four sons got arrested on different occasions, whether they were involved in protests or not. He watched as the only home he had ever known—Gaza—slowly deteriorated under the weight of occupation and inhumane blockade. In 2005, the Israeli forces retreated from Gaza and removed all the settlements. However, this did not really improve the situation for Palestinians in Gaza; in fact, it arguably aggravated it. In the aftermath of its redeployment, Israel maintained control over Gaza's sea, air, and land. The city became a so-called open-air prison for its residents, and my grandfather became a "prisoner" for the third time—this time for life. He passed away in 2010, at the age of ninety-eight.

Gaza never had a poetic name like Jaffa's "beautiful bride of the sea," and it was never considered that special in Palestine. But it was still home to many Palestinians like my Sedo Abu Majed. A home that was assaulted, occupied, and turned into a prison. Yet he never chose to leave because it was the only home he had ever known, the only place he could truly call his own.

Epilogue

Returning to the poem with this chapter opens, Mahmoud Darwish portrays the realm of diasporic consciousness with these lines: "I am from there, I am from here, / but I am neither there nor here." As a Palestinian with a Canadian citizenship, my diasporic struggle lay within defining my national identity. I felt blessed to live in a stable, peaceful environment as a citizen; yet, at the same time, I felt a sense of guilt for being given the opportunity to "escape" life under occupation, and even refugee status. My internal conflict was coming to terms with my new "home" and the feeling that I had abandoned my only "home." I was afraid that acceptance of belonging meant an unconditional betrayal of my homeland and eventual loss of my Palestinian identity.

Initially, my Palestinian identity was cultivated through the stories recited by Sedo Abu Kamal at bedtime, and it continued to develop through my persistent efforts to collect more stories from Sedo Abu Majed. Thus, habitation was not likely a key factor in my journey of self-discovery. I was able to identify with my homeland before I set foot into Gaza; and Gaza mainly unveiled the reality of living under occupation, but did not shape my identity. Therefore, living in Canada could not possibly make me forget where I came from; I am the lineal descendant of these two family histories. My grandfathers' stories opened a window unto my family's past and taught me about the struggles of occupation and exile. My grandfathers' stories taught me about resistance and resilience. But, most of all, their stories helped me envision a place for myself in the broad universe, a starting point for my own journey of self-discovery. And wherever I migrate, my homeland will always live inside of me, in the stories of my ancestors.

AUTHOR'S NOTE
I would like to express my sincere gratitude to my grandfathers' Sedo Abu Kamal and Sedo Abu Majed for sharing their stories with me and allowing me to explore my Palestinian roots. I would also like to thank Fadi Issawi for helping me gather archival material for this story, and the rest of my family for their continuous love and support. Finally, many thanks to Rana El Kadi for her invaluable feedback and editing throughout the writing process.

REFERENCES
Abu Shehadeh, Sami, and Fadi Shbaytah. 2008/2009. "Jaffa: From Eminence to Ethnic Cleansing." al-Majdal 39/40: 8–17.

Badil Resource Center for Palestinian Refugee and Residency Rights. 2009. *Survey of Palestinian Refugees and Internally Displaced Persons, 2008-2009*. Edited by Ingrid Jaradat Gassner. Bethlehem: Badil Resource Center for Palestinian Refugee and Residency Rights.

Darwish, Mahmoud. "Exile." In *If I Were Another: Poems*. Translated by Fady Joudah. New York: Farrar, Straus and Groux, 2011.

Quigley, John. 1990. *Palestine and Israel: A Challenge to Justice*. Durham, NC: Duke University Press.

Rempel, Terry. 2003. "Housing and Property Restitution: The Palestinian Refugee Case." In *Returning Home: Housing and Property Restitution Rights of Refugees and Displaced Persons*, edited by Scott Leckie, 296–305. New York: Transnational Publishers.

———. 2008/2009. "Resolution 194 (III): A Retrospective." *al-Majdal* 39/40: 5-7.

Shehadeh, Raja. 1985. *Occupiers Law: Israel and the West Bank*. Washington, DC: Institute of Palestine Studies.

UNISPAL. 1921. *An Interim Report on the Civil Administration of Palestine, during the Period 1st July, 1920-30th June, 1921*. League of Nations. http://unispal.un.org/UNISPAL.NSF/0/349B02280A930813052565E90048ED1C.

———. 1935. *Report by His Majesty's Government in the United Kingdom of Great Britain and Northern Ireland to the Council of the League of Nations on the Administration of Palestine and Transjordan*. December 31. League of Nations. http://unispal.un.org/UNISPAL.NSF/0/B672DC87B2D50447052565D4005173DF.

3 Palestine

Via Dolorosa

I WOULD LIKE TO SHARE with you 37
the story that we as Palestinians have all experienced in some way
or another—the story of being exiled from our homes, displaced into
nearby Arab countries as refugees with no citizenship, and having
to emigrate in search of a better future. This chapter tells the life
story of two Palestinian families, my mother's family, Awwad, and
my father's family, El-Bekai, both of whom have tasted the bitter-
ness of exile to which we as Palestinians have been sentenced to
experience ever since a foreign colonial entity came from distant
shores to occupy and depopulate our beautiful Palestine.

This story begins before I was born, in a place that would become
a distant memory passed on from my grandparents to my dad to me.
It begins in the beautiful village of Birya, situated north of Palestine
near the city of Safed. My great-grandfather was born in this village
when it was part of the Ottoman Empire. My grandfather, Ibrahim
Ayoub, was born in this same village in 1910 when it was under
British Mandate. My father, Ahmad, was born in this very same
village when the systematic Zionist ethnic cleansing began in 1947.

My grandfather described Birya as a small village situated at the
foothills of Mount Kanaan, five kilometres from the city of Safed.

The villagers were hardworking farmers who relied on the olive trees as their main source of income. He said that a farmer's life was not an easy one, but that he was a happy man since everyone in the village was as one family sharing each other's happiness and sorrows. In the summer, all the weddings would be held and, in the fall, the villagers would celebrate the olive picking harvest with dances and songs. During the festivals, people from all over the village would gather in the centre of the village. They would go early in the morning where they would spread white blankets underneath the trees. Each olive was sacred, so to avoid dropping any on the ground, they would handpick them one at a time. The olives would then be taken to the olive juicer to extract the olive oil. For ten days, people would celebrate this tradition by singing and dancing at night. This is why the olive tree is a strong symbol of the Palestine; it holds within it the lives of Palestinians as it is the main source of income for the villagers. Olives, olive oil, and soap made from the tree are sold in local markets and in nearby countries. Olives are a staple food in any Palestinian household to this day. Thus, there is a strong bond between the Palestinian farmer and the olive tree; the olive tree remains rooted in the land for many decades, passing from one generation to another. The farmers then were a close community working together to build houses, plant olives, grapes, figs, melons, plums, pears, and oranges, and harvest these crops. However, this quiet and peaceful community was shaken up in 1947 with the news of Zionist military units such as the Haganah, the main Jewish paramilitary organization in Palestine, killing defenceless people, including women and children in nearby villages. The infamous Deir Yassin is but one of around sixty-eight massacres that occurred during and after the British Mandate, which was supposed to protect the Palestinian inhabitants (Jawad 2007). News of the massacre travelled to Birya. Fearing for her family, my grandmother, Khadija, fled with my father, who was only seven months old, and sought temporary refuge in Lebanon. Her parents lived in a village there called Al-Manara, located in the District of West Bekaa, south of Anjar, near the Lebanese-Syrian border.

Like many of the refugees, she left with nothing but the keys to her home, believing it would only be a very short time until she returned. Little did she know that this would be the last time she would ever see her beautiful Birya. My grandfather stayed behind, defending his village against the well-trained Haganah units who were more organized and better armed than the Palestinian farmers (see Pappe 1994, 65, 67). He fought with the other villagers until Birya fell into the hands of the Zionist units in May 1948.

The loss of over three-quarters of the land of mandatory Palestine in 1948 and the displacement of three-quarters of a million Palestinians became known as the Nakba (catastrophe). The Nakba also refers to the Palestinians' collective experience of becoming stateless on their land and in exile. It changed the lives of many Palestinians for generations to come. Unlike many Palestinian refugees, my grandparents were fortunate to have family in Lebanon because my grandmother was Lebanese. But the majority of refugees who ended up in Lebanon had to endure the harsh experience of living in one of the twelve refugee camps established by the United Nations to temporarily host them. In these camps, the Lebanese government treated and still treats Palestinian refugees as third-class citizens. The refugees live in ghettos, in homes lacking many of the basic necessities for living. They are forbidden from owning businesses, homes, or land, and from working in any one of twenty professions, including law, medicine, and engineering (UNRWA 2013a). Accordingly, they are deprived of basic human rights under the pretext that the Lebanese government does not want to make them Lebanese citizens. The only hope for these refugees was to liberate Palestine so they could return to their homes and land. For this reason, Fatah, the main Palestinian political party and the largest faction of the Palestine Liberation Organization (PLO) led by the late Yasser Arafat, gained popularity as a resistance movement in 1967.

My dad was one of the many Palestinians who joined Fatah in 1968 at the age of twenty-one. A year later, he got a scholarship through Fatah to study mechanical engineering in the former Soviet Union. There, he met and married my mother, who was studying international law at the same university. She was from the West Bank city of Salfit and a daughter of the exiled leader of the Palestinian Revolutionary Communist Party, Arabi Awwad.

My grandfather Arabi Awwad was born in 1929, while Palestine was under British Mandate, in Salfit, a city well known for its century-old olive trees and olive oil. The family was well educated. My great-grandfather was a well respected and renowned teacher of Arabic, math, and religion for thirty-six villages. To receive his education, my grandfather had to move to Bethlehem and Jerusalem, where he finished high school with honours as one of the top students in Palestine. Upon graduation, he quickly landed a job as a teacher. During his work, he met his cousin, Fahmi al-Salfiti, who would become the most influential person in his life, introducing him to members of the Jordanian Communist Party and their ideology. He became involved in secret political activity against the Jordanian rule in the West Bank. From 1948 until June 1967, the West Bank, including East Jerusalem, was ruled by Jordan, which annexed the area in 1950 and extended Jordanian citizenship to Palestinians living there. For Palestinians to get their rights in Jordan, the communist party ran for office in 1956 and was elected into the Parliament in an election that was considered free and fair. Unhappy with the elections results and the directions of the new government, King Hussein of Jordan moved against the elected members, dissolved the Parliament, declared a martial law, and changed the constitution to ban all political parties, including the communists (NIMD 2014, 12, 13). As a result, a large number of communist members were killed and imprisoned in 1957. My grandfather was chased by the king's soldiers and captured. He was sentenced to nineteen years in prison for being a member of the communist party. My grandmother had two kids at the time—my uncle and my mother—to support on her own.

Like many of the strong Palestinian mothers whose husbands were killed or imprisoned, my grandmother took on the hard task of raising her children on her own. She moved in with her eldest brother in a small house that now sheltered twelve adults and children. As you can imagine, the sleeping conditions were crowded, food had to be shared sparingly, and life, to say the least, was difficult. My grandmother worked as a tailor to help support her family. The only memory my mother has of her father was that of visiting him in prison as a child. He was released from prison after thirteen years in June 1967 when Israel captured the rest of mandatory Palestine—the West Bank and the Gaza Strip along with Golan Heights of Syria and the Sinai Peninsula of Egypt. My grandmother's happiness upon being reunited with her husband was short-lived and ended after the 1967 Six-Day War where the West Bank went from Jordanian rule to Israeli military occupation.

Immediately after that war, the Israelis started to confiscate land, build settlements, and imprison people (MERIP 2001). My grandfather started his political activism against the Israeli occupation through protests, distributing pamphlets, and speaking to civil rights groups all over the world. Because the Palestinians were under brutal military occupation, they had no choice but to defend themselves and their families. My grandfather was a founding member of the National Front, which consisted of members of all Palestinian parties. Israel later arrested and exiled him to Jordan and then to Lebanon in 1974 where he became a member of the Palestine Liberation Organization.

My grandfather travelled throughout the world to give a voice to the Palestinian cause and raise awareness of the struggle of the Palestinian people. In his travels, he met with Fidel Castro of Cuba and Nelson Mandela of South Africa, both revolutionary leaders who were successful in reclaiming their country's independence from colonial powers. He believed that this would also be the case for Palestinians. In 1982, he left Lebanon for Syria where, to this day, he chooses to live among the Palestinian refugees in Yarmouk refugee camp, eight kilometres from the centre of Damascus.

In 2014, as I write this chapter, and the war in Syria continues, yet another story of the plight of Palestinians unfolds where thousands of the Palestinian refugees, including my grandparents, have been forced to leave their homes once again due to the ongoing conflict (MAP 2013). My grandparents call it a second Nakba because their community and home in Yarmouk has now become a battle ground between the Syrian government and opposition militias who are trying to gain control of this strategic area in Damascus. Once again, Palestinians are forced to leave their homes, seek refuge in nearby areas, and leave behind all their possessions. It is as though we were sentenced to become permanent migrants after losing our native land.

After my parents completed their studies in the former Soviet Union in 1983, they travelled back to Lebanon, a country that was recently invaded by Israel and divided by civil war. During this time of unrest, I was born in 1985 in the same village where my grandmother found refuge and settled in after the 1948 Nakba. Shortly after, my parents left Lebanon and headed to Syria where some factions of Fatah had gone. I spent the first three years of my life in the Palestinian refugee camp of Yarmouk. There, my mother faced many hard years raising my older brother and me as we lived in a small apartment in a very poor area of the refugee camp. My dad was politically active at the time and saw little of us. For my mother, history was repeating itself as she, too, saw little of her father when she was young. The burden of the family fell on her shoulders, which meant sacrificing her needs for the family's, giving up any luxuries for necessities, and having strength to withstand these conditions. I believe a big part of my personality was shaped and influenced by my mother and grandmother. I grew up admiring them for the strength, determination, willfulness, and love they had. Many Palestinian women, throughout this struggle, have taken on the role of mother and father during their husband's absence due to imprisonment or political activity or even death.

As Fatah became more and more divided, my dad decided to

take us back to my birthplace, the serene mountainous village of Al-Manara in Lebanon, where we lived for seven years. Along with my older brother and younger sister, we spent many happy years there as children. The mountain was our playground. During the day, we built dreams of castles, slain dragons, and rescued princesses. Nearby, the famous Roman temple ruin, Al Qasr, was our battleground where we slayed our enemies and celebrated our victory by drinking fresh spring water. At night, the sky would be transformed with a million stars and we would dream of becoming astronauts, travelling light years away in our spaceship of hope. In the fall, we would play fishing games with dried leaves, our pretend fish, using our poles made from twigs with strings tied at the end. In the spring, the mountains would come alive with the scent of flowers and fresh grass. In the winter, we would make snowmen and, in the summer, we would bask in the warmth of the sun and play games made from our wild imaginations.

Unfortunately, the reality of Palestinian refugees in Lebanon is one of limited opportunities, so, seeking a better future for his family, my dad decided to immigrate to Canada in 1996. We became uprooted from the place that we wanted to believe was home. It was a hard but necessary move as we were refugees with no passports. All we had was a piece of paper that stated we were refugees from a country that no longer existed in the eyes of the world.

Time and time again, my family faced moves to new cultures and new societies. Integration into a foreign society, which many immigrants face, was difficult for me and my siblings. In Canada, we had to learn a new language and the ways of this new culture into which we were suddenly immersed. But, through perseverance and hard work, my parents built a new life in Canada.

I remember the first time I was asked where I came from. I would answer, "I lived in Lebanon, but I am Palestinian." Some would reply, "Is that a country? I thought it was called Israel." I would get angry and answer back, "No, it's called Palestine; I don't know of a country named Israel." My first report in elementary school about the person I admired the most was not about a pop star or a famous celebrity like the other kids wrote about. Instead, it was about Yasser Arafat, the leader of Fatah, the party my father belonged to. When my brother was growing up, his room was plastered not with sports teams or famous soccer players but with pictures of the Palestinian intifada, of little children throwing rocks at Israeli tanks.

Even though I was only ten years old when we immigrated to Canada, I have never forgotten Palestine. Through the years, I saw images of Palestinians getting massacred, assassinated, imprisoned, continually humiliated at the many Israeli military checkpoints, separated from each other by a concrete wall, and having their homes and land confiscated by Israeli soldiers. These images don't even begin to illustrate the refugees' ongoing struggles, which I saw for myself in 2006 when I visited my mother's parents in the Yarmouk refugee camp.

Unlike the Lebanese government, the Syrian government treats the Palestinians like Syrian citizens, giving them many rights and freedoms, which means that the camps in Syria are in much better shape than those in Lebanon (see Human Rights Watch 2012). There are a couple of facts that I would like to mention here about the Yarmouk camp. First, it is the largest refugee camp in Syria, home to 148,500 registered refugees from northern Palestine (UNRWA 2013b). Second, it has a highly educated population and the largest employment sector is in construction and education. It is also the political hub for left-wing parties and is now a thriving centre for shopping.

When I first arrived at the camp, I saw it as grim and depressing. I saw nothing but concrete houses. There is no way to compare the life we have in Canada to that lived in the refugee camp. The longer I stayed, however, the more I saw how vibrant and alive this place really was. In the morning, I'd wake up to the morning call to prayer followed by loud revolutionary music. Then the shopkeepers would start to open their shops. At noon, lines of taxis streamed into the camp because the Palestinians had made it a place to shop for high quality but less expensive groceries, clothes, and shoes. At night, the camp filled with people laughing, shopping, and eating *shawerma*—the best you will ever have and for only two dollars. And then I started to meet the refugees.

The best place to meet people was grocery shopping. Unlike Canada, in the camp, you buy the food from street vendors. One day, as I was taking photos, people became very friendly because they thought I was a journalist. Some would pose for me or ask me to take their pictures. Others would complain to me about the rising prices of food and living, wanting someone to listen to their concerns. Some walls in the camp were filled with spray-painted slogans, such as "We shall return," "Fatah was here," or "Long live Yasser Arafat." Other walls were filled with pictures of famous martyrs from the past or ones who were recently killed by Israelis. While I was there, I also got to experience the sadness and loss that we experience daily as Palestinians as they held a funeral for a martyr who died in Lebanon from an Israeli airstrike during the 2006 war on Lebanon. He was laid to rest in the graveyard where three generations of Palestinian refugees have been buried.

This experience taught me that regardless of the overwhelming oppression and injustice we face as Palestinians, we continue our struggle to gain back our legal and basic rights, our identity, our freedom, and our right to return home. In short, we resist so we can exist. The best way that I can explain the Palestinian case to a person who argues against it is by putting the person in the shoes of Palestinians. I ask them to imagine the home they live in now and have spent money and labour on—and have many happy memories in. This place is your shelter and part of you. Imagine if one day, a perfect stranger came to your home and decided to take it over because he had a hard life, was victimized by another person to whom you had no relation, and decided that your home would be the perfect compensation. Would you, the owner, stand by and let them take it or would you fight for it? The response would of course be "no." Then I ask them, if you decided to take them to court and the courts did not compensate you and instead they rewarded the aggressor, would you accept that? Again, the answer would be "no." So I say to them, this is why we fight the Israeli military occupation to this day. As the famous Palestinian thinker Edward Said once stated, "You cannot continue to victimize someone else just because you yourself were a victim once—there has to be a limit" (qtd. in Jhally 2005). The Israelis have not reached yet this limit as they continue their apartheid system in the 1948 Palestine and 1967 Palestine, building the oppression wall and illegal colonies in the West Bank and disregarding the right of return of millions of Palestinian refugees all over the world.

As I finished writing this chapter and was searching for a title for it, words such as *path, pain, oppression, struggle, injustice, freedom, overcome,* and *fight* came to mind. However, my mother suggested "Via Dolorosa" as a fitting title. Translated from Latin, it means the "Way of Suffering" or the path that Jesus walked carrying his crucifix. There couldn't be a more fitting title for the Palestinian struggle as we are still walking the painful road, carrying the weight of being refugees and being crucified everywhere we go until we reach the golden gates of return to our Palestine.

I dedicate this chapter in loving memory of my two grandfathers. My grandfather, Ibrahim El-Bekai, passed away in 2007 without seeing his home or land, which he dearly loved. Although my grandfather was physically forced to leave his home in Birya, I always thought he never left it mentally or emotionally. Whenever he spoke of it or described it, it was though he could see it right in front of him. And to my grandfather, Arabi Awwad, who passed away in March 2015 in exile in Jordan. He spent his life fighting for his communist ideology and Palestinian liberation. He led his party and family through many tribulations and left behind a great and honourable history. He was a firm believer that all roads built by the blood and soul of the Palestinian struggle would surely lead us to freedom and self-determination. On a cold and rainy day in exile, he passed away and was buried far from his beloved city of Salfit. Both their memories and stories will be passed on until we return to our beautiful Palestine.

REFERENCES

Human Rights Watch. 2012. "World Report 2012: Israel/Occupied Palestinian Territories." *Human Rights Watch.* http://www.hrw.org/world-report-2012/world-report-2012-israeloccupied-palestinian-territories.

Jawad, Saleh Abdel. 2007. "Zionist Massacres: The Creation of the Palestinian Refugee Problem in the 1948 War." In *Israel and the Palestinian Refugees*, edited by Eyal Benvenisti, Chaim Gans, and Sari Hanafi, 59–127. Berlin: Springer.

Jhally, Sut, dir. 2005. *Edward Said: The Myth of "the Clash of Civilizations."* Media Education Foundation Transcript. https://www.mediaed.org/assets/products/404/transcript_404.pdf.

Medical Aid for Palestinians (MAP). 2013. "Displaced Refugees Face Medical Barriers." *Medical Aid for Palestinians, Notes from the Field,* January 10. http://www.map-uk.org/notes-from-the-field/archive/article/1-displaced-refugees-face-medical-barriers.

Middle East Research and Information Project (MERIP). 2001. "The Occupied Territories /Jerusalem." In *Primer on Palestine, Israel and the Arab-Israeli Conflict.* Washington, DC: Middle East Research and Information Project. http://www.merip.org/palestine-israel_primer/occupied-terr-jeru-pal-isr.html.

Netherlands Institute for Multiparty Democracy (NIMD). 2014. *Maps of Political Parties and Movements, 2013–14.* Kingdom of Netherlands: Netherlands Institute for Multiparty Democracy. Accessed August 12. http://www.nimd.org/wp-content/uploads/2014/01/Map-of-the-Political-Parties-and-Movements-in-Jordan-2013-2014.pdf.

Pappe, Ilan. 1994. *The Making of the Arab-Israeli Conflict, 1947–1951.* London: I.B. Taurus.

UN Relief and Works Agency (UNRWA). 2013a. "Lebanon." UNWRA. http://www.unrwa.org/etemplate.php?id=65.

———. 2013b. "Syria." UNWRA. http://www.unrwa.org/etemplate.php?id=156.

SAMAR EL-BEKAI

RAMZY BAROUD

The Man with
the White Beard

Uniting the Palestinian Narrative

WHAT DO a Palestinian farmer living
in a village tucked in between secluded West Bank hills, a prisoner
on hunger strike in an Israeli jail, and a Palestinian refugee roaming
the Middle East for shelter, however, temporary, all have in common?
They are all characters in one single, authentic, solid, and cohesive
narrative. The problem, however, is that Western media and academia
barely reflect that reality, or intentionally distort it, disarticulate it,
and, when necessary defame its characters.

An authentic Palestinian narrative—one that is positioned within
an original Palestinian history and articulated through Palestinian
thoughts—is mostly absent from Western media, and, to a lesser
degree, academia. If such consideration is ever provided, everything Palestinian suddenly falls into either a side note of a larger
Israeli discourse, or at best, is juxtaposed—often with unconcealed
hostility—with a pro-Israeli plot. The Palestinian story, if it exists,
it is often disconnected, disjoined news items, offering little or no
context, and marred with negative connotation. In this narrative,
a farmer, a prisoner, and a refugee barely overlap. And due to the
deliberate disconnect, Palestine becomes pieces, ideas, notions,
perceptions, but nothing complete, never a whole.

On the other hand, an Israeli narrative is almost always positioned within a cohesive plot, depending on the nature of the intellectual, political, academic, or religious contexts. Even those who dare criticize Israel, within a mainstream Western platform, do so ever prudently, gently, cautiously. The outcome of this typical exercise is that Israel's consecrated image remains largely intact, while Palestinians constantly jockey for validation, representation, and space in a well-shielded pro-Israeli narrative.

To counter these misrepresentations, the pieces must be connected to form a collective, one that would truly epitomize the Palestinian experience—the story, and the history behind it. Once that has been attained, there are chances for greater clarity regarding the roots of the conflict, its present manifestations, and future prospects. That can only happen if we return to the basics of a protracted tragedy that is draped with the names and stories of individuals, which ultimately articulates a consistent, generational discourse, which deserves to stand on its own, without belittling juxtapositions or belligerent comparisons.

Man with the White Beard

In the winter 2012 edition of *Palestine News*—published by the Palestine Solidarity Campaign in the UK—and more specifically on page five, there is a photo of an old man. With a white beard, grey, traditional *jalabiya*, a black belt, and an old blue jacket, he could be any Palestinian's grandfather. In the photo, the man holds broken branches of his olive trees, maliciously destroyed by illegal Jewish settlers in the village of Qusra, in the West Bank.

The old man's name is not provided. He could be Mohammed, George, or Ali. A Muslim or a Christian. His village, Qusra, is located south of Nablus, but that too matters little. It could be bordering Jerusalem, Ramallah, or Jenin. Throughout the years, many men and women in his village must have posed with the remains of their ancient olive trees, conveying a look of sorrow or despair, hoping that maybe, their collective yet often muted cry for justice will bring to an end the heinous and perpetual crime under which they all suffer.

According to the accompanying report, the destruction of Palestinian olive trees by settlers—under the watchful eye of the Israeli army—cost farmers over $500,000 in 2011. Oxfam, the Union of Agricultural Work Committee, and others estimated that olives collected in 2011 would produce half of the oil of the 2010 harvest.[1] But it is not exactly the financial burden that settlers are targeting in their constant rampages throughout the Occupied West Bank and East Jerusalem. They know well that the land is not only a source of income to about one hundred thousand families but also a source of empowerment to the white-bearded old man and many like him. Thus, a repeat of the same sad spectacle was witnessed in the ensuing years, as it was for decades before. The aim is to ultimately break the bond that unites the native inhabitants of Palestine with their land and has since time immemorial. But will they succeed?

Resistance behind Bars

Palestinians who dare resist such injustice, regardless of the method by which they choose to rebel, often find themselves handcuffed and shackled before military judges, or, in most cases, thrown in jail without due process. The agony of Palestinian prisoners is the same as the greater agony of the Palestinian people, all suffering different manifestations of injustice throughout the Occupied Territory, inside Israel, or as refugees in exile. One such prisoner was Raed Abu Hammad, who was found dead on the floor of his cell in an Israeli prison in April 2010. He was ill, but he was kept in solitary confinement. The death of the twenty-seven-year-old inspired little media coverage. "Issa Qaraqi, minister of prisoner affairs in the Western-backed government of Palestinian President Mahmoud Abbas," reported the Israeli daily newspaper *Haaretz*, demanded "an investigation."[2] Israeli Prison Service authorities offered little by way of explanation. And as abruptly as the seemingly negligible news emerged, it disappeared.

Raed's death, of course, is neither the beginning nor the end of a very painful chapter of Palestinian resistance. There are thousands of Palestinian prisoners in Israeli jails, many of whom are held in solitary confinement for resisting the brutal policies of the Israeli occupation, for seeking freedom for their people, for fighting for the honour of their families and all Palestinians. However, they remain faceless and nameless to Israeli and Western media. To the Palestinian people, they represent the finest of Palestine's fighters, a collective retort to injustice, the antithesis to the politicking of the self-serving politicians, and much more.

In a prisoner exchange that saw the release of Gilad Shalit, the only Israeli soldier held by Palestinians in Gaza, on October 18, 2011, a total of 1,027 Palestinian prisoners were released in two phases.[3] These freed prisoners were spared the chains of their small cells, yet found themselves confined to larger open-air prisons, divided between Gaza—placed under a harsh siege since 2007—and the West Bank and East Jerusalem, sliced by the ever-growing apartheid wall and dotted with hundreds of military checkpoints. It was a bittersweet moment, as these men and women emerged from their buses, to be greeted by their families and thousands of cheering Palestinians, only to resume another long-term sentence, behind a wall, or at the other side of a military checkpoint.

While some of these released prisoners were, once again, unlawfully apprehended by the Israeli army, perhaps to return to the very cells in which they lived for many months or years, others carried on with life as best as they could. Hana Shalabi was one of those freed prisoners. Her story is troublingly typical. She spent twenty-five months under what Israel calls "administrative detention," a bizarre legal system that allows Israel to hold Palestinian political activists indefinitely and without charge or trial. She was released in October 2011 as part of the prisoner exchange deal, only to be kidnapped by soldiers a few months later. "She was beaten, blindfolded and forcibly strip-searched and assaulted by a male Israeli soldier," the Palestinian Council of Human Rights Organizations said. With no international action to oblige Israel to accept that "no one shall be subjected to arbitrary arrest, detention or exile,"—as stated in Article 9 of the Universal Declaration of Human Rights— Hana had little choice but to follow the path of other political prisoners. On February 16, 2012, she went on hunger strike. Forty-three days later, Hana was deported to Gaza, and was only allowed to be united with her family under Israeli military supervision, for a tear-filled twenty minutes at the Erez crossing. It will be another three years before they see her again.[4]

Hana's hunger strike followed that of Khader Adnan, who, at the time, had staged the longest hunger strike ever carried out by a Palestinian prisoner. Khader endured sixty-six days without food to send a message to his jailer that life without dignity is not worth living. Neither Hana's case, nor that of Khader is isolated by any means. Charlotte Kates, who is active with the National Lawyers Guild wrote, "Imprisonment is a fact of life for Palestinians; over 40% of Palestinian men in the West Bank have spent time in Israeli detention or prisons. There are no Palestinian families that have not been touched by the scourge of mass imprisonment as a mechanism of suppression."[5] According to the Addameer, "Since the beginning of the Israeli occupation of Palestinian territories in 1967, over 650,000 Palestinians have been detained by Israel. This forms approximately 20% of the total Palestinian population in the Occupied Palestinian Territories (OPT)."[6]

Addameer (Arabic for *conscience*) Prisoner Support and Human Rights Association has enough numbers and figures that would demonstrate without a doubt that Israel has violated every provision of the Geneva Convention relative to the Treatment of Prisoners (known also as the Third Geneva Convention), and every relevant international law. But while there is abundance of numbers, we rarely hear from the Palestinian prisoners themselves. On the other hand, who doesn't know Gilad Shalit, an Israeli soldier who contributed to the successive raids on besieged and impoverished Gaza? In Western media, Shalit was often portrayed as a victim, a hero, or some other positive or non-threatening expression, but never a killer, or a potential one. Khader, on the other hand, was arrested and demonized for "activities that threaten regional security," yet refused a trial, for none was possible with such insubstantial pretenses. As for the Palestinian prisoners, who are now "free," or rather yet to be re-imprisoned, they are the voices of Palestine's finest resisters; they are also the echo of the muted voices of 650,000 Palestinians who were imprisoned since 1967, and the millions who are confined behind menacing and expanding walls.

Refugees on the Run

Palestinian refugees are also prisoners, of a precarious legal status, of Israeli intransigence, of international negligence, and of Arab betrayal. When Israel was established on the ruins of hundreds of Palestinian towns and villages in 1947–1948, nearly a million Palestinians became refugees. Their suffering has not ceased since then, as three generations have now lived in the confines of that original sin, upon which Israel became a country. But the story of the refugees should not merely compel a historical pause, but a deep and profound consideration of the present and the future.

When a war becomes imminent, rich and politically powerful countries swiftly evacuate their citizens from areas of conflict using every means available. Other countries lag behind and often their refugees become stranded for months before they are transported home. And then, there are Palestinian refugees. The adversity of Palestinian refugees merely provides opportunities for political and other forms of exploitation. Few seek actual solutions and one is accused of being too radical for daring to suggest examining the roots of Palestinian statelessness or calling for the repatriation of the refugees to their lands in Palestine according to international law. If any "solution" is offered, they are merely partial solutions, which even then are half-hearted and insincere.

The latest expression of the protracted hardship was witnessed in Syria in its uprising turned regional power play and most destructive civil war. The destitution of hundreds of thousands of Palestinian refugees in Syria—whether they are internally displaced or those who successively braved the journey to Lebanon, Jordan, Turkey, among other places—was reported as a side note. Their suffering was often belittled and lumped into a much larger landscape of destitution. In fact, since the commencement of the so-called Arab Spring early 2011, a pattern of misleading comparisons also has surfaced. Palestinian victimization is juxtaposed in a disparaging way to other tragedies across the Middle East. According to some bizarre logic, Israeli leaders are emerging as more benevolent brutes than Arab leaders. Regardless of the intentions, Palestine and its refugees around the region were being downgraded as if their collective suffering and anguish of nearly seven decades are transitory matters, barely useful for self-indulging contrasts.

Even genuine voices distraught by the plight of refugees seem to echo in the same predictable pattern, a tedious attempt at making political points—organizing conferences, issuing statements—with little practical mechanism, except for the habitual detonations of UN resolutions. In the final analysis, however, nothing changes. The refugees seem destined to move about in an endless odyssey, amid fiery speech and heartening commentary.

While 1947-1948 marked the Palestinian Nakba or catastrophe[7]— initiating a bloody nomadic journey for nearly a million Palestinians— it was not the last exodus as other Nakbas followed and still continue today. Some are well known and others are scarcely discussed, such as the slow ethnic cleansing underway in occupied Jerusalem, West Bank, and the Naqab desert. In Lebanon, there were sub-Nakbas, where the refugees found themselves on an aimless run over and over again.

Syria defines the norm, not the exception. Iraq was another example of the same tragedy, even though refugees there were considered somewhat exempt from further suffering. Before the US invasion of Iraq in 2003, a small community of thirty-five thousand

Palestinians resided there. Following the invasion, they became an easy target for various militias, US forces, and criminal gangs. Many were killed, especially those who could not afford paying heavy ransoms haphazardly imposed by gunmen. Most of the refugees fled, seeking safe havens in Iraq. When that was no longer possible, they sought shelter in neighbouring countries. Allowing Palestinians entry into Arab countries, however, is not so simple. For this reason, thousands were stranded in newly constructed refugee camps at the Jordanian and Syrian borders.[8] They subsisted, some for years, fighting the elements in punishing deserts and surviving on handouts. Finally, many of them were sent to various non-Arab countries. It was a pitiful spectacle of the betrayal of Palestinians. The more passionately Arab regimes seem to speak of Palestine, the more inconsiderate they actually are of the plight of Palestinians. History has been consistently cruel this way.

The point must be repeatedly iterated. Iraq's Palestinian refugees belong in Palestine. For now, however, UN Resolution 194 of December 11, 1948,[9] pertaining to the right of return for Palestinian refugees, remains ink on paper. As long as Israel continues to flout international law, millions of Palestinian refugees will remain captive in regional struggles that use them as political fodder or see them as a demographic problem, or even worse, a threat. And with the United States ensuring that no meaningful action is ever taken to alleviate the suffering of the refugees, thousands will continue to find themselves at some border, queuing for food and pleading their cases to anyone willing to listen.

There are twelve refugee camps in Syria. Nine of them are registered as official camps by the UN Relief and Works Agency (UNRWA) and have a population of more than 496,000 refugees. Yarmouk alone, near Damascus, hosts an estimated 150,000 refugees.[10] This camp has been a recurring target for various militant groups and Syrian forces. Other camps have also been targeted in the brutal conflict, including Dera'a, Husseinieh, and Neirab among others. Hundreds of Palestinians have been killed in Syria.

They were either caught in the bloody conflict between the Syrian government and the opposition, or were purposely targeted under one pretext or another. Both sides of the bloody conflicts are responsible for extending the suffering of the Palestinians in Syria, as Israel remains the main party to blame for their original and continued dispossession. But the Palestinian leadership bears much responsibility as well, as it downgraded the urgency of the refugee crisis, thus the right of return, into something like an enigma that would be unravelled in one way or another during the final status talks between it and Israel. Of course there were no such talks and, according to the leaked Palestine Papers, it appears that the Palestinian National Authority had completely disowned the refugees in secret talks with Israeli officials.[11]

However, there is no changing the fact that most of the Syrian Palestinian refugees were driven from their homes in Palestine. The first wave arrived in 1948, mostly from Safad, Haifa, and Yafa; the second after Israel's occupation of the Golan Heights in 1967; and the third during Lebanon's civil war and Israel's wars on Lebanon. It is a multilayered, protracted tragedy. It demands a serious re-examination of the international community's dismissive attitude towards the refugees. Palestinian refugees are not simply fleeing multitudes caught in Arab conflicts, but they represent a grave political and moral crisis requiring immediate action, guided by Palestinian rights as enshrined in international law.

Demarcating History

All tragic stories of the greater Palestinian narrative—of those enduring the ongoing ethnic cleansing, those who are fighting for freedom, and those who are seeking their right of return have the same a beginning—the Nakba.[12] But no end is yet to be written. The storyline is neither simple nor linear—the refugee is fighting for the same freedom sought by the prisoner, the son of an old farmer, part of whose family are refugees in one place or another. It is convoluted and complex. It requires serious considerations of all of its aspects and characters. Perhaps no other place unites all of these ongoing tragedies like Gaza. Yet, as powerful as the Gaza narrative is, it has been deliberately cut off from urgently related narratives, whether in the rest of the Occupied Territory, or the historical landscape starting with the Nakba. To truly appreciate the situation in Gaza—whether the suffering, the siege, the repeated wars, the struggle, or the steadfastness and the resistance—the Gaza story, like all narratives concerning Palestine, would have to be placed within its proper context, as an essentially Palestinian story, of historical and political dimensions that surpass the current geographic and political boundaries demarcated by mainstream media and official narrators. The common failure to truly understand Gaza within an appropriate context is largely based on who is telling the story, how it is told, what is included, and what is omitted.

But most narratives concerning Palestinians in Western discourses are misleading or deliberately classified into simplified language that bears little resemblance to reality. History, however, cannot be classified in binaries, good vs. bad, heroes vs. villains, moderates vs. extremists. No matter how wicked, bloody, or despicable, history also tends to follow rational patterns, predictable courses. By understanding the reasoning behind historical dialectics, one can achieve more than a simple understanding of what took place in the past; it also becomes possible to chart fairly reasonable understanding of what lies ahead. Perhaps one of the worse aspects of today's detached and alienating media is its reproduction of the past—and mischaracterization of the present—based on simplified terminology. This gives the illusion of being informative but actually manages to contribute very little to our understanding of the world at large. Such oversimplifications are dangerous because they produce an erroneous understanding of the world, which in turn compels misguided actions.

For these reasons, we are compelled to discover alternative meanings and readings of history. To start, we could try offering

historical perspectives that try to see the world from the viewpoint of the oppressed—the refugees, the fellahin who have been
denied, amongst many rights, the right to tell their own story.
This view is not a sentimental one. Far from it. An elitist historical
narrative is maybe the dominant one, but it is not always the privileged who influence the course of history. History is also shaped by
collective movements, actions, and popular struggles. By denying
this fact, one denies the ability of the collective to affect change.
In the case of Palestinians, they are often presented as hapless
multitudes, passive victims without a will of their own. This is of
course a mistaken perception; the Palestinians' conflict with Israel
has lasted this long only because of their unwillingness to accept
injustice and their refusal to submit to oppression. Israel's lethal
weapons might have changed the landscape of Gaza and Palestine,
but the will of Gazans and Palestinians is what has shaped the
landscape of Palestine's history—composed of farmers, prisoners,
refugees, and numerous other manifestations and characters of
oppressed but resilient individuals.[13] It is essential that we understand the complexity of the past and the present to evolve in our
understanding of the conflict, not merely to appreciate its involved-
ness, but also to contribute positively to its resolution.

The Palestinian narrative was long either denied any meaningful access to the media or tainted through the very circles that
propped up and sanctified Israel's image as an oasis of democracy
and a pivot of civilization.[14] Things have begun to change, however,
thanks to developments such as the Internet and various global
civil society movements, although it is yet to reach critical mass or
affect a major paradigm shift in public opinion. But these voices
have been able to impose a long-neglected story that has been seen
mostly through Israeli eyes.

However, a narrative that is centred on the stories reflecting
history, reality, and aspirations of ordinary people will allow for
genuine understanding of the real dynamics that drive the conflict.
These stories that define whole generations of Palestinians are

powerful enough to challenge the ongoing partiality and polariza-
tion. The fact is Palestinians are neither potential "martyrs" nor
potential "terrorists." They are people who are denied basic human
rights, who have been dispossessed from their lands and are griev-
ously mistreated. They have resisted for over six decades, and they
will continue to resist until they acquire their fundamental human
rights. The core of the Palestinian narrative is the one that is least
told. A true understanding would require a greater exposure of the
extraordinary, collective narrative of the "ordinary people."

60

NOTES

1. Lara El-Jazairi, "The Road to Olive Farming: Challenges to Developing the
    Economy of Olive Oil in the West Bank," Oxfam briefing paper, October
    2010, http://www.oxfam.org/sites/www.oxfam.org/files/the-road-to-olive-
    farming_0.pdf.

2. Reuters, "Probe Death of Palestinian Prisoner in Israel Jail, PA Says." Haaretz,
    April 17, 2010, http://www.haaretz.com/news/
    probe-death-of-palestinian-prisoner-in-israel-jail-pa-says-1.284441.

3. "Shalabi's Mother: My Daughter Is Dying in Prison," Ma'an News Agency, March
    8, 2012, http://www.maannews.net/eng/ViewDetails.aspx?ID=466199.

4. Dylan Collins, "Israel's Farcical 'Compromise' with Hana Shalabi," Palestine
    Monitor, April 3, 2012, http://www.palestinemonitor.org/?p=4577.

5. Charlotte Kates, "Israeli Military Courts as Enforcement Mechanism of
    Occupation," Palestine Chronicle, February 23, 2012, http://palestinechronicle.
    com/view_article_details.php?id=19122.

6. Addameer, "Addameer Fact Sheet: Palestinians Detained by Israel," accessed May
    12, 2015, http://www.addameer.org/etemplate.php?id=275.

7. For more on Nakba (catastrophe), see Walid Khalidi, All That Remains: The
    Palestinian Villages Occupied and Depopulated by Israel in 1948, Arabic ed. (Beirut:
    Institute for Palestinian Studies, 1997).

8. UN High Commissioner for Refugees (UNHCR), Update of UNHCR Aide-Memoire
    of 2006: Protection Considerations for Palestinian refugees in Iraq, July 2012,
    http://www.unhcr.org/refworld/pdfid/500ebeea2.pdf.

9. UN General Assembly, Resolution 194 (III), "Palestine—Progress Report of the
    United Nations Mediator," December 11, 1948, http://unispal.un.org/UNISPAL.
    NSF/0/C758572B78D1CD0085256BCF0077E51A.

10. "Syria Camps Profile," UN Relief and Works Agency (UNRWA), n.d., accessed January 8, 2013, http://www.unrwa.org/where-we-work/syria/camp-profiles.

11. Amira Howeidy, "The Palestine Papers: PA Relinquished Right of Return," *Al Jazeera*, January 24, 2011, http://www.aljazeera.com/palestinepapers/2011/01/2011124121923486877.html.

12. For more on Nakba see Illan Pappe, *The Ethnic Cleansing of Palestine* (Oxford: One World Publications, 2006).

13. Ramzy Baroud, *My Father Was a Freedom Fighter: Gaza's Untold Story* (London: Pluto Press, 2010).

14. For more on this, see Greg Philo and Mike Berry, *Bad News from Israel* (London: Pluto Press, 2004).

61

PART II   **Activist Views**

International Solidarity
and the Palestinian
Freedom Struggle

HUWAIDA ARRAF

MY PARENTS made their way to the   65
United States a month before I, the oldest of five children, was born.
They were not kicked out of Palestine, as hundreds of thousands of
other Palestinians were, but, as a young couple, they decided to try
to start their family in a country where they could provide their
children with opportunity and hope, neither of which they saw
possible in Palestine. My father is from the Palestinian village of
Mi'ilya, located in the Upper Galilee, in the Akka[1] District, in part
of what is now Israel. Mi'ilya is one of only two all-Christian—
Melkite—villages left within Israel. Others faced fates like that of
Iqrit (also Ikrit) and Kfar Bir'im, Christian villages that were
depopulated by Israeli forces in 1948, with the promise that their
residents would be allowed to return after a few weeks; they never
were.[2] My mother is from the Israeli-occupied West Bank town of
Beit Sahour, near Bethlehem. Living in Mi'ilya would have meant
living as a second- or third-class citizens in a state that barely
tolerates the indigenous Palestinian inhabitants, and living in Beit
Sahour would have meant living under complete Israeli military
occupation. Neither promised a chance at a dignified life or an
optimistic future.

For the most part, I grew up in an apolitical home but there were some things that didn't escape me, even as a young child. One of these is why, after our 1986 visit, my parents stopped taking us on regular family trips to Palestine. At the time of our last family visit, I was ten years old, and old enough to understand the discrimination and public humiliation that we were subjected to and that ultimately turned my father off from returning. At the airport in Amsterdam, where we had a connection and where Israeli security scrutinize passengers on their way to Tel Aviv, and at the airport coming out of Israel, we were pulled aside and searched for hours. Security separated my father from us and took me, my mother, and my three younger sisters to be strip-searched. The search of our belongings and our persons went on for so long that the plane (in Amsterdam) took off without us.

Through a lot of hard work, my parents were able to provide a comfortable life for five children. I received a good education, earning my bachelor's degree from the University of Michigan, a place where I also became more politicized. I began to ask what my role in my people's liberation struggle was. I realized that because of my parents' decision to leave Palestine, I had a privileged life filled with opportunities that most Palestinians do not have. With that privilege and opportunity came responsibility.

In the spring of 2000 I decided to move to Jerusalem to accept a position with a conflict resolution program working with Israeli and Palestinian youth. Less than six months later, the second Palestinian intifada erupted.

On September 28, 2000, hardline Israeli opposition leader Ariel Sharon made a highly provocative visit to Al-Haram Al-Shareef, the Nobel Sanctuary, which is the site of Al-Aqsa Mosque. It is also known as the Temple Mount to Jews. Palestinian Authority President Yasser Arafat is reported to have pleaded with the Israeli Prime Minister Ehud Barak not to allow Sharon to go through with the visit as Palestinians consider Sharon to have the blood of thousands of Palestinians on his hands from the 1982 massacres at the

Sabra and Shatilla refugee camps.[3] A visit by him to the holiest site in Jerusalem for Muslims for a "political demonstration" to show "that under a Likud government [the Temple Mount] will remain under Israeli sovereignty" would inflame Palestinians and surely cause much unrest.[4] Barak, however, did not stop the visit, and in fact provided Sharon and a Likud Party delegation with hundreds of police and security forces to accompany them.

Predictably, demonstrations ensued that day following Sharon's visit and escalated the next day, after Friday prayers. Israeli forces responded to Palestinian demonstrations with live ammunition and rubber-coated steel bullets, killing seven Palestinians on September 29, 2000 and wounding dozens more. These deaths sparked more demonstrations, or what Israel would call "riots" across the West Bank, Gaza, and in Palestinian communities within Israel, all of which Israeli forces responded to with lethal force. Although Palestinian protesters were unarmed, Israel saw it fit to attack the demonstrators with bullets. According to Israeli sources, Israeli soldiers fired over one million bullets during the first few days of the second intifada.[5] One of those bullets killed a dear friend, one of the youth in the conflict resolution program that I was working for, seventeen-year-old Aseel Asleh, a Palestinian citizen of Israel.[6] According to eyewitness accounts, Aseel was participating in a demonstration at the edge of his village of Arrabeh when he was chased into an olive grove by Israeli soldiers. A bullet to his heel indicates that he was immobilized before a rubber-coated steel bullet was shot into the back of his neck at point-blank range. Aseel had been wearing his Seeds of Peace T-shirt when he was shot dead, and his family decided to bury him in it.

The first month of the second intifada was characterized by popular Palestinian demonstrations—men, women, and children taking to the streets to express their rejection of Israeli occupation policies and their frustration with a "peace process" that for seven years had gone nowhere. Although Ariel Sharon's visit to the Nobel Sanctuary triggered the intifada, the provocation was the spark and not the cause. Rather, the cause was the continued colonization of Palestine under the guise of a "peace process." The Oslo Peace Accords, signed by Palestine Liberation Organization Chairman Yasser Arafat and Israeli Prime Minister Yitzhak Rabin on the White House lawn on September 13, 1993 was received with much fanfare and talk of the "dawn of a new era in the Middle East." The accords, based on UN Resolutions 242 and 338, which called for Israel to withdraw from the territories that it occupied after the 1967 war, provided for the establishment of a Palestinian state, living side by side with Israel, within five years. Although issues of final borders, settlements, water, refugees, and Jerusalem, were not agreed upon and left to "final status" negotiations, the establishment of a viable and independent Palestinian state on the 1967 borders necessarily meant that the illegal colonies Israel had built over the last thirty-plus years would have to be dismantled. However, that is not what happened. In the seven years from 1993 to 2000, Israel not only continued but accelerated its process of settlement expansion and confiscation of Palestinians' land. During that period, the number of illegal settlers in Israeli colonies doubled from 200,000 to 400,000;[7] Israel confiscated and razed Palestinian farmland to build bypass roads—roads connecting the Jewish colonies to each other and to Israel so that settlers would not have to enter Palestinian towns and villages to travel through the Occupied West Bank. From 1994 to 1996 Israel confiscated over 4,300 dunums (4.3 km²) of privately owned Palestinian land for the construction of a network of 17 bypass roads for settlers.[8] From 1996 to 2002, the total land area taken up by such roads in the West Bank increased from 400 km² to 620 km².[9] These roads, though built on occupied Palestinian land, were off limits to Palestinians.

In addition to expansion of its colonial infrastructure during the Oslo era, Israel continued its policy of demolishing Palestinian homes, particularly in East Jerusalem, tightened its control over Palestinian movement, and continued to carry out political arrests. Palestinian complaints about Israeli violations of the Oslo Accords were marginalized for the benefit of sustaining the "peace process." Thus, the outbreak of the second intifada represented a culmination of Palestinian frustration with the sham of Oslo and a statement to the world that "we are no longer willing to be part of this facade of a peace process." Unfortunately, this message was muted as Palestinians were blamed for turning their backs on the peace process and choosing the path of violence.[10]

After a few weeks of violent repression by Israeli forces, the popular demonstrations died down and the second Palestinian intifada took on an armed characteristic. Civilians largely stopped taking to the streets, not because Palestinians suddenly became afraid or unwilling to risk their lives for their freedom but because of a culmination of factors that diminished people's belief that there was any kind of utility to the popular demonstrations.

To understand this, it is important to understand the Palestinian history of non-violent resistance. It's a rich history, scarcely recognized. Most would be surprised to know that many of the tactics used by icons of non-violent resistance throughout history, such as Gandhi and Dr. Martin Luther King Jr., have been used by Palestinians to resist the occupation and colonization of their land. The height of co-ordinated Palestinian non-violent resistance was probably the first intifada, from 1987 to 1993. During that period, Palestinians, organized into local popular committees throughout the West Bank, including East Jerusalem and Gaza, led a popular, largely non-violent campaign to "shake off" the occupation.[11] Thousands of Palestinians were arrested and served many years in prison for their role in the first intifada. But these years in prison were served proudly by a people who had taken their fates into their own hands and believed in the power of their collective action. The first intifada came to an end when the leadership of the Palestine Liberation Organization (PLO), located outside the Occupied Palestinian Territory (OPT), signed the Oslo Accords, an agreement that had been negotiated in secret, without the knowledge of or representation from the Palestinians engaged in struggle on the ground. For those that remembered, or were active in the first intifada, it was hard to overcome a feeling of disempowerment—a feeling that no matter what you did, higher powers were calling the shots.

Add to this Israel's excessive use of force against unarmed protesters and the fact that Palestinians were being blamed for their own deaths. Within the first month of the intifada, by the end of October 2000, 161 Palestinians had been killed by Israeli forces. Twelve Israelis, of which six were soldiers and four settlers, were killed by Palestinians.[12] However, as mentioned above, the prevailing narrative was that Palestinians had abandoned the path of peace; subsequently, the violence was the fault of the Palestinians. As such, demonstrations were not managing to garner international public support for the Palestinian struggle. These and other factors raised serious doubt as to the effectiveness of continued demonstrations. If you don't believe that the actions you are risking your lives to undertake will make a difference, then it does not make strategic sense to engage in them. Yet emotions were running high and the desire to seek revenge for all the killing was strong, and therefore those that had guns in Palestinian society began using them.

Against this backdrop, I searched for my role in what was happening. How could I contribute to my people's liberation struggle? I couldn't pick up a gun, nor did I necessarily believe that an armed uprising was a strategically wise choice for Palestinians. Yet the popular struggle had fizzled and it was difficult to convince most Palestinians that anything we could do would make a difference.

Propelled by a sense of indignation at the thought that Israel could get away with what it was doing and have the full support of the United States, infused with ignorance as to the history of my own people's struggle, and a bit of naïveté, I began to seek out some leaders of the first Palestinian intifada. How did they do it? I wanted to know. And how could we revive the Palestinian belief in our collective power? I threw out ideas for creative actions, only to learn that nothing I was suggesting was new. Palestinians had tried it all before. From strikes and boycotts, to burning ID cards in order to create chaos for the Israeli occupation forces that demanded every Palestinian carry and ID card, Palestinians had vast experience engaging in various forms of civil disobedience. When the Israeli military shut down Palestinian schools and universities during the first intifada, parents organized underground schooling, and professors arranged alternative meeting places with their students so that the learning continued. My mom's town of Beit Sahour organized a tax strike in 1989, with the residents of the town refusing to pay taxes to the Israeli authorities. To break the will of the people, the Israeli military authorities placed Beit Sahour under curfew for forty-two days, blocked the delivery of staples into the town, cut telephone lines, and conducted house-to-house raids seizing millions of dollars in money and property. They also imprisoned forty residents believed to be organizers of the strike, blocked foreign diplomats from visiting to investigate, and tried to bar reporters from entering the town.

How do we bring this spirit back? In one meeting I was told, "Huwaida, you're right, we need to revive the popular resistance as our strength is in our people, but my generation—the generation that lived and was active in the first intifada, we're tired, and we're disillusioned. We led a powerful resistance, only to have the rug pulled out from underneath us. It's your generation, the young and idealistic that need to carry this forward." I thought, "Great! But how?"

One organizer during the first intifada who didn't allow disillusionment turn into disempowerment was Dr. Ghassan Andoni, a resident of Beit Sahour and then director of the Palestinian Centre for Rapprochement. At a meeting organized at the centre, I met Israeli activist Neta Golan, and others with whom I would go on to co-found the International Solidarity Movement (ISM). The idea behind the ISM was to support and strengthen the Palestinian popular resistance by providing the Palestinian people with a resource, international protection, and a voice with which to resist, non-violently, an overwhelming military occupation force.

The launching campaign of the ISM was called for August of 2001. We, or at least I, had visions of thousands of internationals standing with Palestinians, forming a massive civilian army and blocking the Israeli army from invading Palestinian villages. At the same time, we really didn't know if anyone would respond to our call. Reports and images of dozens killed and injured every day had my mother constantly calling me from the United States, urging me to "come home." But for me, I was home. I am Palestinian. Would people who are not Palestinian risk their lives to come stand with us?

Thousands didn't come. Not even hundreds came. For our first campaign, fifty people from various countries, primarily from the United States and the United Kingdom, came to join us for a two-week, co-ordinated campaign of non-violent direct action against various manifestations of the Israeli occupation. Those who joined us returned to their home countries to share their experiences with their friends, family, and colleagues, to engage in education and advocacy initiatives in their communities, and to encourage more volunteers to travel to Palestine. Primarily as a result of encouragement from those first ISM campaigners, we decided to organize another campaign for Christmas 2001.

It is important for internationals to join the Palestinian struggle for four key reasons. The first reason is protective accompaniment: an international presence at Palestinian civilian actions and protests can help provide a certain level of protection for the Palestinian people engaged in non-violent resistance. Palestinians engaging in protest activities alone are often met with harsh and even lethal forms of violence by Israeli occupation forces, including arbitrary, long-term arrest, beating, severe injury, and sometimes even death. Israel has succeeded in labelling every Palestinian man, woman, and child as a potential terrorist to justify its physical and structural violence against us. No one holds Israel accountable for Palestinian lives. Foreign civilians, however, are not so easily labelled "terrorists," and they have governments responsible for them to hold Israel accountable for harm that may come to them.

If for none other than purposes of image and public relations, Israel would rather not injure or kill internationals, and so when they are present, generally orders are for soldiers to be more restrained. This is not a hard and fast rule, however. Palestinians have been seriously injured and killed at demonstrations in which internationals have been present. Internationals have also been seriously injured and killed.

Second, having internationals join the Palestinian struggle sends a message to the mainstream media. The Palestinian struggle is not accurately reported by the mainstream corporate international media. To give one example, back in 2001, I participated in a large demonstration organized by Birzeit University students and staff, under the banner of a right to education. The purpose of the demonstration was to repair the main road from Ramallah to Birzeit (and thirty other villages), in which the Israeli military had dug a huge trench, halting all traffic. Over two thousand people participated in that demonstration, and we repaired the road using only our hands, as to not give Israel the opportunity to claim that any tools we might have used were weapons. As soon as the trench was filled in and the first car was able to pass, an Israeli military bulldozer arrived on the scene to tear up the road again. Soldiers fired tear gas to disperse us so the bulldozer could work, which prompted some students to throw stones at the bulldozer. Israeli soldiers opened fire, killing one and injuring ten. The American media described our action and ensuing events as "clashes" between Palestinians and Israeli soldiers, rather than what it really was—Israeli forces opening fire on a peaceful demonstration of Palestinian university students and staff demanding the right to education.

The mainstream media fails to convey the Palestinian struggle as the struggle for freedom, dignity, and human rights that it is. Rather, Palestinians are inaccurately depicted as a violent people who want to destroy Israel. Or, at best, this is a "conflict" in which two equal sides are fighting over a piece of land. This "conflict" is not Palestinians vs. Israelis, or Muslims and Christians vs. Jews; it is freedom and dignity vs. occupation, apartheid, and oppression. As such, people of various social, national, and religious backgrounds, including Jews, joining Palestinians in the freedom struggle can help us convey this message.

Third, international civilians who join Palestinians on the ground can engage alternative media and advocacy. They can bear witness and return home to talk to their communities about what is happening. This helps create alternative sources of information to the mainstream media. Even if we have to educate people one person at a time, we are working so that one day everyone will know what was happening to Palestinians while the international community was silent. At the same time, we encourage this knowledge to be turned into action. Since Israel could not maintain its occupation and colonization project without the acquiescence of states, corporations, and institutions that maintain regular or enhanced diplomatic and economic relations with Israel, Palestine needs international civilians to advocate for a change in their countries' foreign policy, and for boycott of and divestment from the occupation.

Finally, having internationals join the Palestinian struggle breaks isolation and provides hope. The occupation isolates Palestinians and cuts the Palestinian people off from the rest of the world and from each other. Israel controls all entrances into and exits out of the occupied Palestinian territory,[13] controls almost all movement of Palestinians and, except for moderate relaxing of restrictions on the Rafah border following the ouster of the Mubarak regime in Egypt, can prevent, at will, all access of the international community to Palestinians. This isolation is compounded by a feeling that Palestinians have been abandoned by the international community. The UN and formal bodies commissioned with defending human rights have failed to hold Israel accountable for violations of Palestinian basic rights. In contrast, international civilians coming in despite restrictions (many times volunteers have had to walk hours to get around Israeli roadblocks, checkpoints, and complete closure of Palestinian areas, to get in to Palestinian communities) sends a message to the Palestinian people—"we see, we hear, and we are with you." At the very least, international civilians have been able to raise the morale of the Palestinian people with the powerful message, "you are not alone." One phone call that I will never forget I received in April of 2002. Israel had reinvaded Palestinian cities with ground troops, Palestinians were under house arrest, and the Israeli military was carrying out various operations throughout the OPT. I was based in Jerusalem, training volunteers as they arrived in response to our emergency appeal, and sending out teams to some of the most hard-hit areas. One day I received a call from a man in Nablus. The Israeli army was conducting house-to-house raids in Nablus, blowing up doors, ransacking homes, and rounding up men between the ages of fifteen and fifty. ISM's small team of volunteers was following the soldiers to let them know that someone was watching, and urging soldiers not to use violence against civilians. The man on the other end of the line told me that he was in his home with his family and expecting the soldiers to raid shortly: "I see the internationals on the street. I don't think that they'll be able to do anything to protect me and my family; but I know they are here with us and I just wanted to say thank you." Then he hung up. I never found out the man's name, how he got my phone number, or what happened to him. But his phone call confirmed to me the importance of international solidarity on this very personal, individual level.

While the primary purpose of the ISM has been to engage in and support the Palestinian unarmed, civilian-based freedom struggle, due to the regular and unmitigated aggression of the Israeli military and settlers against Palestinian civilians, the ISM has also had to take up a role in providing humanitarian assistance and protection by using their status as internationals to escort doctors, ambulances, schoolchildren, and other civilians to work, hospital, and school. One of the regions in which accompaniment and a solidarity presence constituted the crux of the ISM's work was in Gaza. From 2001 to 2003, we were able to get volunteers into Gaza through the Beit Hanoun (Erez) crossing. Our volunteers in Gaza spent a lot of time in Rafah, which is on the border with Egypt and the site of frequent Israeli military activity, including demolishing homes to create a "buffer zone." Solidarity actions included visiting schools and community centres, accompanying workers to repair wells and other structures destroyed by the Israeli military, and staying overnight with families whose neighbourhoods and homes would come under constant fire from the Israeli army.

On March 16, 2003, one of our volunteers, twenty-three-year-old American Rachel Corrie, bravely stood in front of an Israeli military bulldozer[14] that had come to demolish the home of Dr. Samir Nasrallah, a local pharmacist—a bullet-riddled home in which Rachel had been staying with Dr. Samir and his family. Donning a bright orange reflective jacket, and carrying a bullhorn, Rachel attempted to reason with the bulldozer driver. The bulldozer driver played "cat and mouse" with her, advancing and then stopping and retreating as Rachel stood her ground in front of the house. Then, at one point, after about two hours, the bulldozer driver decided not to stop and ran Rachel over, crushing her to death under the blade of the armoured vehicle. Three and a half weeks later, on April 11, British photography student and ISM volunteer, twenty-one-year-old Tom Hurndall was shot in the back of the head by an Israeli sniper as he attempted to move Palestinian children out of the line of Israeli fire. Tom was also wearing a reflective vest and clearly not posing any threat to Israeli soldiers when he was sniped. He lay in coma for nine months then passed away on January 13, 2004. Three weeks after Tom's shooting, on May 2, 2003, James Miller, an award-winning British journalist and documentary filmmaker, was shot dead by the Israeli military in Gaza.

The lethal injury and killing of three foreigners in Gaza in less than two months brought scrutiny down upon Israel and led the Israeli government to close off Gaza to internationals, with very few exceptions. No longer could one just show up at the Beit Hanoun (Erez) crossing and seek entry into Gaza. Now one had to submit an application to the Israeli military's Southern Command, with a declared purpose for the visit that Israel considered legitimate, and wait for approval. Approvals were largely limited to individuals who worked for international organizations that Israel condoned and Israeli-sanctioned journalists. Many of these workers and journalists reported being made to sign waivers before entering Gaza stating that they are not going to Gaza to work with the ISM and that the Israeli military cannot be held responsible for their safety. From that point, it became very difficult for the ISM to send volunteers to Gaza and the ISM was largely cut off from Gaza until years later.

The isolation of Gaza continued to grow, with the situation deteriorating following Israel's unilateral "disengagement" in August/ September 2005. In a much heralded "pullout" from Gaza, Israel evacuated approximately nine thousand Jewish settlers from twenty-one illegal colonies in Gaza and redeployed its military from within the Gaza Strip to its borders. It then proceeded to proclaim that Gaza was no longer occupied. However, nothing about Israel's disengagement ended its occupation, or the isolation of Gaza. Israel continued to control Gaza by land, sea, and air, and to enforce a near complete separation of Gaza from the West Bank and from the rest of the world. Under international law, the measure of whether a territory is occupied is not boots on the ground, but rather the measure of "effective control" that a foreign power has over a territory.[15] In addition to control over Gaza's land crossings, airspace, and territorial waters, the Israeli military maintains a buffer zone inside Gaza's borders, covering approximately one-third of Gaza's agricultural land, and shoots at Palestinians who enter this area. Israel controls what goods come in and out of Gaza, including food and medicine, and controls Gaza's access to fuel, water, and electricity, Gaza's economy, and Gaza's population registry. As such, Israel maintains effective control over Gaza and consequently still occupies Gaza.

After elections for the Palestinian Legislative Council in January 2006 saw Hamas win a majority of seats, the United States and European Union countries cut off international aid to the Palestinian Authority, and Israel undertook a series of punitive measures, including withholding tax revenues that Israel collects on behalf of the Palestinian Authority, and severely restricting the movement of goods and labourers in and out of the occupied Palestinian territory. These measures were not only crippling to an economy largely dependent on Israel facilitating movement and trade as well as on foreign aid,[16] but they also represented the collective punishment of a people as a result of their vote in a democratic elections process.

Following internal strife in which Hamas, claiming it was preempting a planned Fatah coup, ousted Fatah officials and took control of Gaza, the international community lifted its sanctions on the Palestinian Authority in the West Bank to boost Mahmoud Abbas's government. At the same time, Israel placed more severe restrictions on Gaza, imposing a near hermetic closure on the territory. The restrictions included a ban on exports from Gaza and a ban on imports, except for humanitarian aid. Truckloads allowed into Gaza were significantly reduced from the required 10,400 trucks per month, according to the average in 2005, to 2,500 truckloads per month,[17] and the kinds of goods allowed limited to an unpublished list. According to Israeli authorities, the entrance of goods into Gaza was limited to a "humanitarian minimum," which includes only those goods that are considered "essential to the survival of the civilian population."[18] As such, a wide range of food items, batteries, toys, certain medical supplies, schools supplies, all raw materials, and much more were banned. Israel also cut fuel and electricity to the Gaza Strip. This policy, declared illegal collective punishment by the UN and human rights and humanitarian organizations, led to a severe decline in the humanitarian situation of the people in the Gaza Strip. Patients died from a lack of access to required medicine and necessary medical care, the majority of

factories shut down, unemployment rose to over 40 per cent, over
80 per cent of the population became food aid dependent, and the
general health and welfare of Gaza's most vulnerable increased,
with a rise in the rate of anemia in children and pregnant women,
as well as instances of malnutrition and stunted growth in
children.[19]

Because Israel banned the import of materials needed to fix
the sanitation system in Gaza, approximately eighty million litres
of untreated or partially treated sewage is dumped into the
Mediterranean Sea every day. Between 90 per cent and 95 per cent
of the water in Gaza does not meet the minimum standard set by
the World Health Organization and is unfit for human consumption. As a result, incidents of water sanitation-related illnesses such
as typhoid fever and diarrhea increased sharply, with cases doubling
in children under the age of three.[20] And the list goes on. Perhaps
this situation doesn't constitute the worst humanitarian situation
in the world, but it is a situation created as a result of a deliberate
policy to punish and break an entire people. It created a crisis of
human dignity and a challenge to the international community to
do something to stop Israel.

Yet, despite the reports, the statistics, the verbal condemnation
of Israel's policy by humanitarian agency representatives, no one
did anything to make Israel stop.

At this time, a handful of former ISM volunteers, dismayed at
the lack of action to force Israel to end its deliberate persecution of
Palestinians in Gaza, began discussing what average civilians could
do.[21] "Let's sail a boat to Gaza," suggested an Australian colleague.
I was initially skeptical—not only did one of the most powerful
militaries in the world have a naval blockade on Gaza, but we did
not have a boat, or the money to get a boat, or know the first thing
about boats! Yet no one had a better idea of something that we
could do to address the severity of the situation, and so we decided
to put our minds to it and make it happen. A year and a half later,
on August 22, 2008, forty-four people from seventeen different

countries boarded two small, refurbished fishing boats in Cyprus and set sail for Gaza. Before voyaging into the Mediterranean, we reviewed every scenario that we could think of, including being sunk, shot at, blockaded, and arrested. With the veracity of Israel's threats against the mission, everyone understood that the undertaking was a dangerous one. In pre-voyage training, we clearly told everyone, "if you're not prepared for the possibility of being seriously injured, or maybe even killed, then don't step foot on those boats." No one turned back. It's not that anyone wanted to die; our group consisted of parents, grandparents, students, medical workers, journalists, professors, and others; all had jobs and families that they wanted to return to. At the same time, we strongly believed in the power and necessity of what we were doing.

We did not expect to actually reach Gaza. Our hope was to expose Israel's closure policy as not about security, as Israeli leaders proclaimed to the world. With two small, Greek registered fishing boats departing from Cyprus, checked by Cypriot port authorities, carrying hearing aids, balloons for children, and people from various religious, cultural, and professional backgrounds, ranging in age from twenty-one to eighty-one, including a Catholic nun and a Greek parliamentarian, we did not constitute a threat to Israel. Therefore, if Israel decided to prevent us from reaching Gaza, it would show to the world that this was not at all about security, but rather to enforce the isolation and strangulation of the people in Gaza. We hoped that the exposure would then compel action.

Within a few hours of setting sail, all of our satellite phone signals were jammed so we lost communication with our land support team and with the media; one by one, passengers fell sick; and the media boat that we had arranged to meet us at sea to document our confrontation with the Israeli navy never found us. Nevertheless, we continued. Then on August 23, 2008, after over thirty-two hours at sea and over thirty sick passengers, including our resident doctor and two nurses, we crossed into Gaza's territorial waters. We couldn't believe it. Despite all the threats, Israel decided not to intercept our boats and we were actually going to make it to Gaza! Palestinian fishermen jumped in their boats and came out to meet us; young boys jumped into the sea to swim out to us; and tens of thousands of elated Palestinians rushed to the port to welcome us with excitement, honour, and humbling gratitude. The mantra became "we broke the siege!" However, we hadn't broken the siege. What we had done was overcome the blockade once. To really break Israel's stranglehold on Gaza, we would have to repeat our action again and again, until we effectively managed to open a sea route to Gaza. This is what we promised the people of Gaza that we would do.

A few days later, we left Gaza the same way that we came. Eight volunteers decided to stay in Gaza to accompany farmers and fishermen who regularly get shot at by Israeli forces, and to restart the ISM in Gaza. In their place, we took out Palestinians. One of the people that we took out was sixteen-year-old Sa'ed Musleh, who was loaded onto our boat in his wheelchair. Two years earlier, Sa'ed had his leg amputated from the hip after being injured by shrapnel from an Israeli tank shell fired into his neighbourhood. After his amputation, Israel denied Sa'ed the permission to seek a prosthetic leg in either Israel or a foreign country.

From October to December 2008, the Free Gaza Movement, as we decided to call ourselves, organized four more successful sea voyages to Gaza, taking in doctors, lawyers, journalists, professors, parliamentarians, a Nobel Peace laureate, and others who could not enter Gaza any other way. We were also able to take out of Gaza dozens of Palestinians who needed to travel for medical purposes or to take up educational opportunities in foreign countries but were prevented from doing so by Israel. On our humble boats, for the first time Palestinians were able to exit and enter their homeland freely. It was beginning to look like a sea route to Gaza had indeed been opened; unfortunately, we were the only ones using it as we had not managed to convince other organizations frustrated by Israel's blockade on Gaza, such as the UN Relief and Works Agency, to follow suit.

Two days after Israel launched massive air strikes on the Gaza Strip commencing Operation Cast Lead—a twenty-two-day assault that led to the killing of over 1,400 Palestinians and the destruction of thousands of homes, schools, hospitals, businesses, and mosques—the Free Gaza Movement organized an emergency mission to Gaza. On a small, twenty-two-metre yacht called the *Dignity*, we loaded three tons of medical supplies and sixteen volunteers, including four doctors, a Cypriot member of Parliament, a former US congresswoman, and journalists from CNN and Al Jazeera. On December 30, 2008, in the dark of night and still ninety miles from the coast of Gaza, an Israeli warship rammed the small vessel three times, and left it to sink. With the help of the Lebanese Coast Guard, the captain was able to maneuver the *Dignity* safely to the southern Lebanese port of Tyre. Two more attempts to reach Gaza via the sea, on January 14 and June 29, were each violently intercepted by the Israeli navy.

In the summer of 2009, after three unsuccessful attempts to reach Gaza via the sea, we were faced with the question of what to do. Some were questioning the utility of continuing to send boats to Gaza, but, for us, giving up was not an option as we refused to give into the notion that military might was stronger than the rights that we were fighting for. However, in order to overcome Israel's apparent determination to put an end to our efforts, we had to make the cost of stopping us much higher for Israel. Instead of sending one small boat with a few dozen people and a symbolic amount of supplies on it, we would need to send many boats! And thus we began organizing. From Chile to South Africa, India to the United States, we recruited community groups, unions, parliamentarians, journalists, and other individuals to support our new, larger-scale, non-violent, direct-action effort to end Israel's strangulation of Gaza—the Freedom Flotilla.

On May 30, 2010, six vessels, carrying approximately ten thousand tons of aid and nearly seven hundred people from thirty-five countries, met in the middle of the Mediterranean Sea and started en route to Gaza. A seventh vessel, a cargo ship named the *Rachel Corrie*, had fallen five days behind due to attempts at sabotage. In the middle of the night, the Israeli navy radioed demanding that we turn around. "We are unarmed civilians, carrying only humanitarian aid for the people of Gaza; we constitute no threat to Israel... don't use force against us," I repeated over and over into the VHF radio. What happened next was witnessed across the globe. At shortly after four o'clock on the morning of May 31, Israel launched a full-scale military assault on the Freedom Flotilla in international waters. Our satellite capabilities were jammed as masked, armed commandos came at us from the air and sea, using sound grenades, tasers, attack dogs, and bullets to raid and overtake all six vessels. The first things the soldiers went for were our communications and recording equipment. They confiscated our phones and cameras, arrested everyone on board, and held us near incommunicado for days, ensuring that the Israel's version of the events dominated the news.

Nine of our colleagues were shot dead and fifty others were injured that night. Israel never returned any of our footage and refused to co-operate with an independent fact-finding mission (FFM) commissioned by the UN Human Rights Council to investigate the flotilla raid. The FFM's final report found that Israel's blockade of Gaza was unlawful, that the flotilla did not constitute an imminent threat to Israel and thus its interception in international waters was unlawful, and that the force used by Israel to intercept the flotilla was unlawful. The report also found that six of our murdered colleagues were most likely executed, and concluded that there was enough evidence to pursue prosecution against Israel for willful killing, torture, and causing great bodily harm.[22]

If Israel's goal in launching such a massive attack on our civilian convoy was deterrence—to break the momentum of the boat missions and scare activists from engaging in similar feats—its strategy of force failed. The brutality of the assault on the flotilla led to an increase of support for this kind of non-violent, direct action. Dozens of new organizations and thousands more people joined efforts to plan Freedom Flotilla II, and impetus was given to the global boycott, divestment, and sanctions movement (BDS).[23] Among other things, Swedish dockworkers refused to unload Israeli cargo ships,[24] American dockworkers in Oakland, California refused to cross a picket line to unload an Israeli ship,[25] and international artists such as the Pixies, Klaxons, and the Gorillaz Sound System cancelled scheduled performances in Israel.[26] Moreover, worldwide condemnation of Israel's actions as well as strong demands coming from Europe forced Israel to ease its closure on Gaza. Even though the easing of the closure was only cosmetic, the fact that civilian action created the necessary pressure on Israel to compel that change was and remains significant.

While ISM and the Free Gaza Movement were ways that international solidarity could be made manifest on the ground in Palestine and in direct-action challenges to Israel's oppressive policies, BDS presented an opportunity for people around the world to take concrete action against Israel's colonial occupation from their own hometowns. Launched in 2005 by over 170 Palestinian civil society organizations, unions, and political factions, BDS called for the isolation of Israel and profiteers from its occupation, much as was done to apartheid South Africa decades earlier. Not surprisingly, at the forefront of many BDS groups around the world are people who had joined us in Palestine—witnessing, breathing tear gas, standing in endless lines at checkpoints, enduring Orwellian questioning by teenage Israeli soldiers, and experiencing the terror of Israeli military operations. Back in their own countries, nearly all were keen to do something to take those lessons and experiences home and challenge international complicity in the daily drumbeat of occupation. BDS has provided an outlet by which this could be done as part of an effective, global campaign led by Palestinian civil society.

For over six decades, Palestinians have and continue to engage in the most powerful forms of resistance—maintaining attachment, in spite of overwhelming forces, to our land, culture, history, and humanity. For the struggle to end in the realization of justice, and a true peace based on freedom, dignity, and equality for all people in the region, global civilian action challenging colonialism, violence, racism, and oppression must continue and intensify. Left to world "leaders," we're bound for more of the same; but in the words of Gandhi, if we "the people lead, the leaders will follow."

NOTES

1. There are various spellings for this district, including Akko and Acre.

2. Israeli forces depopulated the villages "until the security situation allows their return." In 1951, the Israeli High Court ruled that the villagers were allowed to return "as long as no emergency decree" against it has been issued. The government hastened to issue a decree against the Iqrit refugees. Two months later, the Israeli military blew up their houses. In 1953, it blew up the houses of Kfar Bir'im. In 1955, the land of the two villages was expropriated for establishing Jewish settlements. See Ilan Pappe, *The Forgotten Palestinians: A History of the Palestinians in Israel* (New Haven, CT: Yale University Press, 2011), 158–59.

3. From September 16 to 18, 1982, the Israeli military, led by Defense Minister Ariel Sharon, surrounded the Sabra and Shatilla Palestinian refugee camps in Lebanon, while Lebanese Phalangist Militia went in and massacred civilians. See Robert Fisk, "The Legacy of Ariel Sharon—The Butcher of Sabra and Chatila," *Independent* (UK), February 6, 2001, reprinted at http://rense.com/general8/butcher.htm. A UN commission as well as an Israeli commission set up to investigate both found that Ariel Sharon bore responsibility for the attack. See Seán MacBride, et al., *Israel in Lebanon: The Report of International Commission to Enquire into Reported Violations of International Law by Israel during Its Invasion of the Lebanon* (London: Ithaca Press, 1983), 191–92, and Kahan Commission, *Report of the Commission of Inquiry into the Events at the Refugee Camps in Beirut*, February 8, 1983, Council on Foreign Relations, http://www.cfr.org/israel/report-kahan-commission/p15290.

4. Likud spokesman Ofir Akounis qtd. in CNN, "Palestinians Say Opposition Tour of Holy Site Could Cause Bloodshed," September 27, 2000, reprinted at http://journals.democraticunderground.com/Douglas%20Carpenter/356.

5. Reuven Pedatzur, "More than a Million Bullets," *Haaretz*, June 29, 2004, http://www.haaretz.com/print-edition/opinion/more-than-a-million-bullets-1.127053.

6. From October 1 to 8, 2000, Israeli forces killed thirteen Palestinian citizens of Israel in what became known as "Black October." The Israeli government appointed a commission headed by Judge Theodore Or to investigate the events of October 2000. The commission's report, released on September 2, 2003, found

HUWAIDA ARRAF

that Israeli forces were not justified in using live ammunition, rubber-coated steel bullets, and snipers to disperse demonstrations; that none of the protesters constituted a danger to the lives of the security forces to justify their shooting; and in fact that the opening of fire by Israeli forces was not legal. However, the commission was only authorized to issue recommendations and ultimately none of those responsible for the deaths was held accountable. Adalah, "12 Years since the October 2000 Killings and the Victims' Families Continue to Demand Accountability," press release, February 10, 2012, http://www.adalah.org/eng/Articles/1839/12-Years-Since-the-October-2000-Killings:-Adalah-to. See also Seeds of Peace, *Or Commission Materials*, accessed January 20, 2013, http://www.seedsofpeace.org/?page_id=4032.

7.   I use the terms *settlement* and *colony* and their plural forms interchangeably. Israel refers to these illegal presences as *neighbourhoods* or *communities*. Article 49 of the Fourth Geneva Convention, which is binding upon Israel, states, "The Occupying Power shall not deport or transfer parts of its own civilian population into the territory it occupies." International Committee of the Red Cross (ICRC), Geneva Convention Relative to the Protection of Civilian Persons in Time of War (Fourth Geneva Convention), August 12, 1949, 75 UNTS 287, http://www.unhcr.org/refworld/docid/3ae6b36d2.html. Article 8 (2)(b)(viii) of the Rome Statute prohibits "the transfer, directly or indirectly, by the Occupying Power of parts of its own civilian population into territory it occupies." Rome Statute of International Criminal Court, July 1, 2002, http://www.icc-cpi.int/nr/rdonlyres/ea9aeff7-5752-4f84-be94-0a655eb30e16/0/rome_statute_english.pdf.

8.   Souad R. Dajani, *Ruling Palestine: A History of the Legally-Sanctioned Jewish-Israeli Seizure of Land and Housing in Palestine* (Geneva: Centre on Housing Rights and Evictions; Bethlehem: Badil Resource Center for Palestinian Residency and Refugee Rights, May 2005), 116, http://www.ochaopt.org/documents/opt_prot_COHRE_Seizure_Of_Land_And_Housing_In_Palestine_may_2005.pdf.

9.   Ibid.

10.   Deborah Sontag, "And Yet So Far: A Special Report; Quest for Mideast Peace: How and Why It Failed," *New York Times*, July 26, 2001, http://www.nytimes.com/2001/07/26/world/and-yet-so-far-a-special-report-quest-for-mideast-peace-how-and-why-it-failed.html?pagewanted=all&src=pm. Sontag notes how the narrative that took hold in Israel and the United States was that Arafat had rejected a most generous offer by Barak at Camp David in July 2000 and instead chose to start the intifada.

11.   The word *intifada* comes from the Arabic root word *intafada*, which means "to shake" or "to revolt."

12.   *Killing Fields, Day By Day Chronology of the Second Intifada*, website, accessed April 14, 2015, http://194now.net/Killingfields/index.php.

13. Israel maintains roughly five hundred to six hundred checkpoints or road-blocks throughout the West Bank, controlling movement between West Bank cities, towns, and villages, and between the West Bank and Israel. The only land crossing between the West Bank and Jordan is controlled by Israeli authorities on the Palestinian side. There are five land crossings between Gaza and Israel, all of which are controlled by Israel. The only other land crossing with Gaza is to Egypt. This crossing, Rafah, is indirectly controlled by Israel by way of Israeli–Egyptian understandings. Palestinians with Palestinian ID cards are forbidden to use the Israeli airports and are forced to travel via land to Jordan or Egypt to use an airport.

14. The bulldozer was a Caterpillar D9, built to specification and provided by the US-based Caterpillar (CAT) company, then outfitted in armour by the Israeli military. The Caterpillar company, its board, and shareholders have been repeatedly approached by human rights activists and organizations, including by Human Rights Watch, about ceasing sales to Israel because of the various human rights abuses that Israel uses its bulldozers to commit. In addition to killing Rachel, the Israeli military has and continues to use CAT bulldozers to demolish Palestinian homes, sometimes with Palestinians still in them, uproot Palestinian olive trees, and raze Palestinian agricultural land. As a result of its refusal to take action to ensure that its equipment is not used to commit human right abuses, Caterpillar is a target of the global boycott, divestment, and sanctions (BDS) movement. See "Caterpillar Campaign," End the Occupation, accessed April 14, 2015, http://www.endtheoccupation.org/section.php?id=158.

15. See Iain Scobbie, "Is Gaza Still Occupied Territory?" *Forced Migration Review* 26 (2006): 18, http://www.fmreview.org/sites/fmr/files/FMRdownloads/en/FMRpdfs/FMR26/FMR2608.pdf. Scobbie reviews the test employed by international law to determine whether territory is occupied, and determines that, according to international standards, Gaza remains occupied. For more comprehensive law and analysis on the topic of the beginning and end of occupation, see International Committee of the Red Cross (ICRC), *Expert Meeting Report: Occupation and Other Forms of Administration of Foreign Territory* (Geneva: ICRC, March 2012), https://www.icrc.org/eng/assets/files/publications/icrc-002-4094.pdf.

16. According to World Bank estimates, in 2005, Palestinian imports and exports totaled nearly US$3.4 billion—an amount equivalent to 83 per cent of the Palestinian gross domestic product; and donors contributed a total of approximately US$1.3 billion to the Palestinian economy, or some 22 per cent of gross disposable ncome. World Bank, *West Bank and Gaza Economic Update and Potential Outlook*, March 16, 2006, http://siteresources.worldbank.org/

INTWESTBANKGAZA/Resources/WBGEconomicUpdateandPotentialOutlook. pdf.

17. "Two Years of Gaza Closures by the Numbers," Gisha – Legal Center for Freedom of Movement, accessed January 25, 2013, http://www.gisha.org/item. asp?lang_id=en&p_id=1061.

18. Gisha, "Restrictions on the Transfer of Goods to Gaza: Obstruction and Obfuscation," Info sheet, January 2010, 1n2, quoting a January 13, 2010 letter from the Coordinator of Government Activities in the Territories (COGAT) to Gisha, http://www.gisha.org/UserFiles/File/publications/Obstruction_and_ obfuscation.doc.

19. Save the Children and Medical Aid for Palestinians, *Gaza's Children: Falling Behind, The Effect of the Blockade on Child Health in Gaza*, 2012, http://www.savethechildren.org.uk/sites/default/files/docs/Gazas-Children-Falling-Behind.pdf.

20. Ibid.

21. See UN Office of the High Commissioner for Human Rights, "UN Fact Finding Mission Finds Strong Evidence of War Crimes and Crimes against Humanity Committed during the Gaza Conflict; Calls for End to Impunity," press release, September 15, 2009, http://www.ohchr.org/EN/NewsEvents/Pages/ DisplayNews.aspx?NewsID=91&LangID=E. This press release states that Israel's policy, "which deprives Palestinians in the Gaza Strip of their means of subsistence, employment, housing and water, that denies their freedom of movement and their right to leave and enter their own country, that limits their rights to access a court of law and an effective remedy, could lead a competent court to find that the crime of persecution, a crime against humanity, has been committed."

22. UN Human Rights Council, *Report of the International Fact-Finding Mission to Investigate Violations of International Law, Including International Humanitarian and Human Rights Law, Resulting from the Israeli Attacks on the Flotilla of Ships Carrying Humanitarian Assistance*, A/HRC/15/21, September 27, 2010, http:// www2.ohchr.org/english/bodies/hrcouncil/docs/15session/A.HRC.15.21_en.PDF.

23. See www.bdsmovement.net for more information on the BDS movement. Also see the Palestinian Campaign for the Academic and Cultural Boycott of Israel at www.pacbi.org.

24. "Sweden to Boycott Israeli Cargo," *Jerusalem Post*, June 5, 2010, http://www. jpost.com/International/Sweden-to-boycott-Israeli-cargo; Björn Borg and Erik Helgeson, "Swedish Dockworkers: We're Refusing to Handle Israeli Cargo in Support of the Civilian Population of Gaza," *LabourNet*, June 25, 2010, http://www.labournet.net/docks2/1006/sweden5.html.

25. Greg Dropkin, "Dockworkers, Worldwide, Respond to Israel's Flotilla Massacre and Gaza Siege," *Counterpunch*, July 13, 2010, http://www.counterpunch.org/2010 /07/13/dockworkers-worldwide-respond-to-israel-s-flotilla-massacre-and-gaza-siege/.

26. Tom Breihan, "Pixies, Gorillaz, Elvis Costello, Klaxons Cancel Israel Shows as Political Protest," *Pitchfork*, June 7, 2014 http://pitchfork.com/news/39050-pixies-gorillaz-elvis-costello-klaxons-cancel-israel-shows-as-political-protest/; Leah Greenblatt, "Gorillaz and the Pixies Latest to Cancel Concert Appearances in Israel," *Entertainment Weekly*, June 7, 2010, http://music-mix. ew.com/2010/06/07/gorillaz-pixies-cancel-tel-aviv-israel-concert/.

89

Palestine Calling

R A F E E F   Z I A D A H

6

*Notes on the Boycott, Divestment,
and Sanctions Movement*

> As we face the full might of Israel's military
> arsenal, funded and supplied by the United
> States and European Union, we call on civil
> society and people of conscience throughout
> the world to pressure governments to sanc-
> tion Israel and implement a comprehensive
> arms embargo immediately.
> —Gaza civil society organizations'
> statement, 2014[1]

Introduction

In July 2014, Palestinian residents of Gaza lived through yet another
full-scale Israeli military assault, the third since 2008. The United
Nations Office for the Coordination of Humanitarian Affairs in
the Occupied Palestinian Territory (OPT) explained, "the scale of
destruction, devastation and displacement during the 50 days of
conflict is unprecedented in Gaza, since at least the start of the
Israeli occupation in 1967" (UNOCHA 2014).

These repeated military attacks only punctuate the ongoing illegal land, water, and sea blockade of Gaza imposed by Israel since 2007. The siege has had a devastating impact on the population of Gaza with 35 per cent of arable land and 85 per cent of fishing waters inaccessible to residents of one of the most densely populated areas on earth. Electricity and fuel shortages result in power cuts up to twelve hours daily (UNOCHA 2012). In addition to the blockade, the repeated military assaults act to periodically decimate the limited infrastructure in Gaza.

While Israel's military might is most stark in Gaza, its overall system of colonialism, occupation, and apartheid applies to the entirety of the Palestinian people. In the Occupied West Bank and Jerusalem, Israel continues its systematic ethnic cleansing, land confiscation, and brutal military occupation. Palestinian citizens of Israel are treated as second-class citizens and discriminated against in most aspects of life (Adalah 2011). Palestinian refugees displaced in 1948 during the Nakba (catastrophe) and their descendants are denied their right to return to their homes and lands from which they were expelled (Abu-Lughod and Sa'di 2007; Khalidi 1992; Pappe 2007). In contrast, any person who claims Jewish descent from anywhere in the world may become an Israeli citizen under the so-called Law of Return. This form of apartheid is sustained through an elaborate system of laws, policies, and practices that discrimin-ate openly against Palestinians, whether they are citizens of Israel or not (Abu-Laban and Bakan 2008; Davis 2003; Tilley 2012).

Israel is able to carry out this systemic discrimination and mil-itary occupation due to the unequivocal support it receives from Western powers. This support comes in many forms, from the lucrative free trade agreements and a comprehensive arms trade to the diplomatic protection Israel enjoys, which helps to shield it from any responsibility for its illegal actions.

The Palestinian civil society call for an international movement of boycott, divestment, and sanctions (BDS) against Israel until it complies with international law and upholds Palestinian rights in full emerges in this context of Israeli impunity. Seeing the severity of Israel's assault on Palestinian rights and the unwavering international governmental and corporate complicity, Palestinian civil society called for a global citizens' response to hold Israel to account. The call is inspired by the international movement that helped to end apartheid in South Africa but also, importantly, by the longstanding Palestinian tradition of anti-normalization—that is, severing all "normal" relations with the colonizing power so long as the injustices committed against Palestinians remain.

Since its inception in 2005, the BDS movement has gained momentum and achieved significant success across many sectors, including trade unions, faith groups, non-governmental organizations, and grassroots movements around the world. This chapter traces the conditions leading up to the emergence of the call for BDS during the period of the Oslo Accords and the second Palestinian intifada (uprising) in 2000. The chapter then turns to the BDS call itself, its demands and outlook. Finally, it discusses some of the BDS movement's campaigns. The aim is not to give an in-depth analysis of ongoing BDS campaigns within various sectors, but to give an overview of the overall trajectory of the BDS movement in its first ten years.

The Oslo Accords and the Second Intifada

During the years of the so-called Oslo peace process between Israel and the leadership of the Palestinian Liberation Organization, the greater part of solidarity organizing that emphasized the historical injustice against the Palestinian people fell dormant. The Oslo Accords, officially called the Declaration of Principles on Interim Self-Government Arrangements, reconfigured the political struggle for Palestinian rights from a collective struggle for self-determination against a colonial-settler state (Rodinson 1973) to a struggle within a framework that equalized two sides in a "conflict zone." Demands for Palestinian self-determination morphed into a "state-building" project on ever-shrinking slivers of land managed by a narrow coterie of Palestinian officials in the West Bank and the Gaza Strip (see Said 2000). Palestinians were thus stripped of their collective voice while decisions were made at secret negotiating tables. But even with the Palestinian leadership agreeing to give up 78 per cent of historic Palestine in the last round of negotiations, Israel remained invested in holding ultimate power over the area.

The years immediately following the signing of the Oslo Accords were marked by heavy funding of projects promoting reconciliation, dialogue, and peace building. This contributed to what some authors have termed the peace industry (Bishara 2001, 142). These initiatives often emphasized the need for Palestinians and Israelis to "co-exist," while ignoring power relations and de-emphasizing history.

The failure of the negotiations at Camp David and the beginning of the second Palestinian intifada in 2000 was a clear challenge to the formulations of the Oslo process. The violent military reinvasion of the West Bank reinserted "power" as a concept, emphasizing that Israel—even during the "Oslo years"—continued to hold power over Palestinian lives by retaining structural power in the region (Hanieh 2003). Critically, Israel also retained ideological power within Western circles that quickly laid the blame for the failed negotiations on the Palestinian side, claiming it was the Palestinian leadership that refused to accept a "generous" final offer (Ross 2005).

The second intifada, a mass uprising that began in the West Bank and Gaza, spread to Palestinian citizens of Israel and led to mass demonstrations across the Arab world. Political economist Sara Roy argued that, within two years of the second Palestinian intifada, "Palestinians unquestionably face the deterioration of their economy, a humanitarian crisis that is characterized in large part by levels of impoverishment and social decline that have no parallel during Israel's 36-year occupation of wb/g [West Bank/ Gaza], and the destruction of ordinary life. Not since 1948, perhaps, have Palestinians faced such conditions of loss and dispossession" (2004, 366). She emphasized, however, that the "present state of Palestinian life—be it economic, social, or political—derives fundamentally from dynamics institutionalized during and by the Oslo peace process" (2004, 366).

The second intifada breathed life into the solidarity movement internationally. As Israeli human rights abuses against the Palestinian people intensified, the solidarity movement began to orient itself towards mass education, teach-ins, and public meetings. Demonstrations were organized and, importantly, contingents focused on Palestine took place within the broader anti-war movement that emerged over the invasion of Iraq.

The Call for BDS

The 2005 call from all sectors of Palestinian civil society for boycott, divestment, and sanctions against Israel until the realization of Palestinian rights came in this context and helped to provide a strategic impetus to the growth of the Palestine solidarity movement internationally. The BDS call made an explicit connection between South African apartheid and Israel, emphasizing a direction for action similar to that taken by people around the world to end racism in South Africa (Barghouti 2011, 63–84). The Unified BDS Call gave the needed push for a reorientation of the Palestine solidarity movement, away from educational events that left attendants unclear about what to do next to a very specific call for action— and an analysis that included a set of demands that pertained to the entirety of the Palestinian people, not only those living in the West Bank and Gaza Strip. The three demands—ending the occupation, equality for Palestinian citizens of Israel, and right of return—were a reclamation of the Palestinian collective narrative, against erasure and segmentation (Palestinian civil society organizations 2005). Critically, the call for BDS highlights the three broad sections of the Palestinian people: refugees, those living under military occupation in the West Bank and Gaza Strip, and Palestinians in Israel.

While, for decades, Israel denied basic Palestinian rights to freedom and self-determination through an intricate system of racial discrimination, ethnic cleansing, and direct military occupation, and despite abundant resolutions condemning Israel's actions and reports from human rights organizations that meticulously documented Israel's military actions, the international community did very little to hold Israel to account. As a matter of fact, the BDS call was launched exactly one year after the International Court of Justice (ICJ) decision on the illegality of Israel's apartheid wall, as it became clear that governments were not interested in the implementation of the ICJ ruling. The ICJ ruled that Israel is legally obliged to dismantle the wall and to make reparation for all damage caused by its construction; but most importantly the ruling noted that third states are under an obligation not to recognize, aid, or assist the illegal situation resulting from the construction of the wall (ICJ 2004). Yet construction of the wall and the land confiscation continued. In the face of this international inaction, Palestinian civil society clearly articulated BDS as a global citizens' response to Israel's continued impunity.

The main difference between the BDS call and earlier forms of solidarity was that it directly questioned and challenged the corporate and state relations that sustain Israeli actions. It appealed directly to people to act in their own capacity, in their workplaces, universities, etc., to challenge specifically the role of corporations and the state in sustaining Israel's policies against the Palestinian people. The BDS call did away with the Oslo peace process paradigm of equalizing both sides and looked directly at the root causes of the conflict in the region—not seeing Palestinians and Israelis as two peoples that have some intractable historical disagreement, but rather explaining the situation as a colonial conflict between a native population and a settler colonial state, backed and supported by Western powers.

Therefore, the BDS movement was not merely contesting Israeli state actions; it was tackling the underlying international diplomatic, economic, and corporate support that normalizes Israel's actions and positions it as a state above the law, while at the same time holding up standards of international law as a whip by which to discipline other regimes. The BDS call more specifically was not appealing to the benevolence of states that have acted to support Israel; rather, it put the onus on ordinary people to hold their governments accountable. As noted by Palestinian civil society organizations in a call for an international Day of Rage during the 2014 Israeli military assault on Gaza, "while we have to survive this onslaught, you certainly have the power to help end it the same way you helped overcome Apartheid and other crimes against humanity. Israel is only able to carry out this attack with the unwavering support of governments—this support must end" (Palestinian civil society organizations 2014).

What began as a call from Palestinian civil society in 2005 has, in ten years, transformed into an international movement across many sectors, involving students and academics, trade unionists, clergy, and cultural workers, among others. The following section will look at some specific strides the BDS movement has taken in various sectors and campaigns against specific corporate targets complicit in Israel's crimes.

BDS on Campuses

University campuses have long been regarded as a space for critical debate and the building of solidarity with international struggles, although they are also certainly spaces embedded within broader sets of ruling relations (Smith 1999). Despite the fact that the production of knowledge in universities is increasingly linked to the interests of the corporate sector, campuses provide an important space to organize in support of marginalized and oppressed groups (Sears 2003). The gains made by social movements of the 1960s and 1970s around academic freedom and access to campus space, although increasingly under attack, allow for a degree of freedom for political activism. That the university continues to be a contested political space is perhaps nowhere more evident than with respect to the BDS movement.

Across campuses worldwide one finds Students for Justice in Palestine, Palestine Societies, and Students against Israeli Apartheid groups advocating various forms of BDS. Israeli Apartheid Week, a week-long educational series dedicated to promoting BDS that runs in late February or early March and comprises educational lectures, film screenings, and social events organized on university campuses, was held on 250 campuses globally in 2014.[2]

There is limited space to discuss the large number of divestment initiatives across campuses. To highlight but one, on November 20, 2014, the student government of UCLA voted, 8–2–2, for a resolution to divest from eleven companies that are heavily involved in Israel's occupation and human rights violations (Mitchell and Vescera 2014). Although led by the Students for Justice in Palestine campus group, support for this campaign was widespread, with thirty-one student groups signing on. The positive vote happened despite a full-scale campaign by the Zionist group Hillel and other Israel lobby groups. The UCLA Hillel, hired a public relations firm to tackle what they see as a growing problem (Kane 2014), but they were defeated by a committed group of students who dedicated much time and effort to building coalitions with various social justice groups. Significantly, UCLA is the sixth University of California campus to pass a BDS motion. This is quickly becoming the trend across the world, with students activists inspired by each other's successes and taking bolder steps to declare their campuses "apartheid-free."

Trade Union BDS Action

Palestinian trade unions were among the first signatories to the BDS call in 2005. In a historic conference on April 30, 2011, they formed the Palestinian Trade Union Coalition for BDS (PTUC-BDS) as the largest coalition of the Palestinian trade union movement (PTUC-BDS 2011). The response has been increasing support for BDS among trade unions, including motions that advocate BDS and, in some cases, direct actions, as was the case of several dockworker locals that refused to offload goods from Israeli ships.

"BDS principles and tactics have been formally endorsed by national trade union federations in South Africa, UK, Scotland, Ireland, Norway, Sweden, Belgium, the Basque Country, Brazil and other countries across Latin America, in addition to scores of national and local unions" (PTUC-BDS 2012). Due to the prominent position of the Histradrut, Israel's Zionist quasi-state trade union federation, within international trade union structures, there have been significant obstacles to moving BDS motions forward at the international level. However, it is evident the tide is slowly turning with the British Trade Union Congress passing a motion in support of a limited boycott of illegal settlement products in 2009.

At the height of the military assault on Gaza in summer of 2014, the Palestinian trade union movement appealed to the traditions of trade union solidarity and, with support from the Congress of South African Trade Unions and its affiliates, unanimously called on trade unions internationally to take action to hold Israel to account. They urged unions to "(1) stop handling goods imported from or exported to Israel, (2) Divest your trade union pension—and other—funds from Israel Bonds as well as from corporations and banks that complicit in Israel's occupation and human rights violations, and (3) dissociate from Israeli trade unions which are complicit in the occupation" (Palestinian Trade Union 2014). The response to this call was sadly not swift enough indicating that there is still a way to go to move BDS at the trade union levels from motions to more direct actions.

Cultural and Academic Boycott

In the academic and cultural fields, the BDS movement derives its perspective from the Palestinian call for academic and cultural boycott of Israel issued in July 2004 (PACBI 2004). The academic and cultural boycotts of Israel are a crucial element of the BDS movement because of the way in which Israel relies on promoting its academic and cultural production to sanitize its image globally.

Many artists and other cultural figures now speak publicly of their support for BDS: Roger Waters, Alice Walker, Naomi Klein,

John Berger, Judith Butler, Etienne Balibar, Ken Loach, Arundhati Roy, Angela Davis, among others. Hundreds of artists have chosen to support the cultural boycott of Israel by refusing to play shows in Israel (PACBI 2012). Artists Against Israeli Apartheid collectives now exist on nearly every continent, indicating that increasingly playing Israel will be akin to playing Sun City in apartheid South Africa.

On the academic front, world-renowned physicist Stephen Hawking cancelled a scheduled appearance at an Israeli government conference after appeals from Palestinian academics (*Al Jazeera* 2013). Several academic associations are now calling for support for BDS, including the Association for Asian American Studies, the Native American and Indigenous Studies Association, the American Studies Association. It is striking that the first precedent-setting academic boycott initiative came from the University of Johannesburg in South Africa when, in 2010, the university democratically decided to sever ties with Israel's Ben-Gurion University (PACBI 2011).

Targeting Complicit Corporations
One of the major areas of success for the BDS movement has been the consistent targeting of corporations, Israeli and international, that profit from Israel's system of colonialism, occupation, and apartheid. For example, the Israeli-based company SodaStream has lost nearly 50 per cent of its share value in ten months as investment experts warned that the international BDS campaign against the company, which has a factory based in an illegal Israeli settlement, made it a risky investment (Lomax 2014). BDS campaigners have held pickets outside retail stores carrying SodaStream products both in the United States and across Europe.

Another example is French multinational Veolia, which has been targeted by BDS campaigners since November 2008 due its provision of infrastructure services to illegal settlements, including the Jerusalem Light Rail (Global Exchange 2014a). Following BDS campaigns, local municipalities across Europe and Australia decided not to award Veolia contracts worth at least $14 billion (Mantovani and Deas 2011). A number of municipal authorities also implemented policies to exclude Veolia from bidding on local contracts and some European banks have divested from the company as well (Global Exchange 2014b). This consistent campaigning led to Veolia announcing that it will end its involvement in some of Israel's illegal projects, but the campaign is ongoing until full withdrawal.

Finally, British security contractor G4S indicated it will end its role in Israeli prisons, where Palestinian political prisoners are held without trial and subjected to torture. International campaigning brought to light G4S's involvement in Israel's prisons system, provision of equipment to checkpoints across the apartheid wall, and to businesses inside illegal Israeli settlements. Unions and public bodies across Europe cancelled contracts, and mainstream investors such as the Bill and Melinda Gates Foundation and the largest mainline Protestant church in the United States divested from the company in response to BDS campaigning that consisted of both public protests, pickets, media interventions, and creative actions (Abunimah 2014a).

Tireless BDS campaigning has created a new atmosphere whereby Israel is increasingly viewed as a pariah state. Major investors and institutions are being forced to rethink their investments and business dealings in Israel and with Israeli businesses. In 2014, European investors, including Dutch pension giants PGGM and ABP; Danske Bank, Denmark's biggest bank; Norwegian bank Nordea; and state pension funds in Norway and Luxembourg all divested from Israeli military companies, banks, or companies involved in settlement construction (BNC 2014b). Even the EU and some of its member states have taken measures to limit government and private-sector relations with illegal Israeli settlements (BNC 2014a). This has not happened due to the benevolence of these institutions, but the strategic development of BDS campaigns with a focus on achieving specific successes, building coalitions, and using legal mechanisms when possible. There are scores of targeted initiatives across many countries, and with experience BDS activists are building more creative campaigns daily. For a young movement, there have been important successes, although there is more space for co-ordination across and within campaigns.

BDS a "Strategic Threat" for Israel

While each of these individual campaigns do not necessarily mean a massive shift in international support for Israel's policies, an increasing number of them represents a shift in mainstream support for Israel's ongoing crimes against Palestinians. Israeli leaders themselves understand the impact of BDS very well. They have described BDS as a strategic threat and passed a law that allows Israeli businesses to sue Israeli boycott advocates and hired staff in its ministries and embassies to combat BDS. The Israeli Finance Minister Yair Lapid has warned, "The status quo will hit each of us in the pocket" (Abunimah 2014b). Significantly, the White House even warned of the "potential for Israeli isolation" (Weiss 2014). The combined efforts of BDS campaigners, and the modest successes thus far, in the face of very organized opposition highlight that BDS is an important tool for Palestinian national liberation.

Moving Forward

After the failure of the Oslo peace process logic to deliver anything to Palestinians, anti-normalization must once again become the cornerstone of the Palestinian struggle for freedom and justice. Crucially, BDS does not replace the urgent necessity to restructure the institutions of the Palestinian liberation movement, making them more representative of the entirety of the Palestinian people and reorienting them away from symbolic moves for limited statehood.

Importantly, as BDS becomes more mainstream, we need to diligently insure that the demands of the BDS call that pertain to the entirety of the Palestinian people, not only those living in the West Bank and Gaza Strip, remain central to BDS activism. The significance of BDS is not in the individual campaigning successes but in its political framing of Palestinian liberation in terms of justice for all Palestinians and most significantly Palestinian refugees who continue to be the majority of the Palestinian population. As the civil society statement from Gaza in July 2014 stated, "We are not asking for charity. We are demanding solidarity, because we know that until Israel is isolated and sanctioned, these horrors will be repeated" (Gaza civil society organizations 2014).

RAFEEF ZIADAH

NOTES

1. Gaza civil society organizations that have collectively signed urgent calls for international solidarity against Israel's illegal siege and military aggression include the General Federation of Trade Unions, University Teachers' Association in Palestine, Palestinian Non-Governmental Organizations Network (Umbrella for 133 organizations), General Union of Palestinian Women, Medical Democratic Assembly, General Union of Palestine Workers, General Union for Health Services Workers, General Union for Public Services Workers, General Union for Petrochemical and Gas Workers, General Union for Agricultural Workers, Union of Women's Work Committees, Pal-Cinema (Palestine Cinema Forum), Youth Herak Movement, Union of Women's Struggle Committees, Union of Synergies—Women Unit, Union of Palestinian Women Committees, Women's Studies Society, Working Woman's Society, Press House, Palestinian Students' Campaign for the Academic Boycott of Israel, Gaza BDS Working Group, One Democratic State Group.

2. See apartheidweek.org for information about locations, events, and attendance across campuses.

REFERENCES

Abu-Laban, Yasmeen, and Abigail B. Bakan. 2008. "The Racial Contract: Israel/ Palestine and Canada." *Social Identities* 14 (5): 637–60.

Abu-Lughod, Lila, and Ahmand Sa'di, eds. 2007. *Nakba: Palestine, 1948 and the Claims of Memory*. New York: Columbia University Press.

Abunimah, Ali. 2014a. "G4S 'to End' Israel Prison Contracts as Pressure Mounts over Torture Complicity." *BDS Movement*, June 12. http://www.bdsmovement. net/2014/g4s-announces-prison-pull-out-but-campaign-continues-12144.

———. 2014b. "Growing Boycott Will 'Hit Each of Us in the Pocket' Warns Israel Finance Minister." *Electronic Intifada*, January 11. http://electronicintifada.net/blogs/ali-abunimah/ growing-boycott-will-hit-each-us-pocket-warns-israel-finance-minister.

Adalah: The Legal Center for Arab Minority Rights in Israel. 2011. *The Inequality Report: The Palestinian Arab Minority in Israel*. Adalah: The Legal Center for Arab Minority Rights in Israel.

Al Jazeera. 2013. "Stephen Hawking 'Backs Israel Boycott.'" May 8. http://www. aljazeera.com/news/europe/2013/05.

Barghouti, Omar. 2011. *Boycott, Divestment, Sanctions: The Global Struggle for Palestinian Rights*. Chicago: Haymarket Books.

Bishara, Marwan. 2001. *Palestine/Israel: Peace or Apartheid: Prospects for Resolving the Conflict*. London: Zed Books.

Davis, Uri. 2003. *Apartheid Israel: Possibilities for the Struggle Within*. London: Zed Books.

Gaza civil society organizations. 2014. "Gaza Calling: All out on Saturday 9 August Day of Rage." Statement. *BDS Movement*, August 6. http://www.bdsmovement. net/2014/gaza-calling-all-out-on-saturday-9-august-day-of-rage-12423.

Global Exchange. 2014a. "Why Target Veolia?" Accessed November 7. http://globalexchange.org/economicactivism/veolia/why.

———. 2014b. "Veolia Campaign Victories." Accessed November 10. http://www. globalexchange.org/economicactivism/veolia/victories.

Hanieh, Adam. 2003. "A Road Map to the Oslo Cul-de-Sac." *Middle East Research and Information Project*, May 15. http://www.merip.org/mero/mero051503.

International Court of Justice (ICJ). 2004. "Legal Consequences of the Construction of a Wall in the Occupied Palestinian Territory." Press release 2004/28, July 9. http://www.icj-cij.org/docket/index.php?pr=71&code=mwp&p1=3&p2=4&p3=6.

Kane, Alex. 2014. "UCLA Hillel Partners with PR Firm to Fight BDS Movement." *Mondoweiss*, October 27. http://mondoweiss.net/2014/10/ hillel-partners-movement.

Khalidi, Walid. 1992. *All That Remains: The Palestinian Villages Occupied and Depopulated by Israel in 1948*. Washington, DC: Institute for Palestine Studies.

Lomax, Alyce. 2014. "Why I'm Finally Selling SodaStream." *Motley Fool*, July 15. http://www.fool.com/investing/general/2014/07/15/why-im-finally-selling- sodastream.aspx.

Mantovani, Maren, and Michael Deas. 2011. "French Giant Veolia Cut Down to Size for Abusing Palestinian Rights." *Electronic*

Intifada, August 26. http://electronicintifada.net/content/
french-giant-veolia-cut-down-size-abusing-palestinian-rights/10316.

Mitchell, Kendal, and Joseph Vescera. 2014. "USAC Passes Divestment Resolution
with 8-2-2 Vote." *Daily Bruin*, November 20. http://dailybruin.com/2014/11/18/
usac-passes-divestment-resolution-with-8-2-2-vote/.

Mulholland, Hélène. 2009. "Israel: TUC Boycott on Goods Produced in Illegal
Settlements Is 'Slap in Face.'" *Guardian*, September 17. http://www.theguardian.
com/politics/2009/sep/17/tuc-back-boycott-israel-goods.

Palestinian Boycott, Divestment, Sanctions National Committee (BNC). 2014a. "BDS
Timeline." *BDS Movement*, November 3. http://www.bdsmovement.net/timeline.

———. 2014b. "G4S Campaign Timeline." *BDS Movement*, November 9.
http://www.bdsmovement.net/g4s-timeline.

Palestinian Campaign for Academic and Cultural Boycott of Israel (PACBI). 2004. "Call
for Academic and Cultural Boycott of Israel." July 6.
http://pacbi.org/etemplate.php?id=869.

———. 2011. "University of Johannesburg Makes History: UJ Senate Decides to Sever
Links with Israeli Apartheid." March 23.
http://pacbi.org/etemplate.php?id=1526.

———. 2012. "Palestinian Civil Society Salutes Alice Walker." July 1.
http://www.pacbi.org/printnews.php?id=1936.

Palestinian civil society organizations. 2005. "Palestinian Civil Society Call for BDS."
BDS Movement, July 9. http://www.bdsmovement.net/call.

———. 2014. "Gaza Calling: All out on Saturday, 9 August Day of Rage."
BDS Movement, August 6. http://www.bdsmovement.net/2014/
gaza-calling-all-out-on-saturday-9-august-day-of-rage-12423.

Palestinian Trade Union Coalition for BDS (PTUC-BDS). 2011. "Statement of Principles
& Call for International Trade Union Support for BDS." *BDS Movement*, May 4.
http://www.bdsmovement.net/2011/ptuc-bds-formed-6912.

———. 2012. "Palestinian Trade Union Movement Stands in Solidarity with European
Unions Resisting Austerity and Struggling for Social Justice." *BDS Movement*,
June 12. http://www.bdsmovement.net/2012/ptuc-bds-solidarity-9110.

Palestinian Trade Union Movement and Congress of South African Trade Unions.
2014. "Stand with Palestinian Workers in Gaza: A Call for Trade Union
Solidarity." *Congress of SA Trade Unions*, July 29.
http://www.cosatu.org.za/docs/cosatu2day/2014/pr0729e.html.

Palestinian trade unions in Gaza. 2014. "Stand with Palestinian Workers in Gaza:
A Call for Trade Union Solidarity." *BDS Movement*, July 30. http://www.
bdsmovement.net/2014/stand-with-palestinian-workers-in-gaza-a-call-for-
trade-union-solidarity-12404.

Pappe, Illan. 2007. *The Ethnic Cleansing of Palestine*. Oxford: Oneworld Publications.

Rodinson, Maxime. 1973. *Israel: A Colonial-Settler State?* New York: Pathfinder.

Ross, D. 2005. *The Missing Peace: The Inside Story of the Fight for Middle East Peace*. New York: Farrar, Straus and Giroux.

Roy, Sara. 2004. "The Palestinian-Israeli Conflict and Palestinian Socioeconomic Decline: A Place Denied." *International Journal of Politics, Culture, and Society* 17 (3): 365–403.

Said, Edward. 2000. *The End of the "Peace Process": Oslo and After*. New York: Pantheon Books.

Sears, Alan. 2003. *Retooling the Mind Factory: Education in a Lean State*. Aurora, ON: Garamond Press.

Smith, Dorothy E. 1999. "The Ruling Relations." In *Writing the Social: Critique, Theory and Investigations*, 73–95. Toronto: University of Toronto Press.

Tilley, Virginia, ed. 2012. *Beyond Occupation: Apartheid, Colonialism and International Law in the Occupied Palestinian Territories*. London: Pluto Press.

United Nations Office for the Coordination of Humanitarian Affairs. 2012. "Five Years of Gaza Blockade: The Humanitarian Situation in Gaza Factsheet." June. http://www.ochaopt.org/gazablockade/.

———. 2014. "Situation Overview." OCHA Occupied Palestinian Territory, July 7. http://www.ochaopt.org/content.aspx?id=1010361.

Weiss, Philip. 2014. "White House Says US Can't Stop 'Tsunami' of Boycott and Isolation If Israel Won't End 'Occupations.'" *Mondoweiss*, July 9. http://mondoweiss.net/2014/07/boycott-isolation-occupations.

7 Culture of Resistance

TALI SHAPIRO

Why We Need You to Boycott, Divest, and Sanction Israel

I'M A BABY ACTIVIST. I was born in the summer of 2009 with the sounds of the dropping bombs of Israel's Cast Lead military operation against Gaza. Being a citizen of Israel and a state-designated Jew, I've often described it as waking up into a nightmare. The attack left over 1,400 Palestinian children, women, and men dead, and over 5,000 injured.[1] Civilian infrastructure was deliberately destroyed.[2] Watching it on television, along with the media buildup before and throughout and the rampant nationalistic public fervour,[3] I was launched into a tailspin. Many things that I had known instinctively about the conflict came together in my head. All of a sudden, they clicked.

As Cast Lead progressed and Palestinian bodies were amassing, I put aside everything else and sat myself down to learn. I obsessively searched the Internet for what mainstream media was hiding. I grew up fast; one can't stay too innocent after seeing so much death and destruction and starting to understand the system behind it—a system so ingrained in every facet of my life that only a long-term ongoing process of study, action, involvement, and discussion, and the constant writing out of my findings and thoughts, could allow

me to unravel it, subvert it, act against it, and—who knows?—
maybe one day help break it apart altogether.

I have written this contribution as an activist, in the voice of an
activist, while grounding it carefully in rigorous study, which I view
as an integral part of my activism. In my initial research, I quickly
stumbled upon the then budding movement of boycott, divestment,
and sanctions (BDS), an organized effort of Palestinian civil society,
across the Green Line and around the world. The Palestinian
Boycott, Divestment, and Sanctions National Committee (BNC)
called for action:

> *In light of Israel's persistent violations of international law...we,*
> *representatives of Palestinian civil society, call upon international*
> *civil society organizations and people of conscience all over the world*
> *to impose broad boycotts and implement divestment initiatives*
> *against Israel similar to those applied to South Africa in the apart-*
> *heid era. We appeal to you to pressure your respective states to impose*
> *embargoes and sanctions against Israel. We also invite conscientious*
> *Israelis to support this Call, for the sake of justice and genuine peace.*[4]

Following this lead, groups all around the world, made up of people
just like me, take action to stop the occupation and apartheid. The
movement has grown significantly since Palestinian civil society
has united under its banner and issued this rallying call, its successes
measured in numbers and campaign victories all around the globe.

I found the BDS movement about four months into my activism.
Its cause-and-effect analysis appealed to me and has informed my
research and writing in a new action-oriented direction. As Who
Profits, a research organization that documents Israeli and international companies' commercial involvement in Israeli control of
Palestine, already covered extensive economic research, my research
has veered into the less-charted territory of how cultural institutions and corporations in Israel serve its mechanisms of control.

Many of us do not understand or clearly place ourselves within the context of a given matrix of mechanisms of control. In this chapter, I aim to explain one facet of the matrix or system I was born into. Within this system, I am positioned at the top of a ruling class by virtue of my mother's religion, my grandmother's geographical origins, and the colour of my skin. Within this system, if you don't possess these random endowments, you are not only of the lower class but, in some cases, you are virtually non-existent. I'd like to point out that such "non-existence" isn't a merely metaphorical erasure. It's literal. And it constitutes both a final goal of this system and many of its manifestations on the way to this goal. My main aim is to show how Israeli colonial culture, via the government and business, not only erases Palestinian existence but also thwarts any attempts to counter this erasure.

Oppression Is a System

Since 2009 I've been attending the weekly demonstrations in the occupied neighbourhoods of East Jerusalem (smack dab in the centre of the city) and the villages of the West Bank, Bil'in, Nabi Saleh, Ni'lin, Ma'asara, and Kufr Qaddum. All these locations are emblematic of Israel's military occupation of the West Bank and of its policies of apartheid, ethnic cleansing, and genocide (big words that I'll soon define). While these policies have daily manifestations across the West Bank (such as construction of a separation wall that virtually isolates and seals off Palestinian communities, house demolitions, expulsion and displacement, arbitrary arrests and torture of children and adults, constant police and army presence and brutality and the silencing of protest, summary executions and more), it is at these sites, and many others, that acts of resistance have grown into weekly rituals.

I must have taken part in over 250 demonstrations since 2009. From down here, "on the ground," demonstrating, you can't see much through the tear gas and the apartheid wall. But you learn how oppression feels. And with that choking sensation of ever-expanding military control over every aspect of Palestinian life, I go back home to urban, middle-class Israel to try to figure out other ways to make it stop—other than getting shot at and arrested and witnessing the torture, abuse, and incarceration of loved ones.

Activism isn't just about direct action (a loaded term in its own right). It's also about knowing what you're acting against—directly or otherwise. My most highly recommended resource for understanding Israel's system of oppression is the organization Who Profits from the Occupation. Who Profits helps make the vast number and scope of businesses and entire branches of Israel's economy that benefit from military occupation comprehensible. The work of Who Profits underpins countless divestment campaigns around the world, from interfaith initiatives to the beauty industry and bank divestments.[5]

Waging constant war on an indigenous population for over sixty-six years is costly, both economically and politically. To colonize Palestinian land, Israel has to maintain myriad methods of segregation and implement ethnic cleansing and genocide of the Palestinian population. To be sustainable, these endeavours must to be economically worthwhile. Accordingly, Israel has constructed and relies on an economic system that supports this aim.

For example, Israel's one and only water company/authority controls and distributes water resources in the Occupied West Bank, beyond the armistice lines viewed as Israel's borders prior to 1967. Not only does the occupying power keep its hand on the faucet; it systematically abuses this power by favouring its (Israeli Jewish) civilians (illegally transferred into occupied territory) over the indigenous population under occupation ("protected persons" under international law). Israel rations water in favour of its settlers, and at times leaves the occupied community completely dry, especially during the hot summer months. In addition, the Israel water company/authority also dabbles in water technologies in collaborative projects with various corporations. For example, it desalinates water, which it eventually exports for profit.[6]

This is one of many examples that illustrates how a fundamental imbalance of authority and power enables a broad, intricate system of abuse and discrimination. Given enough time (say, sixty-seven years), a power based on the gravest forms of violence against a whole population can and almost inevitably will evolve into an economic system of redistribution, continually dispossessing and exploiting those occupied and profiting those in power. The system encompasses the whole of Israel's economy, including basic utilities (water, electricity, petrol), agriculture, health care, real estate, banks, and investment companies, and, of course, the very profitable and inflated market of "security" products and services.[7]

Oppression Is a Culture

I'll now attempt to unpack the loaded terms *ethnic cleansing, apartheid*, and *genocide*. These are legal terms with legal definitions. They are complex and aim to define systems whose existence relies on cumulative acts rather than individual actions. The real contexts in which these terms are enacted are also complex, and the terms seem to get redefined with every emergence of yet another system of oppression somewhere in the world. Therefore, for the sake of clarity, in my references to genocide, ethnic cleansing, and apartheid, I adhere to the following definitions. Apartheid, as defined by the 1973 UN Convention on the Suppression and Punishment of the Crime of Apartheid, refers to "an institutionalized regime of systematic oppression and domination by one racial group over any other racial group or groups and committed with the intention of maintaining that regime." The Apartheid Convention characterizes crimes of apartheid as "inhumane acts of a character similar to other crimes against humanity."[8] The UN Security Council defines ethnic cleansing as "a purposeful policy designed by one ethnic or religious group to remove by violent and terror-inspiring means the civilian population of another ethnic or religious group from certain geographic areas. To a large extent, it is carried out in the name of misguided nationalism, historic grievances and a powerful driving sense of revenge. This purpose appears to be the occupation of territory to the exclusion of the purged group or groups."[9] Lastly, Resolution 260 (III) A of the United Nations General Assembly, adopted on December 9, 1948, defines genocide thusly:

ARTICLE 1
The Contracting Parties confirm that genocide, whether committed in time of peace or in time of war, is a crime under international law which they undertake to prevent and to punish.

ARTICLE 2
In the present Convention, genocide means any of the following acts committed with intent to destroy, in whole or in part, a national, ethnical, racial or religious group, as such:

(a) Killing members of the group;
(b) Causing serious bodily or mental harm to members of the group;
(c) Deliberately inflicting on the group conditions of life calculated to bring about its physical destruction in whole or in part;
(d) Imposing measures intended to prevent births within the group;
(e) Forcibly transferring children of the group to another group.[10]

Israel, by use of military force, legal policy, and systematic economic oppression, is committing a series of acts of religo-racial discrimination that amount de facto to apartheid. These are carried out with the intent of achieving an end result of tantamount to ethnic cleansing and, in fact, genocide: "Maximum territory with minimum Arabs."[11] Before progressing any further with my argument for seriously considering the possibility that Israel is committing genocide, I'll first provide some background framework and facts.

The Jewish Agency: The Ethos, Mythos, and Pathos Mechanism of the State of Israel

The answer turns, to a large extent, on the natural need to tell personal stories. All social groups possess and practice various forms of ethos, mythos, and pathos (i.e., "culture"), which inform perceptions of the past, present, and future. In the Zionist entity, as in other historically racist and colonial entities, particular spokesmen and spokes-bodies were responsible for addressing both internal needs and foreign powers.[12] This responsibility for forming and relating the master narratives of Zionism preceded foundation of the state by many years. The stories and strategies presented by these spokesmen changed repeatedly, often, to accommodate freshly committed atrocities.[13] It's not in the scope of this chapter to follow the early development of Zionist ideology, but recognizing the original body of the Zionist entity—the Jewish Agency—provides necessary context.

The Jewish Agency's role, as stated on its website, "was paramount in setting up an economic and cultural infrastructure for the country."[14] This formulation distinctly reflects the extent to which Israel's economy and culture have been historically inseparable. Economy, I argue, is always structured on the values and ideologies of those who control it, and Israel is no different in that respect. The Jewish Agency, being the architect of the future-Israel's economic infrastructure is inherently and explicitly responsible for creating an economy abusive to non-Jews in the land formerly known as Palestine. But it is also responsible for creating an exclusionary cultural infrastructure to lead, support, and follow from the abusive economy.

In search of Palestinians on the Jewish Agency website, one finds either a twisted version of the Nakba (the ethnic cleansing of half the Palestinian population within one year, 1947-1948),[15] or a complete denial of responsibility for it. On top of that, the website provides an equally twisted or marginalized version of the political aspirations of an indigenous Arab population (including refugees, survivors of the Nakba).[16] The Jewish Agency was created as "the official representative of the Jewish community and world Jewry" with the clear goal of "establishment of the Jewish National Home... in Palestine." At the time, Middle Eastern Palestine was under British rule (known as the "Mandate Authority"), although, as noted by the Jewish Agency itself, Britain "proposed the creation within ten years of a single state in Palestine." The Jewish Agency, though, perceived this as the "death knell for hopes of a Jewish state" and proceeded to work against it (which it continues to do to this day). The state it envisioned was "synonymous with...the resettlement of the Jewish people in its homeland."[17]

This narrative of "Jewish return," framed as "self-defence," erased the acts of violence and dispossession against a disappeared indigenous Palestinian population. The same narrative still holds sway today, allowing Jewish citizens of Israel to continue justifying Israel's violations of Palestinian identity and human rights, by identifying Palestinians as an "external," Arab/Muslim "threat to Jewish existence."

Today, no longer "the de facto government of the state-on-the-way," handling "immigration—allocating certificates supplied by the [British] Mandate Authority—and resettlement of new immigrants, the building of new settlements, economic development, education and culture, hospitals and health services," the Jewish Agency has shifted some of these responsibilities to Israel's governments. Yet the agency still claims its role as "the only global Jewish partnership organization, linking Jews around the world with Israel as the focal point...facilitating...Jewish Zionist education."[18] Its educational projects include "[improving] Israel's image on...campuses."[19] It's important to note that this Zionist education is actually funded by, and also exempted from, taxes collected by the state of Israel.[20]

Genocide Starts with Incitement

To return, then, to the question of genocide. The crime of genocide isn't confined to a specific time frame; genocide can be a gradual process. The case of Palestine may be the slowest known process of genocide. The intent is documented,[21] but execution has been cautious and deceptive, wary of the eye of the international community. The focus of my activism—namely, culture—reveals an often neglected element of genocide. It allows us to examine the processes through which particular values are embedded in society so that violence is normalized to the extent of achieving genocide. This focus on culture uncovers Israel's role, as a state, in the crime of incitement to genocide.

The Convention on the Prevention and Punishment of the Crime of Genocide (signed by Israel August 17, 1949),[22] identifies the act of "Direct and public incitement to commit genocide" as "punishable," its enactors being "constitutionally responsible rulers, public officials or private individuals." The mandate of the UN Office of the Special Adviser on the Prevention of Genocide includes "alerting relevant actors to the risk of genocide, war crimes, ethnic cleansing and crimes against humanity, enhancing the capacity of the United Nations to prevent these crimes, including their incitement, and working with Member States, regional and sub-regional arrangements, and civil society to develop more effective means of response when they do occur."[23]

Ethnic cleansing, war crimes, and crimes against humanity are already being perpetrated by Israel. Accordingly, the cultural infrastructure of the state and society of Israel is already geared to facilitate these crimes. Beyond enabling the horrific processes listed above, this cultural infrastructure moreover severely diminishes "the capacity of the United Nations to prevent these crimes, including their incitement, and working with Member States, regional and sub-regional arrangements, and civil society to develop more effective means of response when they do occur."[24] In and of itself, this state of affairs is enough to justify and, indeed, demand an inquiry into the question of direct and indirect incitement to ethnic cleansing, war crimes, crimes against humanity, and at the very least the *risk* of genocide.

Genocide Is a Culture

The culture of genocide is served well by the mental, perceptual manifestations of segregation or apartheid. No one really sees Palestinians (or Arabs, as they are commonly referred to in Jewish Israeli society) because the denial of a self-determined, collective identity is central to the culture. An additional enabling layer is provided by the creative output of the culture when it serves as a "state branding" agent. As I've claimed elsewhere,

> *Along with the "standard" "nation branding"...known as Brand Israel, much of Israel's propaganda is based on the blurring of the lines between the individual and the state...As a B D S activist, whose main focus is cultural boycott, I've come up against a very common Israeli claim (individuals, small business, and government officials) that "culture has nothing to do with politics." Most commonly it comes in the form of a puzzled "rhetorical" question: "What does culture have to do with politics?!" As if asking this question closes the discussion, because it's so obvious that art, music, books, films, theatre, and dance are a pure form of entertainment that have no intellectual, political, anthropological value. As if cultural products aren't bought and sold as commodities and status indicators.*[25]

In its current form, the state use of culture by Israel conflates and harnesses Zionism and capitalism. Most of the cultural artifacts promoted, showcased, or even produced by state authorities either altogether ignore (and help obscure) political problems and conflicts, including issues that, on the face of it, have nothing to do with Arabs, or uphold and reinforce the Zionist ethos, mythos, and pathos.

This means that most cultural workers in Israel take part (often without noticing) in the erasure and the facilitation of genocide.

Nevertheless, with regard to Israeli artists and performers and their appearances outside of Israel, the Palestinian Campaign for the Academic and Cultural Boycott of Israel, known as PACBI, points out that "a cultural product's content or artistic merit is not relevant in determining whether or not it is boycottable."[26] In keeping with this, cultural boycott activities outside of Israel are based on, and expose, two forms of state involvement in Israeli culture. The first form includes cultural projects in the more "classical" genres, such as theatre and dance companies, and classical music, often funded, sponsored and exported (PR included) by the Ministry of Tourism and the Ministry of Foreign Affairs as well as the Ministry of Culture, and ostensibly aimed at "exposing Israeli work in many theatres around the world."[27] This form of state involvement takes a revealing turn, in light of a second, explicitly instrumental form of state-exported culture: in quite a few cases, state contracts with Israeli artists cover their trips abroad as long as "the service Provider [the cultural worker] undertakes to mention the name of the Ministry and/or Israeli representation in...[specified] countries in any publication concerning the services provided by him, in Israel and abroad...The service provider is aware that the purpose of ordering services from him is to *promote the policy interests of the State of Israel via culture and art, including contributing to creating a positive image for Israel...*The service provider will not present himself as an agent, emissary and/or representative of the Ministry."[28] Standard contracts further state, "the Ministry will pay...directly to third parties [these include the foreign organizations issuing the invitations, such as film festivals and publishers]... Reimbursement of expenses, or payment to third parties, for advertising, public relations and publications relating to the provision of the services to the Ministry by the service provider, against receipts and up to a sum of – NIS/$US/euro."[29] In other words, international festivals get paid by the state of Israel to host Israeli artists and disseminate state messaging.

The question of foreign artists coming to Israel from abroad subsumes another version of "What does culture have to do with politics?" What could possibly be the connection between these artists and the state, especially as such artists are usually brought in by small "micro corporations" of under ten employees? If this is the case, why do campaigns taking their cue from PACBI and supported internationally by ad hoc groups of activists—campaigns I take part in as a BDS activist focusing on cultural boycott—work to persuade artists from all over the world to cancel performances scheduled in Israel?

In an article called "Israel 2012, the Question of a Nation: What Does Culture Have to Do with Politics?," I examine the accountability of Israeli (and international) production companies. As I conclude there, such corporations do not profit directly from Israel's genocide of the Palestinian people (due to which they fail to fall under the categories guiding the fact finding of Who Profits). They do, however, meet the criteria outlined by PACBI, as they "serve the purposes of the Israeli colonial and apartheid regime...[through] inherent and organic links between them which reproduce the machinery of colonial subjugation and apartheid."[30] Though such links and reproduction don't necessarily require actual financial relations, many state-sponsored events featuring international artists, such as the bi-annual Red Sea Jazz Festival, actually receive state funding.[31]

Also, specific companies in fact collaborate directly with the government in adopting its goals and words. One must remember that these companies and their management are quite distinct from the "wholesome" conservatives of the rather archaic but still highly functional Jewish Agency. The apparatus of production companies bringing in foreign performers is comprised of the middlemen between contemporary culture and the young public. As such, this apparatus amounts to a major educational project.

One could argue that when "micro corporations," such as Shuki Weiss Promotion and Production Ltd., Udi Appelboim, or Plug

Productions Generator, bring international artists to Israel, this is merely and simply the nature of their work, just as it is the nature of the work of the Ministry of Culture to facilitate culture. But when Plug Productions Generator invites the Lollapalooza festival to Yarkon Park, on the remains of the ethnically cleansed Palestinian village, Jarisha, and quotes the ministries of tourism and foreign affairs, Israel's Consulate General in New York, and the Economic Department of the Consulate General of Israel in San Francisco, among others, to promote Israel and Tel Aviv as "widely recognized as an international culture capitol and...known across the world for its art, architecture, and bustling nightlife," this, to me, is a prime example of the unaccountable culture of genocide rampant in Israel. Unsurprisingly extending this failure of accountability, the Lollapalooza festival followed suit, requoting these sources.[32]

Shuki Weiss Promotion and Production Ltd. has taken this a step further. Not only has Weiss issued a dangerous smear against BDS activists, calling us "cultural terrorists,"[33] he also provides Israeli parliament members with free VIP tickets to shows he produces, and takes an active part in Israel's propaganda:

> *Tourism Ministry spokeswoman Shira Koa said that the ministry had agreed with the producers of the concert that the event would be used to promote Israel as a safe tourism destination. "Madonna belongs to an exclusive club of mega stars, who draws thousands of fans from abroad to her concerts."...*
>
> *"For this reason, the ministry authorized an agreement with the producers that would give the ministry video and stills footage of the singer and her entourage, both during the concerts and her visits to tourist sites in Israel, to be used in international marketing campaigns. They also agreed to have four displays at the concert with films promoting Israel, supplied by the ministry, targeting the thousands of foreign tourists..."*
>
> *"Such promotion campaigns are regular occurrences both in Israel and abroad."[34]*

Israel's parliament, in turn, has highlighted Weiss and his warnings at parliament discussions on stifling freedom of speech, heeded his outraged statements against clients' principled cancellations, and outlawed the boycotts with his active contribution.[35] The law now prohibiting "boycotts that harm the state of Israel" enables Shuki Weiss Promotion and Production Ltd. to sue me—an individual—for writing this article, without requiring him to prove actual damages.[36]

The search for accountability among international, corporate productions companies wouldn't be complete without mentioning the unique phenomena of the so-called Creative Community for Peace. This group of top producers in the American music industry and in Israeli communications "[seeks] to counter artist boycotts of Israel" and do it with the help of Jewish Agency partners and funders, such as the Jewish Federations of North America and Stand With Us, quoting verbatim from the self-victimizing, xenophobic language of Israel's propaganda.[37] To understand how far Creative Community for Peace's reach is, one must only follow their own proclamations: "Today, [Creative Community for Peace] say, there is not a single musical act, from Justin Timberlake to the Rolling Stones to Alicia Keys, that they have not approached and coached in advance of their performance in Israel."[38] Recently, Creative Community for Peace enlisted two hundred Hollywood celebrities, including Bill Maher, Ziggy Marley, Seth Rogan, Sarah Silverman, Arnold Schwarzenegger, Sylvester Stallone, Minnie Driver, Tom Arnold, and Roseanne Barr, into signing a letter of support for Israel's third round of wanton destruction of the hermetically besieged Gaza Strip since 2009.[39]

Cultural Accountability in the Twenty-First Century

I hope that it's clear by now that various actors from across the globe have been taking part in what I've described as Israel's culture of genocide. I hope it is equally clear that the state of Israel has made such participation profitable through direct payoffs, through legislation that stifles freedom of speech, and through years of propagating the perception that there is no such thing as a Palestinian people. How, then, do we demand accountability for the complicity of cultural corporations, artists, and brand names?

As in many cases regarding the occupation, Israel lacks the proper effective grievance mechanisms through which victims may seek redress, so I once again turn to international law. After the United Nations realized the inseparability of corporate business and human rights (or, more precisely, of the violations of such rights), it launched the UN Global Compact framework in 2000. This framework comprises a set of standards for corporations in the areas of human rights, labour, the environment, and anti-corruption, with a "ten commandments" flair of sorts.[40] Within the framework of the Global Compact, the UN Human Rights Council endorsed the "UN Framework and the Global Compact" in 2011, elaborating further on actions that corporations *could* take in order to promote human rights.[41]

"Could" is the operative word here, however, because not only does the "UN Framework and the Global Compact" leave the implementation of its directives in the hands of "the courts of public opinion,"[42] but it also stipulates that

companies cannot be held responsible for the human rights impacts of every entity over which they may have some influence, because this would include cases in which they were not a causal agent, direct or indirect, of the harm in question. Nor is it desirable to have companies act whenever they have influence, particularly over governments. Asking companies to support human rights voluntarily where they have influence is one thing; but attributing responsibility to them on that basis alone is quite another...a government can deliberately fail to perform its duties in the hope or expectation that a company will yield to social pressures to promote or fulfill certain rights—again demonstrating why State duties and corporate responsibilities must be defined independently of one another.[43]

While non-binding, then, this infant framework nevertheless affords me some hope that one day in the future the kind of action taken by Shuki Weiss Promotion and Production Ltd., for one, will be subject to victims' demands for redress through appropriate effective grievance mechanisms. The framework goes on to say,

> *Mere presence in a country, paying taxes, or silence in the face of abuses is unlikely to amount to the practical assistance required for legal liability. However, acts of omission in narrow contexts have led to legal liability of individuals when the omission legitimized or encouraged the abuse. Moreover, under international criminal law standards, practical assistance or encouragement need neither cause the actual abuse, nor be related temporally or physically to the abuse.*
>
> *Legal interpretations of "having knowledge" vary. When applied to companies, it might require that there be actual knowledge, or that the company "should have known" that its actions or omissions would contribute to a human rights abuse. Knowledge may be inferred from both direct and circumstantial facts. The "should have known" standard is what a company could reasonably be expected to know under the circumstances.*
>
> *In international criminal law, complicity does not require knowledge of the specific abuse or a desire for it to have occurred, as long as there was knowledge of the contribution. Therefore, it may not matter that the company was merely carrying out normal business activities if those activities contributed to the abuse and the company was aware or should have been aware of its contribution. The fact that a company was following orders, fulfilling contractual obligations, or even complying with national law will not, alone, guarantee it legal protection.*[44]

This still leaves us, civil society, with the brunt of getting justice served. It is our civil obligation to make sure that companies such as those I've described "have knowledge" of their "contribution" to abuse, and that "following orders" will indeed *not* guarantee legal protection. That is, if and when the UN frameworks actually provide a means to redress. This is precisely why we, BDS activists, need everyone to join in. Including you, the reader of this chapter! And why we, BDS activists, have taken it upon ourselves to do the research; to compile it in accessible, readable formats; to make production companies, agents, and artists and brand names aware of the implications of their business transactions; and to move artists and brand names to rethink their complicity with complicit corporations.

BDS is often said by its detractors to inhibit dialogue and freedom of speech.[45] As an anti-occupation activist, I can testify that there has never before been such widespread public discourse on Israel's violations of the human rights of Palestinians. As an anarchist, who doesn't limit her independent studies to the Palestinian liberation struggle, but sees the importance of learning from other struggles and making the connections, I see myself not only as a compiler of information but as a creative creator of culture in the spectrum of the written word. Given my positioning as a registered citizen of Israel, my written word is part of a culture of resistance.

NOTES

1. UN Human Rights Council, *Human Rights in Palestine and Other Occupied Arab Territories: Report of the United Nations Fact-Finding Mission on the Gaza Conflict*, A/HRC/12/48, September 25, 2009, 90, 267, http://www2.ohchr.org/english/bodies/hrcouncil/docs/12session/A-HRC-12-48.pdf.

2. Tali Shapiro, "With a Shield or Upon It—Impressions from the Spartan State," *PULSE*, September 9, 2009, http://pulsemedia.org/2009/09/09/with-a-shield-or-upon-it-impressions-from-the-spartan-state/.

3. Ethan Bronner, "Israel Puts Media Clamp on Gaza," *New York Times*, January 6, 2009, http://www.nytimes.com/2009/01/07/world/middleeast/07media.html?_r=0; Yossi Verter, "Poll Shows Most Israelis Back IDF Action in Gaza," *Haaretz*, January 15, 2009, http://www.haaretz.com/print-edition/news/poll-shows-most-israelis-back-idf-action-in-gaza-1.268162.

4. Palestinian Boycott, Divestment, and Sanctions National Committee (BNC), "Palestinian Civil Society Call for BDS," *BDS Movement*, July 9, 2005, http://www. bdsmovement.net/call.

5. Sydney Levy, "A Moral Choice: Divesting from the Israeli Occupation," *Jewish Voice for Peace*, accessed April 15, 2015, http://jewishvoiceforpeace.org/ content/moral-choice-divesting-israeli-occupation; *Stolen Beauty*, accessed April 15, 2015, http://www.stolenbeauty.org/; Nora Barrows-Friedman, "BDS Victories: Dexia Bank to Sell Israeli Subsidiary; Veolia Loses Another Contract," *Electronic Intifada*, May 20, 2011, http://electronicintifada.net/blogs/nora/ bds-victories-dexia-bank-sell-israeli-subsidiary-veolia-loses-another-contract.

6. Tali Shapiro, "Playing with Water," *PULSE*, October 15, 2010, http://pulsemedia. org/2010/10/15/playing-with-water/.

7. PLO Negotiations Affairs Department, "Fuelling the Fire: Cutting off Gaza's Electricity and Fuel," September 1, 2007, http://www.nad-plo.org/etemplate. php?id=65; Who Profits, "Captive Economy—The Pharmaceutical Industry and the Israeli Occupation," July 2012, http://www.whoprofits.org/content/captive-economy-pharmaceutical-industy-and-israeli-occupation; Who Profits, "Israeli Construction on Occupied Land," accessed May 18, 2015, http://www.whoprofits. org/involvement/israeli-construction-occupied-land; Who Profits, "Financing the Israeli Occupation," October 2010, http://www.whoprofits.org/content/ financing-israeli-occupation. See also, searches for the terms *petrol, agriculture, finance,* and, in the "Involvement Category," *specialized equipment services* at Who Profits' website, www.whoprofits.org.

8. John Dugard, "Convention on the Suppression and Punishment of the Crime of Apartheid," November 30, 1973, UN Audiovisual Library of International Law, http://legal.un.org/avl/ha/cspca/cspca.html.

9. UN Security Council, "Ethnic Cleansing," May 27, 1994, http://www.his.com/~twarrick/commxyu4.htm#r28.

10. UN General Assembly, Resolution 260 (III), Convention on the Prevention and Punishment of the Crime of Genocide, December 9, 1948, http://www.hrweb.org/legal/genocide.html.

11. Stop the JNF Campaign, "The Jordan Valley: 'Maximum Territory for Israel with the Minimum of Arabs,'" 2010, http://jordanvalleysolidarity. org/index.php/home-2/44-english-categories/reports/ reports2010/141-the-jewish-national-fund-in-the-jordan-valley.

12. "David Ben-Gurion," Israel Ministry of Foreign Affairs, May 8, 2003, http:// www.mfa.gov.il/MFA/Facts+About+Israel/State/David+Ben-Gurion.htm; Jewish Agency for Israel, "The History of the Jewish Agency for Israel," accessed April 19, 2015, http://jafi.org/JewishAgency/English/About/ History/?wbc_purpose=basi.

13. Tali Shapiro, "So How Do I Look?—Zionist Self-Righteousness in the Face of Delegitimization," *PULSE*, February 18, 2010, http://pulsemedia.org/2010/02/18/so-how-do-i-look-zionist-self-righteousness-in-the-face-of-delegitimization/.

14. Jewish Agency for Israel, "The History of the Jewish Agency for Israel," accessed April 19, 2015, http://jafi.org/JewishAgency/English/About/History/?wbc_purpose=basi.

15. Ilan Pappe, *The Ethnic Cleansing of Palestine* (Oxford: Oneworld Publications, 2007).

16. Jewish Agency for Israel, "The Palestinians," accessed April 19, 2015, http://www.jewishagency.org/peace-and-conflict/content/23692.

17. Jewish Agency for Israel, "The History of the Jewish Agency for Israel," accessed April 19, 2015, http://jafi.org/JewishAgency/English/About/History/?wbc_purpose=basi.

18. Ibid.

19. Tali Shapiro, "Why Academic Boycott," *PULSE*, December 15, 2010, http://pulsemedia.org/2010/12/15/why-academic-boycott/.

20. Jewish Agency for Israel, *Faces of the Jewish Future, 2012/2013 Performance Report* (New York and Jerusalem: Jewish Agency for Isreal, 2013), http://www.jafi.org/AnnualReports/Annual_Report_2013-2014.pdf; World Zionist Organization, "Jewish Agency (Status) Law, 5713-1952," November 24, 1952, Article 12, *Israel Law Resource Center*, http://www.israellawresourcecenter.org/israellaws/fulltext/jewishagencystatuslaw.htm.

21. Tali Shapiro, "Let's Talk about Genocide: The Case of Palestine," *PULSE*, July 22, 2014, http://pulsemedia.org/2014/07/22/lets-talk-about-genocide-the-case-of-palestine/.

22. UN, Convention on the Prevention and Punishment of the Crime of Genocide, December 9, 1948, *United Nations Treaty Collection*, https://treaties.un.org/Pages/ViewDetails.aspx?src=TREATY&mtdsg_no=IV-1&chapter=4&lang=e.

23. UN Office of the Special Adviser on the Prevention of Genocide, "Mission Statement," accessed April 19, 2015, http://www.un.org/en/preventgenocide/adviser/.

24. Ibid.

25. Tali Shapiro, "Israel 2012, the Question of a Nation: What Does Culture Have to Do with Politics?" *PULSE*, December 12, 2012, http://pulsemedia.org/2012/12/12/israel-2012-the-question-of-a-nation-what-does-culture-have-to-do-with-politics/.

26. Palestinian Campaign for Academic and Cultural Boycott of Israel (PACBI), "PACBI Guidelines for the International Cultural Boycott of Israel," July 31, 2014, http://www.pacbi.org/etemplate.php?id=1047.

27. Ibid.

28. Izhak Laor, "Putting out a Contract on Art," *Haaretz*, July 25, 2008, http://www. haaretz.com/putting-out-a-contract-on-art-1.250388, emphasis added.

29. Ibid.

30. Palestinian Campaign for Academic and Cultural Boycott of Israel (PACBI), "PACBI Guidelines for the International Cultural Boycott of Israel," July 31, 2014, http://www.pacbi.org/etemplate.php?id=1047.

31. Tali Shapiro, "Israel 2012, The Question of a Nation: What Does Culture Have to Do with Politics? (Part 2)," *PULSE*, December 25, 2012, http://pulsemedia. org/2012/12/25/israel-2012-the-question-of-a-nation-what-does-culture-have-to-do-with-politics-part-2/.

32. Boycott! Supporting the Palestinian BDS Call from Within, 2013, "Dear Artists Scheduled to Participate or Considering Participation in Lollapalooza Israel," reposted at Lollapartheid Israel: Artists of Conscience, Respect the Boycott Facebook page, January 17, https://www.facebook.com/notes/lollapartheid-israel-artists-of-conscience-respect-the-boycott/dear-artist-scheduled-to-participate-or-considering-participation-in-lollapalooz/523469381008195.

33. Hazel Ward, "Israel Slams 'Cultural Terrorism' as Pixies Cancel Gig," *Google News/AFP*, June 6, 2010, http://www.google.com/hostednews/afp/article/ALeqM5jnuiLTovjxjwSwo415F9qITUTsZA.

34. Gidi Weitz, "Tourism Minister Given 'Illegal Gift' of VIP Madonna Tickets," *Haaretz*, January 25, 2010, http://www.haaretz.com/print-edition/news/tourism-minister-given-illegal-gift-of-vip-madonna-tickets-1.262006.

35. Max Blumenthal, "News from Chelm: Knesset Discusses Ways to Pressure Performers Not to Cancel Concerts in Israel" (blog post), January 2, 2011, http://maxblumenthal.com/2011/02/news-from-chelm-knesset-discusses-ways-to-pressure-performers-not-to-cancel-concerts-in-israel/.

36. Association for Civil Rights in Israel, "Boycott Prohibition Law," November 9, 2011, http://www.acri.org.il/en/knesset/boycott-prohibition-law/.

37. Tali Shapiro, "Creative Community for Peace: Elite Club for the Endless Cycle of War Profiteering, Whitewashing and Violence," *PULSE*, April 30, 2012, http://pulsemedia.org/2012/04/30/creative-community-for-peace-elite-club-for-the-endless-cycle-of-war-profiteering-whitewashing-and-violence/.

38. Debra Kamin, "To Counter BDS, It's Who You Know (in Hollywood)," *Times of Israel*, August 24, 2014, http://www.timesofisrael.com/to-counter-bds-its-who-you-know-in-hollywood/.

39. Tali Shapiro, "Almost 200 Hollywood Celebrities Sign on to Israel's Genocide of the Palestinian People," *PULSE*, August 25, 2014, http://pulsemedia.org/2014/08/25/almost-200-hollywood-celebrities-sign-on-to-israels-genocide-of-the-palestinian-people/.

40. United Nations Global Compact, "The Ten Principles," accessed April 19, 2015, http://www.unglobalcompact.org/AboutTheGC/TheTenPrinciples/index.html.

41. United Nations Global Compact, "UN Framework and the Global Compact: Guiding Principles on Business and Human Rights," accessed April 19, 2015, http://www.unglobalcompact.org/Issues/human_rights/The_UN_SRSG_and_the_UN_Global_Compact.html.

42. John Ruggie, *Protect, Respect and Remedy: A Framework for Business and Human Rights, Report of the Special Representative of the Secretary-General on the Issue of Human Rights and Transnational Corporations and Other Business Enterprises*, April 7, 2008, UN Human Rights Council, Business and Human Rights Resource Center, Article 54, http://www.reports-and-materials.org/Ruggie-report-7-Apr-2008.pdf.

43. Ibid., Article 69–70.

44. Ibid., Article 77, 79–80.

45. Tali Shapiro, "It Doesn't Take a Nobel Laureate to Understand the Complex and Seemingly Unsolvable Phenomena of Apartheid," *PULSE*, December 9, 2010, http://pulsemedia.org/2010/12/09/it-doesn't-take-a-nobel-laureate-to-understand-the-complex-and-seemingly-unsolvable-phenomena-of-apartheid/.

8

RELA MAZALI

Complicit Dissent, Dissenting Complicity

A Story and Its Context

LET ME TELL YOU A STORY, or, 129
actually, fragments of one. It's a tale about three women, one of
them, me. I am present in the narrative—openly equating narrator
with real-life writer. The narrated events of the story are real,
personally experienced, remembered, and recounted. Their
arrangement in this particular narrative structure isn't mediated
by an imaginary storyteller. It is explicitly my own arrangement.
This is a story, then, but not a fiction. It is framed and positioned as
an account of reality. It is a form of direct speech (on my part),
although this speech is written and read (on your part). I have told
it without distancing (my)self from substance, retaining and
acknowledging my responsibility for the portrayal, for the thinking
and feelings conveyed, for the standpoint from which the events
were lived and retold. Resisting the deeply gendered public–private
divide that structures lives in Western and other cultures, the story
offers a way of enacting some of the moves of political feminist
activism—that is, standing up in public and stating, while openly
owning, my views, knitting into a visible whole my self, voice,
gaze, actions, words. It is a way of transgressing prohibitions, of
crossing lines.

The women in this story are all mothers, two of them forcibly separated from daughters. The physical space lived by each of these two women is severed and circumscribed by the material machinery of repression. The motherhood of each is held hostage. In different ways, both they themselves and their daughters were imprisoned or restrained by the state of Israel. Each came from a very different background that positions her differently vis-à-vis Israeli society and state. On the face of it, only the tale of one of these women, Tahani Abu Dakka from Gaza, promises insight into Israel's prolonged, ongoing dispossession and subjection of the Palestinian people. Like her, however, Bashan Bat-Israel, of the Black Hebrew community was denied the most basic of rights. And each of them stood vividly dignified yet powerless and, for all practical purposes, right-less in face of the military, the security service, the police, and the courts of Israel. And, no less, in face of the sweeping indifference of most of those Israelis (and Europeans and North Americans and others) privileged enough to command a public voice.

The backdrop of their difference highlights similarities in some of the patterns of power wielded against both these women, operating through and upon their spatiality and their motherhood. The similar patterns in turn illuminate some of the common, unified underpinnings of the power acting on or towards the two women. Linking their divergent experiences and intricately intertwined are the racism, sexism, and militarism manifest in government policies in Israel,[1] much of Hebrew media, the state educational system,[2] and the outlook of many Israelis, which was openly, forcefully, and (for some Jewish Israelis) very painfully displayed in the summer of 2014 during Israel's attack against the Gaza Strip and the West Bank. Forming a reciprocal loop, racism and sexism join the fear feeding (most) Israeli Jews' self-perception as threatened victims, a self-perception that is repeatedly employed to legitimize the dehumanization of "others." The militarized result renders warfare an acceptable option, supposedly imposed upon Israel by uncontrollable, external forces.

I watched, cared about, and recorded the repressive machinery applied to these two individual lives, from my position as a relatively privileged, Jewish Israeli woman. My (partial) privilege, which is founded (even if not through my own personal deeds) on the dispossession of the Palestinian people (as well as other, often less obvious, disempowered groups) and maintained through the type of enforced segregation instituted in past in South Africa under apartheid, requires continual reproduction and reinforcement by the colonizing group. The narrative of danger and threat that upholds ongoing militarization and a continuous, racist "othering," serves to obscure, and thus to facilitate, both privilege itself and the ongoing active maintenance of privilege. A key form of privilege in Israel's society is delineated and positioned relative to two types of "others" projected as either threats to this society or its inferiors. In the process, society's most privileged are constructed as both powerful adversaries facing dangerous enemies and strong protectors of the weak inferiors. The latter, the group perceived to require protection, is feminized: women and femininity, as perceived and prescribed in Israeli Jewish society, are cast as the vulnerable other. Despite the relative privilege of many of its constituent women, myself included, the society I live in devalues and disempowers us as a means of creating the cohesive consent that upholds militarization (Halperin-Kaddari 2004).

While deceptively modernized, by and large, women of the Jewish hegemony in Israel are systematically "kept in place," for instance, through severely gendered and discriminatory laws and practices regulating marriage, abortions, fertility, divorce, and adoption (Adelman 2000; Fogiel-Bijaoui 2003). These measures clearly reveal the state's programmatic work to conscript central aspects of women's lives into "the service of the national cause," as Fogiel-Bijaoui puts it (38), projecting women as bearers and embodiments of the ethnic-national collective and, accordingly, controlling our sexuality and fertility.

Taking a close look at my privilege and my relative freedom as I wrote about two women who were forcibly denied these, I found my own to be dependent on and enmeshed with my complicity, my compliance with power systems. Witnessing, thinking, and writing about their incarceration and/or restriction, I was sensitized to my own. Alongside the state's abuse of their motherhood in particular, mine stood out as a core area of my compliance, generating my (partial) self-imprisonment. A potent, insidious vehicle for the (partial) imprisonment of relatively privileged women, the prescribed concept of "good mothering" has long served to control women in Western and other cultures. Psychologists, educators, and our own mothers teach the imperative of a mother's predominant presence, conjoining good mothering with staying home. My motherhood is employed to keep me occupied in both senses of the word: both busy, distracted *and* subject to control and surveillance. In particular, my motherhood is deployed to circumscribe my space and bar me from the public sphere. It thus factors strongly into both geography and voice and plays out distinctly along borderlines: Should I, can I, for instance, cross into Gaza (referring here to the years when this was still possible for Israelis), knowing that timetables are unpredictable and arbitrary, that I may not be able to get back in time to collect my kids from respective day care arrangements? Should I, can I, cross out of consensus, publicly state dissenting views, knowing that not only I but my children too will be sanctioned for them, via various channels? Should I, can I, transgress the contours of "good mothering," with the painful results this entails?

The story fragments below are a tale of the complicity embedded in my resistance and dissent, embedded perhaps in all resistance and dissent. Of the movement—spatial and emotional, mental, very personal, and political—between these two points: complicity and dissent. They are a tale about negotiating this movement.

The relatively comfortable routine that structures my middle-class life subjects me to a specific type of occupying forces, then.

Largely my own jailer, I am vulnerable—like other women of the dominant group in Israel—to both the incentives and the pressures of state, society, and culture, to stay put and comply; to scale down movement and mute public voice. This same matrix—state, society, and culture—forcibly disallows and dismembers "good mothering" among women from groups whose oppression is less subtle, more open, and far more severe. The prescribed, elusive, somewhat flexible confinement of "good mothering" is reserved, it seems, for women who are neither poor, nor disenfranchised (Hager 2012). "Other" women can be and are violently separated from their children (DCI 2013; Robbins 2012; Nesher 2012; Leichtentritt, Davidson-Arad, and Peled 2011). My experiences from a position of relative privilege are in *no way* comparable to the ordeals faced by the two women with whom I share the story space below. It is this stark disparity that highlights the story as an account of how of militarized racism and sexism operate on very different women through the highly effective, interconnected channels of motherhood and spatiality.

In a culture that is aggressively, though selectively, pronatal (Hashash 2010; Eyal 2009; Birenbaum-Carmeli 2009; Remennick 2006) and that mythologizes, romanticizes, and essentializes motherhood, I'm looking at differential methods of exploitation and repression via motherhood, in particular through its links to spatial existence, that is, through the significance of a mother's spatial proximity to her daughter (or son) vs. its forceful denial. Within that context, I'm touching on the racialization of motherhood(s) and its divergent but related manipulations by the state.

Paradoxically, in the mainstream, largely secular, Jewish society of Israel, the compliance of "good mothering" also includes raising children to enlist—raising them to deem military conflict an unfortunate but inevitable imperative, to view soldierhood as a worthy, normal, *healthy*, actually attractive endeavour. Good mothers among Israeli Jews (and good educators, the vast majority of whom are women in Israel) are meant to raise children to comply with mobilization law (Mazali 1998).[3] In encouraging or even allowing this, as a mother, I am complying with my child's and my own mental and emotional restriction. Raising willing conscripts requires perpetuating (or at least not contesting) a polarized, threatened world view that naturalizes prolonged warfare and denies that it is a policy choice.

At (my child's) conscription age, I am complying with a form of enforced separation, denying my daughter and myself direct mutual access and seriously circumscribing both my authority and my support. So while keeping children healthy and safe is a predominant requirement of parenting or mothering, good mothering in Israel implies raising a child to trustingly place her or him in harm's way, while sufficiently desensitizing myself to do so.

The fragment selection below doesn't unpack the tale of this particular strain of complicity—that is, complicity through privileged motherhood. Although it is absent from the story, this strain is highly pertinent to the tale's study of other aspects of privileged complicity among dissenting activists who are working to resist state crimes and injustices.

After it was written and outside this story space, a group of feminist activists, including me, began to recognize and seek ways to reject the subtle, powerful occupation of our minds and lives via the nexus of motherhood–femininity–spatiality. In 1998, New Profile, a feminist group of men and women, stated in our founding document,

> We understand that the state of war in Israel is maintained by deci-
> sions made by our politicians—not by external forces to which we are
> passively subject. While taught to believe that the country is faced by
> threats beyond its control, we now realize that the words "national
> security" have often masked calculated decisions to choose military
> action...We are no longer willing to take part in such choices. We will
> not go on enabling them by obediently, uncritically supplying soldiers
> to the military which implements them. We will not go on being

mobilized, raising children for mobilization, supporting mobilized
partners, brothers, fathers.

As I perceive them, the group's long years of anti-militarist, anti-occupation work constitute a recognition of privilege and a persistent scrutiny of its components and workings. Though the privilege is partial, given my distinct devaluation as a woman in Israel, I nevertheless count myself lucky and—no less—accountable for it. I hold myself responsible for putting this privilege to use in an attempt to change the very structure of privilege. In doing so, I cross geographical and social, cultural, political lines, to find, listen to, and learn from women for whom my privilege entails deprivation and oppression. My capacity to resist complicity, to broaden and sustain resistance, depends, at least partly, on the experience, knowledge, and support of these women—on their solidarity with me, on mine with them. The following are fragments of that search for solidarity.

Three Daughters and Neveh Tirtzah[4]

A lot of times we work at Auwni's office furniture and human rights store. It's convenient because it's a fairly large off-the-street space with assorted desks for a few Israeli volunteers to sit at beside Palestinian interpreters and take testimonies....The shadow-bureaucracy of human rights work aptly in motion in a clumsy take-off on the offices of the ruling bureaucracy. Which dictates the contents and form of the shadow anyway....Like true bureaucrats we always make a point of explaining very clearly that we can't promise anything.

It's 1992 and I am going into Gaza. Jewish Israelis go to Gaza in 1992 either because they are soldiers or because they are radicals. I choose to leave out merchandisers because they are essentially soldiers too—conquerors—in Gaza, and journalists because they are essentially either one or the other. While I go in, a Jewish Israeli woman in 1992, I am a radical.

Gaza is in my head. It's a dark dream place, not a concrete and corrugated-tin town spread over ground. In my body, at the flick of the name, it's a reflex of dilated pupils and gland dread, an unretrievable shard of nightmare. Maybe faces closing in, foreign silent language, sweating, lostness, palpitations, sweating, imminent danger for my life....The military checkpoint just north of Gaza has already come to be known as "Erez" in Palestinian as well as Hebrew. For other places, many inside Israel, Palestinians make a point of using the Arabic. But this site, set by Israelis, is pinpointed in their Hebrew name for it as the end limit of that language's domain. It is the mental point at which my simple personal sense-knowledge is checked and my fear erupts. And my elation.

"You see Jerusalem when you die." Bashan says. "And you be buried in the ground. And you...Gonna raise up, gonna get your wings and you could fly on to Jerusalem....'I want to be ready, I want to be ready,'" she is singing fast just to outline the tune, in only a rough draft of the rich deep voice she lends regularly to the spirituals choir in her community—the Black Hebrew congregation living in an enclosed neighborhood in an Israeli desert town....

Bashan was born in Georgia under a familiarly American name in August 1944 and lived on her parents' farm till she was about seven, when they moved to Indiana and later broke up. In the house where she lived with her mother and seven sisters and brothers in the 1950s on the outskirts of Gary, Indiana, USA, over a generation after her ancestors were freed from slavery, she says, "We had like a pot-belly stove and this is back in uh the late uh fifties! You know, we didn't have plumbing. We had to use the pump where you go outside and pump the water up and in the winter time it'll freeze. And it just it never was enough to eat in the house, you know."...

In Africa, in the mandatory term of wilderness, mapped onto Liberian jungle, which the community leaders allotted to the first Black Hebrews who made their way to the promised land, Bashan bought a house...."[I]t was like basically I was work...but then I think by the time Ketura was born," her second daughter, "ah we were all together. Yeah. Me, Avi," her oldest daughter,..."and Meshulam was together 'cause then we had got the house yah."

The night before the deportation—to America, where she had never been before—Avigail phoned from prison. She was held there for about six months, maybe longer....Avi, the first born to the community after their exodus, was the youngest of the Black Hebrew women that the Israelis were holding. Bashan says, "I was what like it'd be like three months pregnant when I when I left America I was pregnant with her you know. And then in my in my saying was so strong a belief hey that this is one hey this is a chi— hey I'm gonna have my child is not gonna be born here in America you know. My child is gonna be gonna be born in Africa or Israel or wherever we's we were going. But this one in particular she's gonna have a very you know different type of life from what I've had you know. And then the fact that she was the first one born when we got to Africa you know when we got to L—uh to Liberia she was the she was the first child born there you know...our first child born out of cu—born out of captivity you know. Born into the land of you know freedom. You know free mind, free thoughts, a free life you know and everything."

The police in Tel Aviv had picked Avi up with an unrenounced American passport. Outside the bounds of the community. The community and the embassy hadn't yet had a chance to—Bashan calls it process—it. Making Avi suitable for deportation to the US. "She was on the verge she was close to turning eighteen at this time, right it was—'cause it just was a couple of weeks or so bef— before her birthday. And uhm she hadn't had uhm time to you know she hadn't it hadn't came up her time to go down to begin processing her dep—her uhm what do you—her citizenship you know to her renunciation papers right." Later on Bashan's voice gets even deeper and very quiet. She clears her throat a lot. There are long pauses in the middles of sentences and in some places she's audibly fighting to get the words out unbroken. "And uh then when she did uh she spent her—was it her eighteenth birthday in uh prison you know she was in they locked her up in Abu Kabir. Then they sent her on to uh uhm Neveh what is it Neveh uh—"...

"On the night that on her last night here in Israel," Bashan says, "it was raining and uh she had she had called me from uh fro—from the prison and when and the connection was so baaayudd," she says in a voice which has almost faded to silence. "I could just hardly hear. "But I knew it was her on the other end 'cause all I could hear was this you know imaaa you know ima and and the phone was it was oh that connection was so terrible. And I'm just trying to Avi, Avi you know. And we couldn't you know we couldn't talk and then she only had what about three minutes you know on the then the phone cut off and I'm but then you know she managed to tell me let me know that she was leaving that morning you know."

"If I had really been uh conscious. But uh I wasn't uh you know I was I you know I wasn't aware of the you know danger that uh that uh she was in," Bashan explains. Later she says, "I mean you know as as the mother you know and everything hey you felt that uh somehow another that uh everything may—maybe just happened you know because of like like I say I wasn't you know in tune with what was really going on.".....

She says, "It's a race that you been running you been running running running you know. And finally you know you pah-pah-pah you know look up where you, you look like it seems to me you win it and boom boy all of a sudden you know you fall down. And everything that you done you know you worked you done tried to achieve, everything that you believe in...and everything you can just see it just you know just flying you know just flying off you know." She says, "I thought I had excaped. I had gotten out. I thought I'd really had excaped. You know. But then what happened. I look up, oh wow. Here it is I turn around and I lost you know my first you know Avigail my firstborn...An—and it was like hey I was saying hey uh so uh they didn't get me you know but then they went they came and got the they got they got the uh they got the closest thing to me."

Today, almost nine years later, Bashan, like the rest of her community, is an American citizen again, a temporary resident in Israel. She can open a bank account. She can work. She can travel. And return. She still hasn't been able to get Israeli medical insurance. She says, "If you had a vision, a thought, then you were able to make, to manifest this thought, to make this thought become real you know instead of just imagining or dreaming. But you know you were able to make it exist. And then too I mean you have to understand how brainwashed the black man was concerning Jerusalem, concerning Israel and everything. To us well Israel it was just always like stories. Things you read in the bible you know and things that uh, you know, you hear tales passed on and on and on, but you never could connect yourself with it. Until you found out that hey uh you can be a part of it too."

When I go into Gaza I do it along with one or two other people, radicals, to meet some of the people who live there, with whom we collect and record the details of abuses of their rights. These we then cross back to take to court or to the press or to some officer of the abusing party, that is, of my government. In 1992 we are still at liberty, as the people who live there are not, to come and go, cross in and out. And even though we do it a lot, I can still feel in the people doing it with me and in myself a feeling that verges on exhilarated freedom at crossing into the fearzone and emerging unscathed.

Even though it gets increasingly mapped. Onto just dusty streets in the sun and stale unfull grocery store fronts and the bare concrete steps without banisters that we climb up to cramped lawyers' offices. It is meted out in compressed but different living-cubicles in Jabaliah refugee camp and in our acquaintance with the red dirt lot in between its open sewage pool and the Israeli army post, where the gangs can get pretty rough sometimes. But also with the fringes of the central business area that are usually calm. Or the intersection across from the military government headquarters and the central prison that is often volatile and our escorts know when to skirt. The scented gardens of fruit but mostly citrus trees in the rich residential neighborhood where we're sometimes graciously received and fed are always protected and quiet. The garbage piled gorgeous beach is consistently empty.

Still we feel the power of entering and leaving the locus of fear in our minds. We too covert conquerors, our self-concepts built on images and illusions fed by Gaza's subjection. And still, in spite of mappings that have filled a lot of detail into our blank white mind-spaces, we come clearly excited at crossing in to meet "a density that marks the ruin of the known or the beginning of the unknow-able," as Adrian Rifkin calls it on page 218 of Travelers' Tales, in his piece titled Travel for Men: From Claude Levi-Strauss to the Sailor Hans. "The desire for this [meeting] point or punctum," he says, "is the motive behind that all-pervasive journeying of modern class societies called slumming." Which besides the excitement of the mind's unknown also offers a compelling ritual atonement for richer people's economic guilt.

And the added political oppression of Gaza makes it just that much more magnetic to the slummers....Passing south through Erez changes breathing patterns to deep, free, lung-filling breaths. It straightens spines....

I can see it in the way the radicals greet each other when they happen to or intentionally meet somewhere on their various itiner-aries. Hugs and strong handshakes and warm words and voices stylized in their openness and bluntness along the lines of Israeli pioneer images. Acceptable gestures of emotion. Often between people who know very little of each other, tokens of a quasi-military camaraderie of arms against the subjectors. Travel by slumming, selfhood by dissent, both assign individuals a group. The use of first person plural becomes unavoidable. And it is subtly a male plural, even though the majority of those doing the work are women.

I can see it in the real but overacted warmth of their meet-ings with each one of the hosts. From the gas-station worker who keeps an eye on the Israeli car, parked just a few metres south of the checkpoint, through the visibly overstressed lawyer who tells us the usable details of the latest court hearing, to the known but undeclared party leader whose wife serves us lunch in his garden. I follow our body language. It's serious, important, time-watchful, implying a scale of doings much bigger than the one reflected in their minuscule media-presence. Or even in the warm thanks we get on paper or faces.

I find our self-images often bloated and our self-moral-satisfaction repulsive, even though I agree it's probably vital to the work, which I agree is often good. We are merchandisers too in our subtle way. *Our* personal liberation through uncommon conduct existing by courtesy of, even if not causing, even if trying to end, *their* subjection. We are ingeniously netted in the web of complicity by the mental and emotional benefits of our dissent....

In fact going into Gaza isn't my going. I move in the fearzone by leave of Palestinians who live there and consent to have us. They pick us up just inside the checkpoint and escort us wherever we're going, pre-arranging cars and drivers to take us from one meeting to another. We know we won't be assaulted by any of the rival factions barely avoiding open warfare in 1992, out of deference to the power of our escorts, who are, we have been able to find out, recognized seats of power implicit inside the collective powerlessness. Almost all of them men, one or two women. One of whose very bright and very alive and very black eyes and power of presence I know I've seen before at close range and for a long time, when I meet her in the furniture shop. She's wearing a yellow and black and soft kerchief tucked around her hair. She is slight and small. I talk with her interpreted through her sister in law, who speaks a near-perfect Hebrew, and watch her closely, trying to place our previous meeting. After a while I remember. A hall in East Jerusalem, Israeli mothers and Palestinians whose fathers, mothers, brothers, wives, children, husbands weren't allowed to live here. Each Israeli participant would follow and plea the case of one of the Palestinian families. I was there with Yuval, a friend, and a video camera, to attend and to record, and I followed Tahani, that's her

RELA MAZALI

name, for a long time with my eyes. She came to Auwni's store over two years later about the same thing. She had no way of seeing her father. Aging. He wasn't allowed in, she wasn't allowed out.

She is one of the leaders of a Palestinian women's organization. In that position, if I'm not mistaken, she managed a bakery, drove a pickup truck, managed a nursery school or a network of nursery schools. I also knew vaguely but understood better only later, from a book called *Making Women Talk*, which was written by Teresa Thornhill and published by Lawyers for Palestinian Human Rights, that she had been in prison. For several weeks of the two and a half months of administrative detention without charges or trial, imprisoned along with her daughter, ten months old at the time, at her request. In May 1988. A year after my daughter was born. A few months after the rainy night that had interfered severely with Avi's call from the same prison. In the book Tahani calls it by the Arabic name of the city that was already there before Israel, Ramla. In an affidavit given by her and quoted by Teresa, she describes the miscarriage that she has no doubt was induced against her wishes when she was forced to take unidentified pills in prison. "It is important," she says on page 98, "to mention that I was not provided with sanitary towels" during the entire first night. "I either used paper napkins or borrowed towels which other prisoners had brought from the canteen."...

South of Erez we are by courtesy of our hosts. We're safe because they're vouching for us. The freedom we feel ourselves exercising consists entirely of deciding to trust and listen to them. This is the key to how we position ourselves beyond the dictates of our community.

By which we will nevertheless not be too seriously harassed in the person of Israeli soldiers because we are Jewish Israelis, answerable only to the laws and rules that hold only for the rulers here. These we don't break. We stretch them a little when we try to offer a couple of their protective measures to people for whom they were never meant, and probably won't serve. But the freedom

we feel ourselves exercising in fact consists of deciding to obey and
apply these laws and rules. Which is the key to how we position
ourselves beyond the dictates to their community.

So my liberty or strength come of crossing. Back and forth. As if
I were subject to neither community while I am actually subject to
both. My independence is no more and also no less than crossing
a mental fearplace. Than deciding to rely on the representatives
and rules of a foreign public, known to be dangerous by my own,
on whose rules and representatives I still, in spite of this, continue
to rely. And imprinting this compound decision onto the physical,
geographical place, the territorial signifier. Gaza.

NOTES

1.   On varying and intersecting manifestations of racism and sexism in Israel/
     Palestine, see, for instance, Elias and Kemp 2010; Hassan 2005; Anteby-Yemini
     2004; Shalhoub-Kevorkian 2004.

2.   On systemic educational discrimination against Israel's Palestinian citizens, see,
     for instance, Jabareen and Agbaria 2011; Coursen-Neff 2001. On racism towards
     Palestinians in general in Israel's Jewish schools, see, for example, Peled-
     Elhanan 2010. On state discrimination and racism against Ethiopian-descended
     school children, see Velmer 2011; Nesher and *Haaretz* 2011. On racism in state
     birth control, see Eyal 2009. On discrimination against African refugee children,
     see Cohen 2012.

3.   On the militarization of education in Israel, see Kashti 2012; Gor 2005.

4.   "Three Daughters and Neveh Tirtzah" was written in Hebrew in the course of
     my work on *Maps of Women's Goings and Stayings* (Stanford: Stanford University
     Press, 2001). The short story was published in *Noga Magazine* 32, Autumn (1997).
     See the *Noga* archive at http://www.noga-magazine.org/Olive/FileCabinet/
     Noga/. The story fragments below appeared in English in Chapters 1, 2, 6, and
     8 of *Maps of Women's Goings and Stayings*, quoted here by permission of the
     publisher.

REFERENCES

Adelman, Madelain. 2000. "No Way Out: Divorce-Related Domestic Violence in
     Israel." *Violence Against Women* 6 (11): 1223–54.

Anteby-Yemini, Lisa. 2004. "Promised Land, Imagined Homelands: Ethiopian Jews' Immigration to Israel." In *Homecomings: Unsettling Paths of Return*, edited by Fran Markowitz and Anders H. Stephansson, 146–63. Lanham, MD: Lexington Books.

Birenbaum-Carmeli, Daphna. 2009. "The Politics of 'the Natural Family' in Israel: State Policy and Kinship Ideologies." *Social Science and Medicine* 69: 1018–24. http://www.deepdyve.com/lp/elsevier/the-politics-of-the-natural-family-in-israel-state-policy-and-kinship-W30X97tmRq.

Cohen, Gili. 2012. "Israel to House African Migrant Children in Prison, Not in Facility for Minors." *Haaretz*, August 10. http://www.haaretz.com/news/national/israel-to-house-african-migrant-children-in-prison-not-in-facility-for-minors-1.457255.

Coursen-Neff, Zama. 2001. *Second Class: Discrimination against Palestinian Arab Children in Israel's Schools*. New York: Human Rights Watch.

Defense for Children International (DCI), Palestine Section. 2013. "Freedom Now: Campaign to Release Palestinian Child Prisoners." Accessed January 17. http://www.dci-pal.org/english/camp/freedom/display.cfm?docid=244&categoryid=14.

Elias, Nelly, and Adriana Kemp. 2010. "The New Second Generation: Non-Jewish *Olim*, Black Jews and Children of Migrant Workers in Israel." *Israel Studies* 15 (1): 73–94.

Eyal, Hedva. 2009. *Depo Provera A Contraceptive Method Given via Injection: A Report on its Prescription Policy Among Women of the Ethiopian Community in Israel*. Haifa: Isha L'Isha Feminist Center.

Fogiel-Bijaoui, Silvia. 2003. "Why Won't There Be Civil Marriage Any Time Soon in Israel? Or: Personal Law, the Silenced Issue of the Israeli–Palestinian Conflict." *Nashim: A Journal of Jewish Women's Studies and Gender Issues* 6 (Fall): 28–34.

Gor, Haggith, ed. 2005. *The Militarization of Eductaion*. Tel Aviv: Babel. [Hebrew]

Hager, Tamar. 2012. *Malice Aforethought*. Or Yehuda: Kinneret, Zmora-Bitan, Dvir Publishing.

Halperin-Kaddari, Ruth. 2004. *Women in Israel: A State of Their Own*. Philadelphia: University of Pennsylvania Press.

Hashash, Yali. 2010. "Medicine and the State: The Medicalization of Reproduction in Israel." In *Kin, Gene, Community: Reproductive Technologies among Jewish Israelis*, edited by Daphna Birenbaum-Carmeli and Yoram S. Carmeli, 271–95. London: Berghahn Press.

Hassan, Manar. 2005. "Growing up Female and Palestinian in Israel." Translated by Sharon Ne'eman. In *Israeli Women's Studies: A Reader*, edited by Esther Fuchs, 181–89. Piscataway, NJ: Rutgers University Press.

Jabareen, Yousef T., and Ayman Agbaria. 2011. *Education on Hold: Israeli Government Policy and Civil Society Initiatives to Improve Arab Education in Israel*. Nazareth: Dirasat, The Arab Center for Law and Policy.

Kashti, Or. 2012. "Drafting Them in Kindergarten" *Haaretz*, June 12. http://www. haaretz.com/opinion/drafting-them-in-kindergarten.premium-1.435811.

Leichtentritt, Ronit, Bilha Davidson-Arad, and Einat Peled. 2011. "Constructions of Court Petitions in Cases of Alternative Placement of Children at Risk: Meaning-Making Strategies that Social Workers Use to Shape Court Decisions." *American Journal of Orthopsychiatry, Mental Health and Social Justice* 81 (3): 372–81.

Mazali, Rela. 1997. "Three Daughters and Neveh Tirzah." *Noga Magazine* 32 (Autumn): 47–52. [Hebrew]. http://www.noga-magazine.org/Olive/FileCabinet/Noga/.

———. 1998. "Parenting Troops: The Summons to Acquiescence." In *The Women and War Reader*, edited by Lois Ann Lorentzen and Jennifer Turpin, 272–88. New York: New York University Press.

———. 2001. "Sixth Visit: The Indian in the Longing." In *Maps of Women's Goings and Stayings*, 158–89. Stanford: Stanford University Press.

Nesher, Talila. 2012. "NGOs to Court: Prohibit Mass Imprisonment of Sudanese Migrants." *Haaretz*, October 4. http://www.haaretz.com/news/national/ngos-to-court-prohibit-mass-imprisonment-of-sudanese-migrants-1.468147.

Nesher, Talila, and *Haaretz*. 2011. "Ethiopian Israelis Accuse State of School Segregation." *Haaretz*, September 1. http://www.haaretz.com/news/national/ethiopian-israelis-accuse-state-of-school-segregation-1.381933.

New Profile. 1998. "Charter." http://www.newprofile.org/english/?p=21.

Peled-Elhanan, Nurit. 2010. "Legitimation of Massacres in Israeli School History Books." *Discourse and Society* 21 (4): 377–404.

Shalhoub-Kevorkian, Nadera. 2004. "Racism, Militarisation and Policing: Police Reactions to Violence against Palestinian Women in Israel." *Social Identities* 10 (2): 171–93.

Remennick, Larissa I. 2006. Introduction to *Nashim: A Journal of Jewish Women's Studies and Gender Issues* 12 (Fall): 5–9.

Robbins, Annie. 2012. "Arrests of Palestinian Children—'A Boy in Leg Irons'—Is Becoming a Big Story in UK." *Mondoweiss*, June 29. http://mondoweiss.net/2012/06/arrests-of-palestinian-children-a-boy-in-leg-irons-is-becoming-a-big-story-in-uk.html.

Velmer, Tomer. 2011. "Report: Schools Discriminate Against Ethiopians." *Ynet*, July 28. http://www.ynetnews.com/articles/0,7340,L-4088147,00.html.

PART III

Academic and Expert Insights

KEITH HAMMOND

9 Israel's Legitimacy?

Time for a European Moratorium

The occupation is not just the domain of   149
government, army and security organiza-
tions. Everything is tainted: institutions
of justice and law, the physicians who
remain silent while medical treatment is
prevented in the territories...And also the
university lecturers who do nothing for
their imprisoned colleagues in the territo-
ries, but conduct special study programs
for the security forces. If all these boycotted
the occupation, there would be no need
for an international boycott.

—GIDEON LEVY,
   "With a Little Help from Outside"

BRITISH HOLOCAUST SPECIALIST
Cesarani notes that "Britain has probably had a longer continuous
engagement with Zionism than any other country in the world"

(2006, 131). During the period of that engagement, the "politics" have been mediated through a number of forms, with more and more public participation. Engagement now means constant reports on the web of house demolitions and settlement expansions. For many in the UK, this reads as over sixty years of ethnic cleansing. Much of this would have been unimaginable just a few years go. Even though Arab delegations visited the UK soon after the Balfour Declaration, it would not be until well into the second intifada that broad British opposition really stepped up and different forms of solidarity emerged right across the UK. Universities have played an open role in these new forms of solidarity.

Different sorts of literature were available throughout the nineteenth century, giving the ever-growing reading public a presence in the public imagination. Literature was not limited to academic literature, but Palestine was never really represented *as* Palestine. Representation was fixed in exotic imagery that played to the whims of the European (colonial) imagination. Any image of Israeli violence had to be controlled. With the emergence of the Internet that control has slowly given way to a vibrant discourse, in clear consideration of the Palestinian experience. All sorts of solidarity actions now call for a moratorium on the future of European research collaborations with Israel. This is now a standard call on most British campuses, and indeed it is particularly strong in Scotland and Ireland.

Rose and Rose (2008) claim that Israel's footballers play in the UEFA; its singers compete in the Eurovision Song Contest; and its research scientists participate in the European Research Area. They ask why. Many others ask exactly the same question. After all, Israel's record of violating international human rights law prompts this sort of questioning. Maybe Europe's specific relationship to Israel really should be spelled out to the electorate and decades of "diplomatic" compromise brought to an end. As more questions are asked of the Israel project, an altogether different sort of politics has emerged with the violations of Palestinian individual and collective rights being narrated as the ongoing concern. Why then is the relationship continued? What is the history behind support for Zionism?

The land theft that began before 1948 was encouraged by Britain. Its result was the Nakba. The land theft has continued ever since, increasing with the increase in settlements during the Oslo years. The details are clearly on record, giving a history of ongoing dispossession that has known few compromises. Rarely has that strategy changed, regardless of the political party in the Knesset. It has taken a long time for the facts of the offensive to reach the British public but those facts are now in full circulation (see Pappe 1988, 2007; Shlaim 1988, 2007). With full cognizance of the historical facts have come ethical discussion; a rigorous discourse is especially found in student groups. Students are particularly active, and as a result there is a whole new sort of politics emerging that floods way beyond campus life. This follows from the work of New Historians like Pappe (2007) who showed that three-quarters of the indigenous Palestinian population were ethnically cleansed from their land in 1948. This sort of revelation inevitably has an impact on the way Europeans think about Israel. It challenges founding myths about Israel being a land without people for a people without land.

Interestingly enough, the same ideological apparatus swung into action to sell a particular view of tragic events in 2010 on the *Mavi Marmara*. But for the British public, the impact was not the same. The whole episode came to be seen as yet another example of Israeli violence that went back years. Few now believe a word Israel puts out. Israel has claimed "self-defence" in far too many situations and has stretched its credibility beyond repair.[1] The loss of life in international waters, as the Israel Defense Forces (IDF) mounted the *Mamara*, consolidated an already horrendous view of the Zionist project that seems to get more dangerous as the years go by. Images in the memory of the British public are now indelible. Everywhere the call for a boycott has taken on new energy with the further call for a European moratorium. Solidarity, however, has changed; it now works around considerations of political association with the aims of Palestinian justice that is framed within new angles on moral fact that in the past would never been possible. The new politics go way beyond the pre-1948 British labour movement.

The Labour Movement between the Wars

Contradictions between endorsing anti-imperialism and Zionism have never really been thrashed out in the mainstream British labour movement (see Bhambra 2007). Iraq was probably the nearest that the British public came to disagreeing with government on war in the Arab world. Within the labour movement the first historic compromise with Zionism came in the August 1917 when an announcement was made of wholehearted support for a Jewish "return." This move came with the War Aims Memorandum, which A.J.P. Taylor described as having "a remarkable success" (1957, 156). Allied Socialist groups adopted the document with only slight modifications. The memorandum did not go as far as the Balfour Declaration, but it did sell the same politics to a broader working-class audience. Without any real discussion, War Aims aligned the will of the working people in Britain to that of Zionist organizations. This has had an ongoing impact on subsequent policies. Kelemen describes a prospective Labour Party candidate, M. Fogerty, arguing in a letter to the party headquarters in 1939 that the Arab case had not been put to the members (1996, 86). "Excellent," Fogerty wrote, "as the Jewish case is, it will not be possible to get a final settlement in Palestine until some understanding of the Arab case is shown." The party line on Palestine, he concluded, "seems to deal with the Arabs exactly as the English line on Ireland used to deal with Home Rulers—to put it crudely, that they are silly children misled by capitalist agitators into misunderstanding their own true interests" (Ibid.).

Going back further to 1897 in the East End of London, Zionism had not been instantly accepted by working-class Jews. Jewish politics are very different to Zionist politics, as Alderman points out with reference to Chief Rabbi Hermann Adler, who openly denounced Herzl and everything he stood for publicly. Addressing the Anglo-Jewish Association in July 1897, Adler said the forthcoming First Zionist Congress would be "an egregious blunder" along with the whole project of a Jewish state because it was "contrary to Jewish principles" (1983, 35). Change only came about as East European Jews came to London, quite rightly fleeing Russian and Polish pogroms. Even though anti-Semitism was rife at all levels of British society, these new arrivals were the first to feel its punch. It could hardly be surprising then that Herzl's message was heard with new appreciation by the new arrivals, who simply wanted an end to persecution and wandering. By 1914 Zionist influence was growing. Zionist rhetoric flourishes in the promotion of war.

Zionist groups mobilized pressure around parliamentary candidates, proving to be very effective well before anyone had heard of the Israel lobby. But interventions did not promote discussion outside of Jewish circles and it was noteworthy that Jews were not of one position. Since then, of course, lobbying techniques have become much more sophisticated and the focus has shifted to American politics (see Mearsheimer and Walt 2008). But it might be argued that many of the moves that later came to be associated with the Israel lobby had already made an appearance and been tested in these early days. Almost never have the aims of Zionism been subjected to broader democratic debate. Time and time again, Zionist policies are supported only when they conceal or move away from any disclosure of their essential aim. A case in point is shown in a letter to the *Times* of May 24, 1917 signed by David Lindo Alexander, who was, at the time, president of the Board of Deputies of British Jews, and C.G. Montefiore, president of the Anglo-Jewish Association. The letter attacked the political concept of Zionism. It caused eruptions not because of its anti-Zionist content but because Alexander had not been authorized to sign the letter on behalf of his organization. Protest completely bypassed discussion of the letter's content and brought about a dramatic change on the Board of Deputies. Political criticism had been completely avoided.

With the exception of a handful of individuals, the most effective opposition to Zionism in the UK before 1948 came from those inside Jewish communities. On many occasions, the right-wing press threw up anti-Semite editorials. Beatrice Potter argued that anyone supporting the rights of Jews to return to Palestine should then be able to argue that Kenya belonged to white settlers. She labelled the historic right of the Jews to "return" as sheer nonsense (Schindler 2012). But there was a lack of any real support for the Palestinians. Even during the Mandate period, when many would have seen and participated in the negation of Arab Palestine, there was still acceptance of the keeping Palestinians outside of broader representation. A pattern soon emerged where every expression of Palestinian autonomy was seen as a challenge to the idea of Europe. All this has gradually started to change as young people mobilize through the facilities of global communication. The consequences have been significant for a civil society that refuses to look away from Palestinian suffering. Church groups and the arts have been in the thick of it. No longer are discussions of Israeli actions limited to Labour Party and trade union meetings.

New Alliances around Justice

British academics and members of the labour movement now communicate on a regular basis with their Palestinian counterparts. This has been the case especially since 171 organizations of civil society in Palestine issued a call for an international boycott of Israel in 2004—which included the Palestinian General Federation of Trade Unions, the General Union of Palestinian Teachers, and the Federation of Unions of Palestinian Universities' Professors and Employees. At the same time, British academics have come under more pressure from students who, since the second intifada, have followed events on the ground very closely. Independent filmmakers and freelance journalists have become involved. Academics from Scotland and Ireland were amongst the first to enter Jenin refugee camp after the massacre of March 29 to April 13, 2002. The UN Security Council formed a committee to investigate the massacre but Israel's military refused to co-operate on terms not defined by their aims. In the end, alleged crimes in Jenin were never properly investigated and once again the Israeli military avoided international censure. Many questions about Jenin were left unanswered. The British public felt dissatisfied with the blanket denials.

Amidst this climate of denial, a very different sort of politics, one that moves around issues of representation, had to become more important. Nothing like this existed in the run up to the 1922 General Election when it was noted that the Labour Party candidates were so close to the local Zionist organizations that they actually distributed Zionist pamphlets throughout the East End of London as they distributed their own party material. But it was towards working-class politics, rather than Zionist politics, that the East End electorate moved when it came to the vote, even though the Zionist narrative denied the swing and claimed that the East End had moved towards Labour *because* of Labour's support for Zionism. This sort of linguistic conflict has become central to Israeli politics since November 1930. Alderman said of the occasion,

KEITH HAMMOND

The Zionist movement was in a ferment over the White Paper on Palestine which the minority Labour government of Ramsay MacDonald had issued a month previously, for this document envisaged the cessation of Jewish immigration to the Holy Land. When news of the impending by-election broke, the East London Young Zionist League announced that local Zionists would officially campaign against the government candidate; a Palestine Protest Committee was formed to undertake this work. (1983, 37)

Much of this showed the Zionist movement to grasp the nature of British politics very quickly. Again however, it has to be noted that there was little involvement of a public sphere. Few of those campaigning before the Second World War had not been previously committed to the Zionist cause for many years. In the 1930 elections, Liberals chose a local Zionist solicitor, Barnet Janner, as their candidate. The *Jewish Chronicle* of the time was over the moon, writing that there was now "a real Jewish candidate." Their editorial advised that "no Jewish vote need be lost" (Alderman 1983, 37). When the polls closed on December 3, 1930, there was a swing of 18 per cent towards the Zionist candidate and away from Labour. Labour thus held the seat but only because Labour Zionism (*poale zion*) had enlisted the pro-Zionist general secretary of the Transport and General Workers Union (Ernest Bevin) to make sure of the win. Banner campaigned almost exclusively around opposition to the October white paper prepared by Lord Passfield. The paper had demanded a limitation on Jews moving to Palestine. Subsequently, it was revoked and replaced by Churchill's earlier white paper, which had no similar limitation on Jews moving to Palestine. The Zionist lobby had clearly and very effectively made its point through the likes of Churchill.

Through similarly successful political campaigns, the number of Jews moving to Palestine increased. Activities were focused on specific clubs where Zionism could exploit anti-Semitism. Later, however, the British watered down their attitude to the new Jewish state. Politics were very much conditioned by postwar oil needs, which encouraged Bevin to talk about the interests of two hundred thousand traumatized Jews coming before two hundred million oil-producing Arabs (Zakheim 1999, 330). Typically, however, the British government still supplied Israel with arms right up to 1967. A cold period then followed that only warmed up with the appearance of Margaret Thatcher, the member of Parliament for Finchley. She became prime minister in 1979 and would become particularly close to Israel, as indeed the man who followed her and now has a website titled *Office of the Quartet Representative - Tony Blair*.[2]

1967 Leading back to 1948

With 1967 everything changed and yet politics remained somehow
very much the same. Not only did 1967 further displace the
Palestinians, it raised moral questions about the initial land theft
of 1948. The Nakba became very much alive in re-examinations
of Zionist politics driving *both* 1948 *and* 1967. After all, nothing
had emerged in 1967 that had not already made an appearance in
1948. With the rise of the Left, there came renewed interest in the
Palestinian cause. The French Marxist historian Rodinson wrote,
"Wanting to create a purely Jewish, or predominantly Jewish, state
in Arab Palestine in the twentieth century could not help but lead
to a colonial type situation and to a development of a racist state of
mind, and in the final analysis, to [more] military confrontation"
(1973, 77).

Also on the Left, Jim Allen and Ken Loach created something of
a stir with the play *Perdition*, which used the courtroom model to
represent the Kastner case that had been heard in Israel between
1953 and 1954. The play claimed no correspondence with real events
but its fictional representation gave a devastating picture of collaboration between the Zionists and Nazis as a possibility that fed into
the way Israel's actions on the West Bank and Gaza could be seen.
Allen openly claimed a subtext to the play that discredited Zionism
(Cesarani 2006, 147). Allen and Loach made no claims on historical fact, but the play was still cancelled by the management of the
Royal Court Theatre, and as a result became something of a cause
célèbre for intellectuals and activists. Merits of the play aside, the
general debate showed that the Palestinians of 1967 were not the
Palestinians of 1948. Palestinians had far more support. Edward
Said added to support whilst first serving as a consultant to the
United Nations and advising on an International Conference on
"The Question of Palestine." In preparation for the conference,
Said put together a brief narrative intended for display in the foyer
of the conference hall along with photographs by Jean Mohr that
could be seen as a historic briefing for the delegates attending.

The images showed the Palestinians were not a one-dimensional people, present only by being "outside" official Zionist narratives. Palestinians are a people just as complex as any other. Said and Mohr showed the Palestinians were not without their differences, living in a number of neighbouring states after the creation of Israel. Yet they also showed they were all connected in one way or another through relationships to 1948. For this reason, the texts and pictures were not allowed on display as had been planned. Later, they were put together again to form *After the Last Sky* (1999),

which along with other publications argued the Palestinians were one people, which led a whole new discourse on Palestinian dispossession.

Derogatory images of Palestinians as a terrorist people were discredited in new representational modalities that created endless debates, much of which moved for the first time to the ethics of what had happened in 1948. Gilo Pontecorvo's film *Battle of Algiers* had been released in 1966 and, though banned in France, it was shown for many years after in various university cities around the UK. 1967 saw the discourse being raised to a whole new level where it was repeated that nothing had happened in 1967 that had not happened on a much larger scale in 1948. From the late 1960s to 2012, one discussion of the Palestinians led to another, busting open the founding myths of Israel and creating new ways of thinking about and expressing political histories. At the same time, constant reports came out of Palestine, encouraging new angles on solidarity movements. For the first time, Palestinian scarves appeared on the British High Street as not just a fashion accessory but as a subtle indication of support for the Palestinian cause. One iconic image after another created all sorts of associations. Then, almost ten years after *Algiers*, Roy Battersby directed the *The Palestinian* (1977), the first film to show Palestinians as a people with a well-defined identity. The film gave a representation of the Palestinians from their point of view. For many in the English-speaking world, this was the first time the Palestinian cause was explained in ordinary terms. It was narrated and supposed to have been financed by Vanessa Redgrave. She appeared in one scene dancing with a Kalashnikov, which added to the film's appeal amongst the New Left.

Throughout the 1980s accounts of Israeli horror fed into the imaginary of the Nakba as never before. The ethnic cleansing of Palestine proved to be a constant in the UK discussions. At the height of the Israeli violence, in putting down the Palestinian uprising, the UN Security Council gave a clear condemnation of Israel's persistent ethnic cleansing. In Resolution 636, on July 6, 1989, the council noted the Geneva Convention and said it deeply regretted the deportation of Palestinians and called upon Israel to ensure the safe and immediate return of all those expelled from Palestine. Then, in Resolution 641, the Security Council reaffirmed its commitment to the protection of all Palestinian civilians.

Return of the Soul

Jane Frere's 2008 exhibition at the Edinburgh International Arts Festival, *Return of the Soul*, took on the politics of representation with little equivocation.[3] *Return of the Soul* contained thousands of fleeing Palestinian models made by Palestinians in some of the refugee camps, which had emerged because of 1948. The exhibition was packed out day after day and became one of the talking points of the festival. The installation represented Palestinian history as it had never been seen, or made, before, and it had a huge impact on visitors.

With thousands of tiny figures, suspended by almost invisible precarious threads, an entire people refused to be silenced. The impact was deafening. Figures made by the descendants of 1948 carried bundles of clothes and young children; old people hung on to what they could as though they were holding historic Palestine in their arms. Frere's installation was haunting in creating a political form, millions of miles away from Labour Party resolutions. Frere gave history made by those who had been at the centre of that history and had continued thereafter and refused to be marginalized.

Jane Frere, Return of the Soul: The Nakba Project, *Edinburgh International Arts Festival, 2008. Photo used with permission of the artist.*

Ordinary people filled the Patriothall Gallery. No one left the gallery unaffected by questions about justice for the Palestinians. Why were they still being denied the right of return? Few within British academia did not hear the call to action in support of Palestine. Palestinian trade unions and organizations of civil society had called for a boycott. Bishop Desmond Tutu said after visiting some of the camps where Jane Frere's models had been made that he had been deeply distressed because "it reminded me so much of what happened to us black people in South Africa. I have seen the humiliation of the Palestinians at checkpoints and roadblocks, suffering like us when young white police officers prevented us from moving about" (BRICUP 2007).

Lasson (2006) suggests that the call for an academic boycott and moratorium on European support for Israeli research is shocking—especially for Americans and those outside the ivory tower. That shock should be placed in context alongside the shock that Palestinians endured in 1948. It should be put alongside the shock of seeing Frere's moving representation of the Nakba. Indeed, that shock should be discussed in the different networks for communicating information and points of view that now contour the Palestinian solidarity movement, where Israel's policies of dispossession have come under rigorous review in a much more varied discourse of representational forms. Debate, says the British public, is finally listening to the Palestinian story and not just accepting any old myths inspired by the guilt of a labour movement that first did not support Jews fighting anti-Semitism and then did support the reactionary politics of Zionism. The labour movement in Britain has had to move on. We need a moratorium on all European research links with Israel. Right now Europeans should expect nothing less. It is only in a moratorium that pressure can be put on Israel to change its persecution and dispossession. The right of return for Palestinians has to be honoured and the whole nature of politics in Israel shifted. This will not come by itself. It will only come after there has been a moratorium and more informed debate and discussion.

KEITH HAMMOND

NOTES

1. See Schachter 1989.

2. See *Office of the Quartet Representative - Tony Blair*, http://www.quartetrep.org/ quartet/.

3. See *Return of the Soul: The Nakba Project* at http://returnofthesoul.wordpress.com.

REFERENCES

Alderman, Geoffrey. 1983. "The Political Impact of Zionism in the East end of London Before 1940." *London Journal* 9 (1): 35–38.

Bhambra, Gurinder, K. 2007. *Rethinking Modernity — Postcolonialism and the Sociological Imagination*. Basingstoke: Palgrave Macmillan.

British Committee for the Universities of Palestine (BRICUP). 2007. *Why Boycott Israeli Universities?* London: BM BRICUP.

Cesarani, David. 2006. "Anti-Zionism in Britain, 1922–2002: Continuities and Discontinuities." *The Journal of Israeli History* 25 (1): 131–60.

Hamzeh, Muna, and Todd May, eds. 2003. *Operation Defensive Shield—Witnesses to Israeli War Crimes*. London: Pluto.

Kelemen, Paul. 1996. "Zionism and the British Labour Party: 1917-39." *Social History* 21 (1): 71-87.

Lasson, Kenneth. 2006. "Scholarly and Scientific Boycotts of Israel—Abusing the Academic Enterprise." *Pouro Law Review* 21: 989-1076.

Levy, Gideon. 2006. "With a Little Help from Outside." *Haaretz*, June 4. http://www.pacbi.org/etemplate.php?id=216.

MacKenzie, John M. 1995. *Orientalism—History, Theory and the Arts*. Manchester: Manchester University Press.

Mearsheimer John J., and Walt Stephen M. 2008. *The Israel Lobby and US Foreign Policy*. London: Penguin Books.

Morris, Benny. 1988. *The Birth of the Palestinian Refugee Problem, 1947-1948*. Cambridge: Cambridge University Press.

Pappe, Ilan. 1988. *Britain and the Arab-Israeli Conflict, 1848-51*. New York: Palgrave Macmillan.

———. 2007. *The Ethnic Cleansing of Palestine*. Oxford: Oneworld Publications.

Rodinson, Maxime. 1973. *Israel: A Colonial-Settler State?* Translated by David Thorstad. New York: Monad Press.

Rose, Hilary, and Stephen Rose. 2008. "Israel, Europe and the Academic Boycott." *Race & Class* 50 (1): 1-20.

Said, Edward W. 2003. *Orientalism*. London: Pantheon Books.

Said, Edward W., and Jean Mohr. 1999. *After the Last Sky: Palestinian Lives*. New York: Columbia University Press.

Schachter, Oscar. 1989. "Self-Defense and the Rule of Law." *The American Journal of International Law* 83 (2): 259-77.

Schindler, Colin. 2012. *Israel and the European Left: Between Solidarity and Deligimization*. New York: Continuum.

Shlaim, Avi. 1988. *Collusions Across the Jordan: King Abdullah, the Zionist Movement and the Partition of Palestine*. Oxford: Clarendon Press.

———. 2007. "The Debate about 1948." In *Making Israel*, edited by Benny Morris, 124-46. Ann Arbor: University of Michigan Press.

Taylor, Alan John Percivale. 1957. *The Trouble Makers* London: Random House.

Zakheim, Dov S. 1999. "The British Reaction to Zionism: 1895 to the 1990s." *The Round Table* 350: 321-32.

ABIGAIL B. BAKAN &

YASMEEN ABU-LABAN

10

Israeli Apartheid, Canada, and Freedom of Expression

> *I believe this [Harper Conservative]*
> *government is more Israeli than the Israelis,*
> *more settler than the settlers...I think they*
> *have disqualified themselves from playing*
> *any role in the Middle East peace process.*
>
> — SAEB EREKAT,
> Palestinian chief negotiator [1]

Introduction

On November 29, 2012, the United Nations General Assembly voted overwhelmingly in favour of granting Palestine the status of "non-member observer state." Amongst only nine countries opposing this resolution were Israel, the United States, and Canada. Although Canada has had a long history of supporting the state of Israel (Abu-Laban and Bakan 2009), analysts in Canada have consistently noted the more overtly pro-Israel position taken under the Conservative Government of Stephen Harper, first elected in 2006 (Barry 2010). Indeed, just eight weeks prior to the vote, Prime Minister Harper was reported to have explicitly pressured Palestinian Authority President Mahmoud Abbas to drop the observer state bid, threatening the president that "if you keep doing what you are doing, there will be consequences" (Harper qtd. in Clark 2012). Canada's Foreign Affairs Minister John Baird also attended the General Assembly meeting and spoke out against the resolution on grounds that it was a unilateral move by the Palestinian Authority, meaning that it was not negotiated with Israel. Baird further ominously warned, "as a result of this body's utterly regrettable decision to abandon policy and principle, we will be considering all available next steps" (2012). The most immediate "next steps" included contemplating withdrawing Canadian aid and/or diplomatic representation vis-à-vis the Palestinian Authority. It is therefore understandable that Saeb Erekat, who played a key role in the observer state bid, described Canada as too partisan—even extreme—to play a constructive role in building peace; after all, Canada could have voted against the proposal without delegating Baird to speak out against the resolution, or continually issuing threats to the Palestinian Authority (Clark and Martin 2012).

When viewed from an international perspective, there is certainly considerable evidence that the Harper government is adopting pro-Israel positions with a level of fervour uncharacteristic of Canada's postwar reputation and image as "peacekeeper" in the international community. For example, in addition to its staunch support for Israel during the 2008–2009 Israeli military offensive on Gaza, Canada was the only country on the United Nations Human Rights Council to vote against a resolution condemning the ongoing military operation. Similarly, in November 2012, when Israeli military attacks were again being launched against Gaza, former Foreign Minister John Baird gave a speech in which he sought to explain "why Israel holds such a special place in my heart" (qtd. in Blanchfield 2012). Here Baird leant his support to an explicitly Zionist narrative by speaking of

Israel's "phoenix-like rising...from a barren desert to the dynamic country we see today," and elaborating that "it's simply a miracle to behold what people like Theodor Herzl, Elizer Ben-Yehuda and Chaim Weizman accomplished against all odds" (qtd. in Blanchfield 2012). In January 2014, Stephen Harper visited Israel and gave the first speech ever delivered by a Canadian prime minister to the Israeli Knesset (parliament). Harper notably avoided any critique of settlements, and instead lambasted university campuses where "most disgracefully of all, some openly call Israel an apartheid state"—a position that in Harper's words reflected "outright malice" because the state was based on "freedom, democracy and the rule of law" (Harper 2014).

In an age of "post-Zionist" Israeli historiography that has clearly documented the ethnic cleansing of Palestine (Pappe 2006), and at a moment when Palestine solidarity is growing in Western countries, the unbridled enthusiasm with which the Harper Conservatives have supported Israel is notably out of synch. Moreover, the excessive vitriol of this administration belies the multiplicity of Canadian views on Israel/Palestine; it further belies the human rights abuses and policies adopted by Israel that have reinforced popular and scholarly comparisons with apartheid South Africa (Bakan and Abu-Laban 2010). It is significant, for example, that in Quebec—Canada's province with a majority of francophones—the provincial legislature (National Assembly) passed a motion on December 4, 2012 recognizing the right of Palestinians to self-determination and statehood. The motion also called on the Government of Canada to note the UN position to grant Palestine non-member state status, and to continue its aid to Palestinians (Québec solidaire 2012). It is equally significant that the annual Israeli Apartheid Week (IAW) educational event, which takes place internationally on universities and colleges, was initiated in 2006 at Canada's University of Toronto (Ziadah and Hanieh 2010). Israeli Apartheid Week aims to increase public understanding of the history of the Palestinians as well as the racialized inequalities they experience (whether in the diaspora, under occupation, or as residents of Israel). IAW also aims to build support for the Palestinian-led boycott, divestment, and sanctions (BDS) movement, which challenges Israel's policies that violate international law.

There are, in sum, a number of complex, and contradictory, political realities governing Canada's relations with Israel and the attendant domestic responses to the Israel/Palestine conflict. The resulting tensions have given rise to a pattern of attempts to regulate the public space and discourse on Israel/Palestine. Specifically, we argue that as the economic and security dimensions between Canada and Israel have intensified, so too has broad coalitional support for Palestine solidarity. In this chapter, we attempt to explain these complex realities, proceeding in two parts. First, we consider the growing economic and security ties between Canada and Israel, and demonstrate how this has been adopted as a surveillance model. Second, we focus the use of the term *apartheid* when applied to Israel, and consider how it has been met with more overt attempts to regulate free expression at the national, provincial, and municipal levels. As we detail, these tensions are most graphically demonstrated in the attempt to ban the group Queers Against Israeli Apartheid (QuAIA) from Toronto's Pride celebration, and the ensuing resistance to this ban, significantly in a space particularly noted for its inclusiveness and embrace of difference.

Israeli Apartheid as a Surveillance Model: Economic and Security Dimensions

Racialized inequality and intense regulation of public space and free expression inform the surveillance and security dimensions advanced by the state of Israel. Particularly since September 11, 2001, this model has also been increasingly embraced by Canada through growing economic and security arrangements. As a consequence, there are close linkages between the realities of apartheid in Israel/Palestine and surveillance, security, and freedom of expression. A specific focus on public space in relation to surveillance in Israel/Palestine has been addressed in the context of the Israeli military-industrial complex (Gordon 2011). It is notable that Palestinian exile is itself constructed through the prohibition of access to public space within Palestine, due to Israel's denial of the right of return of Palestinian refugees despite recurrent recognition of this right in international law (Amit and Levit 2011, 135–36). The Israeli state has also been at pains to silence expressions of what Palestinians refer to as the Nakba (catastrophe) of 1948, in reference to their collective experience of becoming stateless in and outside of mandatory Palestine. To this end, the Israeli Ministry of Education banned the word *Nakba* in Israeli schoolbooks, and the Israeli government passed a bill that denies state funding to any Israeli non-governmental organization (NGO) that commemorates the Nakba (Zureik 2011, 17). There are also ongoing discussions regarding insistence that Palestinian Christian and Muslim citizens of Israel declare an oath of loyalty to Israel specifically as a "Jewish, Zionist and democratic state" (Zureik 2011, 17).

We suggest that these features are elements of a particular type of racialized social sorting. Social sorting, a concept introduced by David Lyon (2007), indicates state-led surveillance practices that go beyond traditional notions of managing privacy, which differentially target specific groups. Social sorting is institutionalized in Israel in specific ways. Despite claims of increased liberalization of state practices that mitigate racialization, in fact racialization in the name of security has intensified. Further, these practices find strong reverberations in the contemporary post-9/11 Canadian context, indicated by increasing regulation of discourse regarding Israel/Palestine (Abu-Laban and Bakan 2012). While not unique to the Israel/Palestine context, a specific configuration of the relationship between the Israeli state and society with homeland security domestically and on a global scale (Gordon 2011, 160–61) demands particular attention to the regulation of public space and freedom of expression. Our focus on public space, while similarly rooted in the surveillance industry and addressing the Israeli connection, is however concerned with the context of Canada. The links between the governments of Canada and Israel have parallels with the regulation of public space in Israel and the Occupied Territory, where social sorting between Israeli "Jewish nationals," who receive inordinate privileges, and Arab Palestinians (Muslim and Christian), who are treated as racialized others subject to extra-ordinary measures of control, is deeply entrenched (Lyon 2011; Zureik 2011). This process is manifest not least in a racialized stereotype of the diasporic Palestinian, and an extended racialized stereotype of the "Arab terrorist" in a global context well beyond the Middle East region (Bakan 2014).

In this context, growing economic and security ties between Canada and Israel are relevant. While the United States is Canada's largest trading partner, as Kole Kilibarda notes, what is significant is the pattern of increasing volume and links between Israel and Canada (2008, 6). A series of bilateral trade and security agreements between Israel and Canada have been renewed or enacted in the post-9/11 period, including the Canada–Israel Industrial Research and Development Fund, which was originally established in 1994 and renewed in 2006; the Canada–Israel Free Trade Agreement, established in 1997 and continually supported since then by trade missions (Government of Canada 2015); and, in 2008, the *Declaration of Intent between the Department of Public Safety and Emergency Preparedness of Canada and the Ministry of Public Security of the Government of the State of Israel* (Kilibarda 2008). In 2014, the Canada–Israel Strategic Partnership was advanced with a detailed memorandum of understanding, which included "four pillars": "diplomatic partnership," which stresses government-to-government collaboration; "defence and security," which emphasizes "counter-terrorism collaboration"; "economic prosperity," which attends to trade relations; and "science, culture, education and sport," which emphasizes exchange in each area and specifically attends to academic research (Government of Canada 2014).

The close links between the Canadian and Israeli governments have also led to increasing regulation of public space within the Canadian domestic context. For example, the links between global security claims and Israeli policy have accorded specific priority to an "Israeli approach" to the regulation of air space and airline travel. Accordingly, social sorting in the name of security has been conducted with the aim of "identification and interdiction of dangerous *persons*" rather than the conventional approach directed towards "dangerous *objects* on passengers and their belongings" (Whitaker 2011, 371, italics in original). This approach has been embraced by the Ministry of Transport in Ottawa, indicated in "an undercurrent of support...since 9/11, with much of it inspired by Israeli methods of passenger profiling, as implemented at Ben Gurion International Airport in Tel Aviv" (Whitaker 2011, 376). More broadly, as noted, in 2008 Canada signed a "Declaration of Intent" to "manage co-operation" with Israel, including in areas relating to security, immigration and border management (Government of Canada 2014).

Against this backdrop, there is evidence that popular support for Palestine solidarity has, perhaps paradoxically, grown over the course of the 2000s. This is evidenced, for example, by the expansion of Israeli Apartheid Week referred to above. Moreover, organizations such as the Coalition Against Israeli Apartheid and Independent Jewish Voices have actively campaigned to support the Palestinian civil society BDS movement (Bakan and Abu-Laban 2009). Major labour organizations, such as the Canadian Union of Public Employees of Ontario, and the Canadian Union of Postal Workers have also endorsed the BDS call (Hanieh 2008). It is in response to such alliances, with broad links advanced between Palestinian and Canadian civil society groups, that the regulation of free expression has intensified at federal, provincial, and local levels of government in Canada. Such regulation is reflected in the varied institutional settings in which there have been attempts to ban the use of the word *apartheid* from being used in relation to Israel.

Israeli Apartheid as Contested Discourse: Federal, Provincial, and Local Settings

As a federal state, it is relevant to consider Canada not only in relation to national politics but also in relation to the provinces. Moreover, local politics have also been sites of contention. In this section, we consider how the attempts to ban the use of the term *apartheid* have been advanced by the Conservative federal administration at the national level, in the most populous province of Canada—Ontario—and that province's and the country's largest city—Toronto.

Starting at the federal level, it is notable that in 2009, Jason Kenney, then minister of citizenship and immigration, stated that he was "deeply concerned" by Israeli Apartheid Week events on Canadian university campuses. He rhetorically asked "whether these activities are beneficial or are simply an effort to cloak hatred and intolerance in an outward appearance of 'intellectual inquiry'" (Government of Canada 2009). In 2010, Conservative backbench Member of Parliament Tim Upall attempted to pass a motion as a point of order in the Canadian House of Commons that held "That this House condemns Israeli Apartheid Week for seeking to delegitimize the State of Israel by equating it with the racist South African apartheid regime" (Government of Canada 2010, 1520). While this motion ultimately failed, it is relevant to note that the leaders of each of the two main political parties in Canada, the governing Conservative Party under Stephen Harper, and the Liberal Party when it was in Opposition, then under the leadership of Michael Ignatieff, made a point to go on public record, again unusually, to challenge the student-led IAW event on Canadian university campuses. In each case, the grounds was of the application of the apartheid analysis to the Israeli state.

The Harper government further indicated its intent to regulate public discourse at the federal level through its advance of the quasi-parliamentary body, the Canadian Parliamentary Coalition to Combat Antisemitism (CPCCA). Though the CPCCA had no formal government standing, between its initiation in March 2009, and the issue of its final report in July 2011 (cpcca 2011a), many parliamentarians participated and endorsed this body. Its self-described purpose was to investigate the constructed phenomenon of a "new anti-Semitism." The cpcca defined its mandate as forwarding "evidence of a global rise in anti-Semitic incidents and a return to traditional antisemitic themes in international discourse" (cpcca 2011b, 1). Significantly, one of its named ex-officio members was Jason Kenney, minister of citizenship and immigration in Prime Minister Stephen Harper's government. Kenney's department was responsible for providing $451,280 to the cpcca's operating budget, a substantial contribution not least in a period of austerity and government cutbacks (Geddes 2011). The findings of the cpcca were arguably politically suspect, and contradictory. As a number of university professors noted in a media opinion piece regarding the report, "The coalition urges critics to commit to serious and rigorous debate, but it avoids engaging in debate. It relies on hearsay, anecdotes and cherry-picked testimony while ignoring a wealth of research countering its claims. The report asserts that iaw should not be banned, but then asks university presidents to condemn iaw and calls on government to legislate this new criminalizing definition of anti-Semitism" (Ferguson et al. 2011).

The cpcca's operation and findings signal this moment of increased regulation and surveillance in the Canadian public discourse regarding freedom of expression to challenge Israel's violations of Palestinian human rights, including refusal to adhere to international law. This has also happened at the provincial and municipal levels. For example, in the Ontario provincial legislature, a private member's bill condemning iaw was passed in 2010, which was endorsed by members of the provincial Conservative, Liberal, and New Democratic parties. The condemnation was on the grounds that iaw purportedly "serves to incite hatred against Israel...and the use of the word 'apartheid' in this context diminishes the suffering of those who were victims of a true apartheid regime in South Africa" (Ontario, Legislative Assembly 2010). Moreover, the municipality of Toronto, not coincidentally then under the leadership of ultra-conservative Mayor Rob Ford, became a particularly important test case for state repression of freedom of expression. Prior to the finding of Justice Charles Hackland that the mayor was guilty of violating the Municipal Conflict of Interest Act in November 2012 (Rider, Dale, and Doolittle 2012), Ford's government and the city council of his predecessor were the subjects of considerable national attention regarding another matter connected to free expression on Israel/Palestine—Queers Against Israeli Apartheid (QUAIA).

The specific case concerned the right of QUAIA to participate in the city's annual Pride march. Toronto's Pride celebration had emerged by 1981 as an important annual city festival aimed to redress a long history of discrimination experienced by gays and lesbians and other sexual minorities (bisexuals, transgender people, etc.). The event has grown into a diverse public space affirming the rights of those historically excluded from the mainstream on grounds of sexual difference, and celebrating and valuing diversity. Moreover, it has proven to be a lucrative tourist site, broadly supported not only by social movement advocates but also significant sections of the business community and the state (Pride Toronto 2012). The lessons of this moment of Toronto political history are therefore instructive in highlighting the linkages between Israeli apartheid and surveillance of freedom of expression.

QUAIA's participation in the annual event was consistent with Pride Toronto's mandate and history, but its links to the apartheid analysis of Israel rendered its participation the subject of a targeted campaign. According to QUAIA, "Queers Against Israeli Apartheid formed to work in solidarity with queers in Palestine and Palestine solidarity movements around the world. Today, in response to increasing criticism of its occupation of Palestine, Israel is cultivating an image of itself as an oasis of gay tolerance in the Middle East, a practice that is called pinkwashing. As queers, we recognize that homophobia exists in Israel, Palestine, and across all borders. However, the struggle for sexual rights cannot come at the price of other rights" (2015).

The Toronto City Council entertained a motion in May 2010, tabled by Councillor Giorgio Mammoliti, proposing to withdraw city funding from Pride Toronto if QUAIA was allowed to participate. Later in the month, Pride Toronto's board voted to ban the use of the phrase *Israeli apartheid* at all Pride events, a decision made public by then Councillor Kyle Rae (Dale 2010). Rae in turn ensured, "in an 11th-hour intervention" (Dagostina 2010), that the controversial motion was moved from the whole council to the Toronto executive, where it was to be voted on in June. However, this motion was withdrawn on the grounds that "Pride Toronto's decision to censor any 'Israeli apartheid' messaging rendered the motion redundant" (Dagostino 2010).

As news of the ban became known, a surge of public opposition within and beyond the Toronto lesbian, gay, bisexual, transgendered, and queer/questioning (LGBTQ) community emerged, expressed as a counter-response to the decision of the Pride board of directors. In a groundswell considered comparable only to events dating back to the 1970s when gay bathhouses were subject to surveillance and police raids, pressure for reversal of the ban on grounds of freedom of expression mounted. According to one media report of June 6, 2010, the "outcry against Pride Toronto's ban of the phrase 'Israeli apartheid'" continued to swell as over twenty high-profile event participants and award winners declined to participate unless the decision was reversed (McLean 2010).

The pressure was successful, and ultimately the ban was dropped. QUAIA was permitted to march in July 4, 2010 Pride parade, along with a newly constituted ally, the Pride Coalition for Free Speech (McLean 2010). The emergent legitimacy, given license at the federal state level, and echoed provincially, of associating the term *apartheid* when applied to the state of Israel as equivalent to anti-Semitic hate speech, continued to embolden new voices. This was now expressed in recurrent attempts to regulate the nature of LGBTQ freedom of expression, at an annual event designated specifically to celebrate this public discursive space (Houston 2010). The challenge continued after the October 2010 election, which saw the election of the ultra-conservative Rob Ford to the office of mayor. Once again, motions to ban QuAIA's participation came to the Toronto City Council. An effort to render Toronto City Council funding conditional for the annual Pride Toronto event—a space known to be contrary to the socially conservative views of the Ford administration—was again placed in the context of purported humanitarian grounds.

In this next phase of the conflict, City Council waited for the findings of a report from the office of the independent city manager, Joseph Pennachetti, "to review Pride Toronto's compliance with the City's Anti-Discrimination Policy and whether the participation of Queers Against Israeli Apartheid (QuAIA) including carrying banners in the Pride Parade constitutes a violation under the City's Anti-Discrimination Policy" (Pennachetti 2011, 1). The conclusion, notably, was definitively in favour of QuAIA's right to participate in Pride: "City staff have determined that the phrase 'Israeli Apartheid' in and of itself does not violate the City's Anti-discrimination policy as it does not impede the provision of services and employment provided directly by Pride or the City to any group on any grounds provided for in the Policy...To date, the phrase 'Israeli Apartheid' has not been found to violate either the Criminal Code or the Human Rights Code (Ontario)" (Pennachetti 2011, 1). This report did not, however, satisfy the opponents of QuAIA's right to participate in Pride. A debate regarding acceptance of the report followed, including the presentation of public deputations for and against the findings. One such deputation was presented by QuAIA in the form of a short video accessible to the public (QuAIA 2011a).

Though the report was ultimately adopted, and QuAIA permitted to participate in the 2011 events, funding for Pride Toronto continued to be threatened by the Toronto Ford administration.

Once having won the right to participate in the annual event, in a strategic response to this continuing contest for free expression in public space, Qu A I A opted to remove itself from Ford's line of fire. An April 15, 2011 press release titled "Qu A I A to Mayor: Find Another Pretext for Your Anti-Pride Agenda" announced, "Rob Ford wants to use us as an excuse to cut Pride funding, even though he has always opposed funding the parade, long before we showed up," says Elle Flanders of Qu A I A. "By holding our Pride events outside of the parade, we are forcing him to make a choice: fund Pride or have your real homophobic, right-wing agenda exposed" (Qu A I A 2011b).

In 2013, Toronto's city manager and city solicitor reported that since the term *Israeli apartheid* did not constitute a breach of anti-discrimination policy, the council could not de-fund Pride on that basis (Moore and Hains 2014). Thus, in 2014, Qu A I A participated in Pride, and in fact there was no explicit opposition to their participation by other groups (*Haaretz* 2014). However, Qu A I A's continued participation remains politically charged as indicated in the 2014 Toronto mayoralty race, when candidate Olivia Chow, and the eventual Mayor-elect John Tory, both condemned the term *Israeli apartheid* (Shupac 2014). Chow, however, argued to respect the previous process of the city council, while John Tory specifically pledged that he would support changing the city's anti-discrimination policy to include the term *Israeli apartheid* if elected (Moore and Hains 2014).

Though this particular example of contested public space is occurring through the local Toronto municipal state in relation to the Pride Toronto events, the controversy around Qu A I A has received wider attention in Canada. These local events have been shaped by the provincial and federal Canadian contexts, where the very word *apartheid* in relation to Israel has come under intensive scrutiny. Events, organizations, and individuals that dare to express such words have come under new forms of surveillance and censor (Abu-Laban and Bakan 2012).

Conclusion: Contested Public Space

This chapter has addressed the growing economic and security ties between Canada and Israel, the growing forms of resistance to and contestation of Israeli apartheid as expressed by Palestine solidarity activists, and the complex ways in which attempts to ban the word *apartheid* have found institutional expression at national, provincial, and local levels, as seen in the case of Ontario and Toronto. The example of Queers Against Israeli Apartheid in Toronto Pride is particularly stark. It underscores the extreme nature of the repression experienced by Palestine solidarity activists seeking to defend Palestinian rights, even in a space that was explicitly formed in opposition to the historic regulation of public space. Despite these attempts, it is important to note that solidarity for Palestine continues to build in Canada as in other countries internationally. There is no reason to expect that mobilizing around opposition to *Israeli apartheid* will diminish.

Returning to where this discussion began, it can also be noted that the outcome of the United Nations General Assembly vote on granting Palestine the status of "non-member state observer" is an indication of support for Palestine internationally. This includes support from such European countries as Sweden, Norway, France, Ireland, Spain, and Belgium. Canada's negative position in this UN debate, advanced particularly by the Conservative administration of Stephen Harper, is clearly in contradistinction to the dominant views expressed in the Quebec National Assembly, as well in the wider context of Canadian public opinion. Indeed, days after Baird's statement in the UN, the administration was compelled to withdraw the threats on behalf of Canada, following intense high-level discussions of the implications (Canadian Press 2012). Notably, a 2011 poll conducted for the British Broadcasting Corporation found that 46 per cent of Canadians supported this recognition, and only 25 per cent of Canadians opposed it (CBC News 2011). In this sense, the position of the Harper Conservatives is far from being the sum total of how Canadians view Israel/Palestine, even if it has led to

Canada being viewed as "more Israeli than the Israelis and more settler than the settlers."

AUTHORS' NOTE

This chapter is equally and jointly written by the authors. We would like to acknowledge the support of the Social Sciences and Humanities Research Council of Canada for our project on "Debating Racism and Framing Anti-Racism." We note, too, that ideas for this chapter also benefitted from the SSHRC Major Collaborative Research Initiative, "The New Transparency: Surveillance and Social Sorting," and our participation in a workshop called "The Expanding Surveillance Net: Ten Years After 9/11" held at Queen's University, Kingston, ON (September 8–10, 2011).

177

NOTE

1. Qtd. in Campbell Clark and Patrick Martin, "Palestinians Paint Canada as Too Extreme," *Globe and Mail*, November 30, 2012.

REFERENCES

Abu-Laban, Yasmeen, and Abigail B. Bakan. 2008. "The Racial Contract: Israel/ Palestine and Canada." *Social Identities: Journal for the Study of Race, Nation and Culture* 14 (5): 637–60.

———. 2011. "The 'Israelization' of Social Sorting and the 'Palestinianization' of the Racial Contract: Reframing Israel/Palestine and the War on Terror." In *Surveillance and Control in Israel/Palestine: Population, Territory and Power*, edited by Elia Zureik, David Lyon, and Yasmeen Abu-Laban, 276–94. London: Routledge.

———. 2012. "After 9/11: Canada, the Israel/Palestine Conflict and the Surveillance of Public Discourse." *Canadian Journal of Law and Society* 27 (3): 329–40.

Amit, Zalman, and Daphna Levit. 2011. *Israeli Rejectionism: A Hidden Agenda in the Middle East Peace Process*. London: Pluto Press.

Baird, John. 2012. "Address by Minister Baird to United Nations General Assembly in Opposition to Palestinian Bid for Non-Member Observer Status." Speech, November 29. *Foreign Affairs, Trade and Development Canada*. http://www.international.gc.ca/media/aff/speeches-discours/2012/11/29a. aspx?lang=eng&view=d.

Bakan, Abigail B. 2014. "Permanent Patriots and Temporary Predators?: Post 9/11 Institutionalization of the Arab/Orientalized 'Other' in the United States and the Contributions of Arendt and Said." In *Liberating Temporariness?: Migration, Work, and Citizenship in an Age of Insecurity*, edited by Leah F. Vosko, Valerie Preston, and Robert Latham, 60–75. Montreal and Kingston: McGill-Queen's University Press.

Bakan, Abigail B., and Yasmeen Abu-Laban. 2009. "Palestinian Resistance and International Solidarity: The B D S Campaign:" *Race and Class* (July–September): 29–54.

———. 2010. "Israel/Palestine, South Africa and the 'One-State Solution': The Case for an Apartheid Analysis." *Politikon: South African Journal of Political Studies* 37 (2–3): 331–51.

Barry, Donald. 2010. "Canada and the Middle East Today: Electoral Politics and Foreign Policy." *Arab Studies Quarterly* 32 (4): 191–217.

Blanchfield, Mike. 2012. "John Baird Hails 'Miracle' of Israel as Ceasefire Negotiated with Gaza." *Huffington Post*, November 20. http://www.huffingtonpost.ca/2012/11/20/john-baird-israel-miracle-speech-gaza-ceasefire_n_2168866.html.

Canadian Parliamentary Coalition to Combat Antisemitism (C P C C A). 2011a. *Canadian Parliamentary Coalition to Combat Antisemitism Releases Final Inquiry Panel Report.* Press release. July 7.

———. (2011b). *Report of the Inquiry Panel.* July.

Canadian Press. 2012. "Canada's Aid to Palestinians to Be Maintained." *C P24.com*, December 4. http://www.cp24.com/news/canada-s-aid-to-palestinians-to-be-maintained-1.1065675.

C B C News. 2011. "Most Back Palestinian State, Poll Suggests." *cbc.ca*, September 18. http://www.cbc.ca/news/world/story/2011/09/18/poll-recognition-palestine.html.

Clark, Campbell. 2012. "Harper Took Steps to Stifle Palestinian Statehood Bid." *Globe and Mail*, November 26. http://www.theglobeandmail.com/news/politics/harper-took-steps-to-stifle-palestinian-statehood-bid/article5655676/.

Clark, Campbell, and Patrick Martin. 2012. "Palestinians Paint Canada as Too Extreme." *Globe and Mail*, December 1: A3.

Dagostina, Scott. 2010. "Toronto City Council Dodges Responsibility for Pride Censorship." *Xtra.ca*, June 14. http://www.xtra.ca/public/printStory.aspx?AFF_TYPE=1&STORY_I D =8777.

Dale, Daniel. 2010. "Pride Prohibits Phrase 'Israeli Apartheid.'" *Toronto Star*, May 21. http://www.thestar.com/printarticle/813053.

Ferguson, Sue, and Mary-Jo Nadeau, Eric Shragge, Abby Lippman, Gary Kinsman, and Rubin Roth. 2011. "Debate: Report on Anti-Semitism Seeks Only to Protect Israel." *National Post*, July 21. http://news.nationalpost.com/full-comment/debate-report-on-anti-semitism-seeks-only-to-protect-israel.

Geddes, John. 2011. "Follow the Money." *Macleans.ca*, July 28. http://www2.macleans.ca/2011/07/28/follow-the-money-2/.

Gordon, Neve. 2011. "Israel's Emergence as a Homeland Security Capital." In *Surveillance and Control in Israel/Palestine: Population, Territory and Power*, edited by Elia Zureik, David Lyon, and Yasmeen Abu-Laban, 153–70. London: Routledge.

Government of Canada. 2015. "Canada–Israel Free Trade Agreement (CIFTA)." March 12. http://www.international.gc.ca/trade-agreements-accords-commerciaux/agr-acc/israel/index.aspx?lang=eng.

———. Citizenship and Immigration Canada. 2009. "Minister Kenney Issues Statement on 'Israeli Apartheid Week.'" Media release, March 3.

———. Foreign Affairs, Trade and Development Canada. 2014. "Canada–Israel Strategic Partnership: Memorandum of Understanding." http://www.international.gc.ca/name-anmo/canada_israel_MOU-prot_ent_canada_israel.aspx?lang=eng.

———. House of Commons. 2010. *Hansard*, March 11. (Mr. Tim Upall). http://www.parl.gc.ca/HousePublications/Publication.aspx?DocId=4342803&Language=E&Mode=1.

Haaretz. 2014. "Queers Against Israeli Apartheid to March in Toronto's Pride Parade, This Time Unopposed." June 25. http://www.haaretz.com/jewish-world/jewish-world-news/1.601228.

Hanieh, Adam. 2008. "Building Labour Solidarity with Palestine." *The Bullet* 108 (May 20). http://www.socialistproject.ca/bullet/bullet108.html.

Harper, Stephen. 2014. "Text of Harper's Historic Speech to Israel's Knesset." *Globe and Mail*, January 20. http://www.theglobeandmail.com/news/politics/read-the-full-text-of-harpers-historic-speech-to-israels-knesset/article16406371/?page=all.

Houston, Andrea. 2010. "Drawing Battle Lines: Pride, QuAIA and Toronto Council." *Xtra.ca*, November 20. http://www.xtra.ca/public/printStory.aspx?AFF_TYPE=3&STORY_ID=9458.

Kilibarda, Kole. 2008. "Canadian and Israeli Defense—Industrial and Homeland Security Ties: An Analysis." Working Paper. The New Transparency: Surveillance and Social Sorting Project, Queen's University, November. http://www.sscqueens.org/resources/online-reports.

Lyon, David. 2007. *Surveillance Studies: An Overview*. Cambridge: Polity Press.

McLean, Jesse. 2010. "Backlash Grows Against Pride's 'Israeli Apartheid' Ban." *Toronto Star*, June 6. http://www.thestar.com/printarticle/819813.

Moore, Oliver, and David Hains. 2014. "Tory Targets Queers Against Israeli Apartheid in Two Debates." *Globe and Mail*, September 19. http://www.theglobeandmail.com/news/toronto/tory-targets-queers-against-israeli-apartheid-at-latest-debate/article20711803/.

Ontario. Legislative Assembly. 2010. "Israeli Apartheid Week." *Hansard*, February 25. http://www.ontla.on.ca/web/houseproceedings/house_detail.do?Date=2010-02-25&Parl=39&Sess=1&locale=en#P609_160349.

Pappe, Ilan. 2006. *The Ethnic Cleansing of Palestine*. Oxford: Oneworld Publications.

Pennachetti, Joseph P. 2011. "Compliance with the City of Toronto's Anti-Discrimination Policy—Pride Toronto." Toronto City Council, April 2. http://app.toronto.ca/tmmis/viewAgendaItemHistory.do?item=2010.MM51.3.

Pride Toronto. 2012. "History." http://www.pridetoronto.com/about/history/.

Québec solidaire, Parliamentary wing. 2012. "L'Assemblée nationale du Québec reconnaît pour la première fois le droit des Palestiniens à l'autodétermination." Press release, December 4. http://www.fil-information.gouv.qc.ca/Pages/Article. aspx?lang=en&motsCles=palestine&listeThe=&listeReg=&listeDiff=&type= &dateDebut=2012-12-04&dateFin=2012-12-05&afficherResultats=oui&idArt icle=2012046305.

Queers Against Israeli Apartheid (QUAIA). 2011a. "QUAIA Deputation—Pride 2011." *rabble.ca*, May 27. http://rabble.ca/print/rabbletv/program-guide/2011/05/ best-net/quaia-deputation-pride-2011.

———. 2011b. "QUAIA to Mayor: Find Another Pretext for Your Anti-Pride Agenda." April 15. http://queersagainstapartheid.org/2011/04/15/ quaia-to-mayor-find-another-pretext-for-your-anti-pride-agenda/.

———. 2015. "Who We Are." Accessed April 20. http://queersagainstapartheid.org/ who/.

Rider, David, Daniel Dale, and Robyn Doolittle. 2012. "Rob Ford Out: Toronto Heads into Uncharted Territory." *Toronto Star*, November 26. http://www.thestar.com/ news/gta/article/1293531--rob-ford-out-toronto-heads-into-uncharted-territory.

Said, Edward. 1992. *The Question of Palestine*. New York: Vintage.

Shupac, Jodie. 2014. "Tory, Chow Diverge on Funding Pride if QUAIA Allowed to March." *Canadian Jewish News*, September 19. http://www.cjnews.com/canada/ tory-chow-diverge-funding-pride-if-quaia-allowed-march.

Whitaker, Reg. 2011. "Behavioural Profiling in Israeli Aviation Security as a Tool for Social Control." In *Surveillance and Control in Israel/Palestine: Population, Territory and Power*, edited Elia Zureik, David Lyon, and Yasmeen Abu-Laban, 371–85. London: Routledge.

Ziadah, Rafeef, and Adam Hanieh. 2010. "Collective Approaches to Activist Knowledge: Experiences of the New Anti-apartheid Movement in Toronto." In *Learning from the Ground Up: Global Perspectives on Social Movements and Knowledge Production*, edited by Aziz Choudry and Dip Kapoor, 85–99. New York: Palgrave Macmillan.

Zureik, Elia. 2011. "Colonialism, Surveillance, and Population Control: Israel/ Palestine." In *Surveillance and Control in Israel/Palestine: Population, Territory and Power*, edited by Elia Zureik, David Lyon, and Yasmeen Abu-Laban, 3–46. London: Routledge.

Political Truths

JAMES CAIRNS &

SUSAN FERGUSON

11

The Case of Pro-Palestine

Discourse in Canada

> *The ability to go beneath the surface of*
> *appearances to reveal the real but concealed*
> *social relations requires both theoretical*
> *and political activity.*
>
> — NANCY HARTSOCK,
> *The Feminist Standpoint Revisited*

Palestine Solidarity under Attack

In July 2010, University of Toronto master's student Jennifer Peto submitted her thesis, "The Victimhood of the Powerful: White Jews, Zionism and the Racism of Hegemonic Holocaust Education," to the Department of Sociology and Equity Studies in Education (SESE).[1] Her thesis examines two Holocaust education projects and argues that they draw on and extend an ideology of Jewish victimhood. In so doing, Peto argues, they perpetuate a form of Jewish racism and deflect criticism of the Israeli state project and its internationally condemned violation of Palestinian human rights.

Within months, Peto, her supervisor, her department, and the Ontario Institute for Studies in Education (OISE, the U of T school that houses SESE) came under attack. Members of the media, the academy, and even the provincial legislature lambasted the thesis, calling it a form of anti-Semitic hate literature.[2] But they did not just attack the substance of the research. They also attacked the system that nurtures and legitimizes political work such as Peto's under the name of rigorous, detached inquiry. York University history professor and former Canadian Jewish Congress president Irving Abella's assessment of Peto's thesis was typical: "It's not scholarship, it's ideology...I'm appalled that it would be acceptable to a major university."[3] University of British Columbia Professor Emeritus Werner Cohn accused Peto of "emotion" and "holy rage," and labelled her methodology "purely subjective."[4]

The attack on Peto's thesis is but one example of a series of similar attempts to discredit and therefore silence scholarly and activist work done in solidarity with Palestinian struggles on the basis of its political character. That is, claims to knowledge that support the Palestinian side in the struggle against Israel—that question the legitimacy of the Israeli occupation and refusal of the right of return, the liberal democratic nature of the Israeli state or the tenets of political Zionism on which that state is based—are regularly deemed *political* and thus lacking in integrity (or objectivity). In this view, politicized knowledge is, ipso facto, biased, and therefore cannot be trusted as truthful.

Another recent example concerns the final report of the Canadian Parliamentary Coalition to Combat Antisemitism (CPCCA). Its authors accept the view that proponents of Israeli Apartheid Week (IAW) "have tended to hijack any open and honest dialogue regarding the Middle East," and the week-long series of lectures, workshops, and social events "is antithetical to academic debate and devoid of the integrity and nuance that should govern the Canadian university system."[5] A column in the *National Post* states that "If the goal were actual education and informed discussion about the Arab–Israeli conflict, IAW programming would incorporate competing points of view."[6] The fact that IAW organizers develop a clear political position in opposition to the Israeli state leads many critics to label IAW "nothing but a thinly veiled hate fest."[7] Most witnesses invited to speak at CPCCA hearings dismissed pro-Palestinian scholars and activists for being extremists, "anti-logical," wrathful, "pathological," warped by "bias and prejudice," and incapable of "thoughtful criticism."[8] The political nature of IAW, in other words, prevents it from revealing anything truthful about the world.

York University administration's response to a conference titled "Israel/Palestine: Mapping Models of Statehood and Paths to Peace" is yet another case in point. Despite the conference having been vetted by a peer-review process to obtain funding, the administration charged that it lacked appropriate "balance." One of its main concerns was "with the fact that some of the participants are 'activists, NGO workers and polemicists'" whose work was clearly grounded in solidarity with Palestinian struggles.[9] In the eyes of the university administrators, as well as the extraordinary after-the-fact inquiry into the conference, the perceived pro-Palestinian character of the event placed it beyond the bounds of legitimate debate.[10]

As Nadeau and Sears argue, the push to silence pro-Palestinian research and activism "has deep roots in the specific history of Palestinian unfreedom, which has centred around sustained efforts to erase Palestinian existence."[11] This history runs from the violent displacement of hundreds of thousands of Palestinians by Zionist forces during the Nakba of 1948, through Israel's brutal occupation of the West Bank and Gaza in 1967, through the present-day buildup of apartheid Israel in the form of illegal settlements in the Occupied Territory, an extensive network of Jewish-only roadways throughout Israel/Palestine, severe restrictions on Palestinian movement enforced by hundreds of Israeli checkpoints and the siege on Gaza, constant attacks on Palestinian students and schools, the demolition of Palestinian homes and agricultural lands, and regular military assaults on Palestinians throughout the region.

The history of apartheid, exodus, and expulsion described in this book powerfully shapes the terrain upon which Palestinian solidarity struggles are waged. Such a history of erasure and silencing, and the normalization of Israeli apartheid that it invites, is precisely what allows for the charge of *bias* and *politicization* to undermine any perspective that pushes against the dominant narrative depicting Israel as a victim state that encapsulates and protects the collective interests of Jewish people around the world.[12] This criticism resonates widely in liberal democracies, and lends strength and legitimacy to those seeking to shut down debate on Palestinian history and the Palestine solidarity movement. Palestine solidarity becomes at best a passionate opinion, at worst a racist, manipulative lie.

A growing literature exposes the weakness of this charge.[13] This chapter confronts it on its own terms. Specifically, we address the question: If pro-Palestinian research and activism is "political" (a claim we do not deny), how should we as activists and scholars defend the legitimacy of our work? We suggest that not only can our claims about Israel/Palestine be defended as valid and valuable knowledge, but also—if the movement for justice and against oppression is to prevail—they *must* be defended as such. It is in this spirit that we offer an argument in support of political truths.

The Limitations of Liberal-Pluralist Defences

To assert that something is both true and political at the same time generally invites two equally troublesome responses: (1) the positivist response that greeted Peto's thesis, which views all "political" positions as biased (and therefore untrustworthy and needing to be discredited), or (2) the liberal-pluralist response, which defends the right of all "political" positions to be heard, so that one has the right to assert one's (inevitably biased) viewpoint, just the same as everyone else has. The latter has been a common response to the controversies around the silencing campaign. University administrators, media pundits, politicians, and activists weighing in to support Peto's thesis, Israeli Apartheid Week, or the Mapping Models conference, for instance, have largely argued for the validity of the political critique of Israel on the basis of freedom of expression, noting that this freedom is meaningless unless the right to air views that are unpopular is strongly upheld.[14] The philosophical and strategic virtues of this response are straightforward: not only is free speech a fundamental tenet of democracy but it is only through the airing of all positions that one can determine the "truth" or the best resolution. As Herbert Marcuse argues, the "telos of tolerance is truth."[15] That is, tolerance of diverse and conflicting ideas is not an end in itself but a precondition to freedom. Only by debating our differences can we determine which claims are false or unacceptable and must be rejected, and thus organize society according to those ideas that support freedom, justice, and equality.

But, as Marcuse also notes, the liberal-pluralist commitment to dialogue invariably loses sight of this purported end. To begin, it too easily shades over into liberal-relativism, in which knowledge claims, because they inevitably reflect the social positioning of the knower, cannot be analyzed against a standard outside of subjective experience. Thus, from this perspective, no claim is more truthful than another, as all claims are equally valid. In Marcuse's language, such "pure" or "repressive" tolerance is tantamount to refusing to adjudicate between competing knowledge claims.[16]

Liberal-pluralism is thus easily commandeered by those who espouse the positivist response, as the experience of organizing in the Palestinian solidarity movement has shown. While explicitly anti-liberal attempts to shut down criticism of Israel continue unabated at the level of the state, academic administration, and media, there is another, more subtle, strategy that pro-Zionist forces are now deploying: calls for balanced "dialogue." As Saifer, Nadeau and Sears, and Masri have documented, the anti-Palestinian "silencing campaign" in Canada has made a virtue of "dialogue" (albeit defined in a way that excludes criticism of Israel).[17]

With both counter- and pro-hegemonic forces espousing
the free exchange of opinions and ideas, the question of which
positions *ought to* prevail, which narrative is more *true* (in the sense
of promoting understanding through compelling explanation,
or revealing something accurate and valid about the world), is
positioned outside the bounds of reasonable debate. In other
words, the defence of freedom of expression and the call for
dialogue can lead us down a troubling path. Insofar as conflicting
positions are treated as just so many particular truths, they can
work to undermine or deflect—rather than advance—the quest
for knowledge. Yet the progress of movements for social justice in
general, and of the Palestinian solidarity movement specifically,
depends upon activists' and scholars' capacity to convince others
not just of their right to tell their counter-hegemonic or subaltern
story because it is *their* truth, but of the legitimacy of the claims
of that story—as well as the distortions of the pro-hegemonic or
dominant story.

The Power of Historical Materialism

In contrast to liberal-pluralist defences of pro-Palestine discourse,
we argue for an approach to claiming political truths guided
by the tradition of historical materialism. The liberal-relativist
approach helpfully identifies the contingent nature of knowledge,
insisting that we can only know the world through our particular,
historically specific, experience of it. But it misses the ways in
which our diverse experiences are embedded in—and are partial
expressions of—a wider social whole. The notion of a dialectical
interplay between the particular and the whole is captured by the
Hegelian-Marxian conceptualization of "internal relations."[18] From
this perspective, we can and do come to know the world through
its "diverse aspects."[19] But because our particular and diverse
experiences are always socially mediated (that is, inflected in and
through the wider social dynamics of which they are a part), our
situated knowledge also reveals something real or true about that

wider social totality. It follows then that some knowledge claims are "more true" than others because they more fully grasp and articulate the social whole.

This conceptualization of knowledge and truth as historically and socially mediated helps us move beyond the limits of the liberal-pluralist defence toward a stronger basis for advocating political research and activism. To begin, it accepts the partiality, but not the radical relativity, of knowledge. Not every position is equally true (even if subjectivity is an essential part of rigorous truth-telling).[20] Interpretation—our capacity to identify and theorize the connections between what we know through experience, and what we know of the social totality—is a critical step in arriving at truth or understanding.[21] And insofar as the social is a complex and contradictory totality, interpretation can either obfuscate or clarify. Pro-Palestinian research and activism must be defended (and tested) against this standard: To what extent does it reveal something true about (and thus help us to better understand) the nature of the social relations in which the experiences of not only Palestinians, but also Israelis, Jews, and Arabs are embedded?

Here it is helpful to turn to the Russian literary theorist Mikhail Bakhtin. In Bakhtin's schematic, there are two dominant, broadly defined, ways of coming to know and express the world.[22] Each emerges from different positions within the social whole, and each expresses and defends different social interests. On one hand, there is the official, dreary *monologic* perspective of the dominant order. On the other hand, there is the *dialogic*, the unofficial, often profane and ribald perspective of subaltern communities. The knowledge claims they produce are neither equivalent nor complementary. While monologic knowledge *abstracts* from the complexity of embodied reality in the name of asserting a partial truth that represents itself as being universal, dialogic knowledge *emerges* from that embodied reality.[23] Both are inevitably partial, but only the dialogic is capable of expressing and the rich and complex experiential diversity of the world, knowledge that can reveal truths about the social whole that a monologic perspective obscures.

The authenticity of dialogue stems from the rootedness of the dialogic in the embodied, always-changing, complex, and contradictory experiential realm, which Bakhtin theorized in relation to the carnival (popular celebrations of the Middle Ages). The carnival's diversity and bawdy elements called attention to specific ways in which human bodies of medieval Europe were socially constituted, and as such, manipulated, repressed, and harmed. The behaviours it spawned—grotesque acts of eating, rollicking laughter, and public displays of typically private areas of the body—were certainly transgressive, but they could only be so within a set of social relations in which the norm was hunger, drudgery, and sexual repression. Thus, the truth-telling capacity of the carnival stemmed from the fact that it both celebrated the undeniably diverse and embodied nature of authentic human experience and, in doing so, highlighted the deprivations and dysfunctions of unequal power relations.[24]

For Bakhtin, then, subaltern experiences are true insofar as they can expose an otherwise obscured truth: that is, that the social whole is unequal and unjust. As Hartsock argues about the power of a distinctly materialist feminism, a subaltern standpoint on social relations, "by drawing out the potentiality available in the actuality and thereby exposing the inhumanity of human relations...embodies a distress which requires a solution."[25]

And it is precisely this that allows us to move beyond the liberal-relativist position that sees all knowledge as equally biased on account of being politically interested, and toward theoretical grounds for adjudicating among inevitably "political" accounts. All knowledge is "political" in the sense that it upholds and/or challenges broader relations of power;[26] but some (monologic, that which is often held up as "objective" knowledge) denies and invisibilizes the *real and partial* nature of all knowledge, while other (dialogic, that which is often dismissed as politicized knowledge) insists upon the real, viewed crucially as a partial reflection of the social whole. Guided by historical materialism, we can defend not only the right of subaltern voices to make their claims, but, insofar as they are interpreted in terms of the dialectical relationship between the particular and the universal, experience and social relations, we can also defend the (inevitably partial) truth content of those claims.[27]

Facing up to Political Truths

An example from debates about Israel/Palestine helps to demonstrate the relevance of historical materialism. Ilan Pappe's book *The Ethnic Cleansing of Palestine* explains numerous ways in which the official narrative that supports Israel's privileged place in the eyes of the West depends upon the active suppression of the history of Palestinian people and the crimes against Palestinians perpetrated by the Israeli state.[28] Pappe uses the word "memoricide" to refer to the murder of memories required to maintain the perception of Israel as a liberal, democratic country. The book details how, contrary to official Israeli historiography, Israel's founding in 1948 occurred in tandem with—and was contingent on—a massive ethnic cleansing operation designed and directed by the Zionist leadership. He documents the founding and execution of a specific plan to remove hundreds of thousands of Palestinian people from their traditional lands through their forced expulsion, the destruction of houses, marketplaces, and other infrastructure, and the summary execution of large numbers of innocent people. In Pappe's words, which are corroborated by a range of Palestinian oral histories, when this mission concluded in the fall of 1948, "more than half of Palestine's natural population, close to 800,000 people, had been uprooted, 531 villages had been destroyed, and eleven urban neighbourhoods emptied of their inhabitants."[29]

In order for the new state of Israel to assume the character of a legitimate, democratic nation, it would need to repress knowledge of the real experiences upon which it was founded. One of the earliest instruments of this "memoricide" was the Israeli government's "Naming Committee whose job it was to Hebraize Palestine's geography," replacing the Arabic names of Palestinian towns with Hebrew names.[30] Another example is the massive forestation project carried out by the Jewish National Fund (JNF). Pappe explains that quite apart from the environmental concerns indicated in the official explanation of the forestation project,

> the true mission of the JNF...has been to conceal [the] visible remnants of Palestine not only by the trees it has planted over them, but also by the narratives it has created to deny their existence. Whether on the JNF website or in the parks themselves, the most sophisticated audiovisual equipment displays the official Zionist story, contextualising any given location within the national meta-narrative of the Jewish people and Eretz Israel [the name for Palestine in the Jewish religion]. This version continues to spout the familiar myth of the narrative—Palestine as an "empty" and "arid" land before the arrival of Zionism—that Zionism employs to supplant all history that contradicts its own invented Jewish past.[31]

These examples of memoricide are instructive because they help to think concretely about some of the theoretical problems raised in this chapter. Specifically, they provide an example of the dominant narrative in action, the monologic discourse of official culture. Israel's official history erases the actual history of ethnic cleansing and builds up the myth that the Zionists settled an empty land. Doing so, as Pappe explains, means erasing its treatment of Palestinians from the collective consciousness, a project that involves mythmaking, as well as erasing physical signs of Palestinian pre-1948 existence—in particular, the embodied experiences of Palestinians who variously fought, died, and fled. This is what we mean by official history that abstracts from embodied reality, denying the truth-telling potential of specific partial experiences. Israel's ongoing refusal to negotiate with the Palestinian people about claims to their traditional lands (claims recognized by the United Nations in December 1948) means that the country's official history depends upon the erasure of embodied reality both in the past and the present. The monological Zionist narrative excludes the rich history of the Palestinians in what is now Israel, the Occupied Territory, and the Palestinian diaspora.

This official narrative has achieved the status of truth within mainstream Western consciousness. Of course, the Zionist story is itself political: it is a particular way of conceiving of and organizing social relations that privileges some and excludes others. But as this story has achieved the status of truth, its political character has been hidden under the taken-for-grantedness of Israel's present power.[32] As Gramsci explains, part of achieving the kind of hegemony that Israel and its Western allies enjoy is making historical relations appear as matters of "common sense."[33] Social relations become so naturalized that people have a hard time imagining how things could ever be otherwise. It is, therefore, counter-hegemonic to question the legitimacy of common sense, an act that gets interpreted as "political" by those who accept the status quo.

This takes us back to the importance of embodiment and inter-pretation in defending political truths. If claims to truth are to avoid falling into the trap of liberal-relativism—claiming to be true only inasmuch as they have the right to be heard alongside any and all other competing "truths"—political truths must claim not only that they reflect a particular experience or individual subjectivity, but that their particularity is internally related to the wider social whole, and as such, have the potential to illuminate something real about the oppressive nature of social relations more generally. As such it is *partial* for sure, but it also shines a light on the diverse unity that comprises the real. In the case of Palestine solidarity work, the argument against silencing can thus move beyond the liberal claim to free speech. Thoughtful and rigorous pro-Palestine research and activism highlights not only those embodied experiences the official Israeli account denies and erases, but situates these within the wider unequal and exploitative set of social relations in which they are embedded. Thus, campaigns such as Right to Education, which publicizes firsthand accounts of Palestinian students' daily struggle to attend classes, or IAW and other such events that feature films and discussions about the humiliations Palestinians endure at checkpoint crossings, the difficulties they encounter supplying medical services, the destruction of their livelihoods and homes in a Gaza under siege, all can be defended to the degree that they uphold the historical materialist standard of truth: To what extent do they collectively reveal and articulate a fuller understanding of the Israel/Palestine conflict, and clarify (rather than obfuscate) the nature of the wider social relations in which these experiences are embedded? The same can and must be said for Peto's thesis and the presentations at the Mapping Models conference. It is not simply that as pro-Palestinian researchers and activists, we have a right to tell these stories. More importantly, we can and must insist that they contribute to our understanding, our knowledge about a conflict that is too often understood from the official culture's point of view—a point of view that obscures the inequality and injustice of the imperialist-colonialist reality that inflects all these experiences.

This does not mean that every claim made by a pro-Palestinian activist or researcher is beyond challenge simply because it contests the official view. On the contrary, facts should be verified against experiential accounts, and their contextualization should be logical and coherent. Of course debates should be had. But their political character must not be the thing that delegitimizes them.[34] A claim can be political at the same time as it insists upon being the best possible, partial, representation of the social whole.

It is not in fact the political character of research and activism that dominant voices object to (as all accounts are political); it is, rather, the idea that particular social locations are capable of viewing and articulating something truthful about the world. It is the subaltern position of particular groups of people that make them a problem, as opposed to the fact that they make political arguments whereas others ostensibly do not. This is part of the disadvantage subaltern groups must struggle against within existing relations of power. In one sense, no matter how correct their arguments are, when these groups seriously challenge the legitimacy of hegemonic power relations, they inevitably face hostility from those who hold power. Accusations of political bias are an effective way of dismissing subaltern claims from mainstream public debate. And yet, counter-hegemonic movements ignore mainstream culture at their peril.

If it is to grow in size and strength, a counter-hegemonic movement must engage people who tend not to conceive of the world in counter-hegemonic terms. This requires critical scholars and activists to convince others of the justice and truth of their claims—and effectively repel accusations of illegitimacy due to political bias. Our argument has been that an emphasis on the relationship between embodiment and narrative in (the always partial) representations of the social whole contributes to the challenging task of arguing that political research and activism can also be true. We are not so naive as to suggest that this theoretical framework is all-powerful in defending against the attacks of hegemonic forces. But in light of the subordinated position from which subaltern groups struggle, we would suggest that concentrating on the real material circumstances of social experience, understood from within the overarching system of unequal social relations, is a promising way of defending against the delegitimation tactics of an official culture whose "truth" depends upon hiding aspects of embodied existence.

1. Jennifer Peto, "The Victimhood of the Powerful: White Jews, Zionism and the Racism of Hegemonic Holocaust Education" (MA thesis, University of Toronto, 2010).

2. David P. Hornick, "U of Toronto Posts Anti-Semitic Tripe," PJ Media, November 19, 2010, http://pjmedia.com/blog/u-of-toronto-posts-anti-semitic-tripe/; Jonathan Kay, "Jennifer Peto and the New Breed of Self-Hating Jews," National Post, December 8, 2010, http://fullcomment.nationalpost.com/2010/12/08/jonathan-kay-on-jennifer-peto-and-the-new-breed-of-self-hating-jews/; Jonathan Kay, "Wow—Even Ultra-Politically-Correct Lefties Are Throwing Jennifer Peto under the Bus," National Post, December 9, 2010, http://fullcomment.nationalpost.com/2010/12/09/wow-%E2%80%94-even-ultra-politically-correct-lefties-are-throwing-jennifer-peto-under-the-bus/); Ontario, Legislative Assembly, Hansard (December 7, 2010), 4016, http://www.ontla.on.ca/house-proceedings/transcripts/files_pdf/07-DEC-2010_L080.pdf.

3. Abella qtd. in Daniel Dale, "U of T Slammed Over 'Jewish Racism' Thesis," Toronto Star, December 7, 2010, http://www.thestar.com/news/article/902572--u-of-t-slammed-over-jewish-racism-thesis.

4. Werner Cohn, "The Frauds of OISE," FringeGroups, November 8, 2010, http://www.fringegroups.com/search/label/Peto%20Jennifer.

5. Canadian Parliamentary Coalition to Combat Antisemitism, Report of the Inquiry Panel, July 7, 2011, 54, https://www.jewishvirtuallibrary.org/jsource/anti-semitism/canadareport2011.pdf.

6. Catherine Chatterley, "A Hateful Pedigree: On the Eve of 'Israeli Apartheid Week,' a Canadian Scholar Traces the Event's Roots to Two Sources: Classic Anti-Semitism and Stalinist-Era Soviet Propaganda," National Post, March 3, 2011, A14.

7. Frank Dimant qtd. in "Arab Events Draw Ire," Toronto Star, January 22, 2005, B02.

8. See James Cairns and Susan Ferguson, "Human Rights Revisionism and the Canadian Parliamentary Coalition to Combat Antisemitism," Canadian Journal of Communication 36 (2011): 427–28.

9. Mazen Masri, "A Tale of Two Conferences: On Power, Identity, and Academic Freedom," Journal of Academic Freedom 2 (2011): 21.

10. Although Masri rejects the administration's conception of "balance," he also points out that the conference included participants from a variety of political viewpoints ("A Tale of Two Conferences," 2011, 7–13).

11. Mary-Jo Nadeau and Alan Sears, "The Palestine Test: Countering the Silencing Campaign," Studies in Political Economy 85 (2010): 7.

12. See, for example, Irwin Cotler, "Global Antisemitism: Assault on Human Rights," submission to the Canadian Parliamentary Coalition to Combat Antisemitism, November 2, 2010, Ottawa, http://www.cpcca.ca/Cotler.pdf.

13. See, for example, Yasmeen Abu-Laban and Abigail Bakan, "The Racial Contract: Israel/Palestine and Canada," *Social Identities* 14 (2008): 637–60; Abigail Bakan and Yasmeen Abu-Laban, "Israel/Palestine, South Africa and the 'One-State Solution': The Case for an Apartheid Analysis," *Politikon* 37 (2010): 331–51; Cairns and Ferguson, "Human Rights Revisionism"; Nadeau and Sears, "The Palestine Test."

14. See, for example, the defence made by University of Toronto vice-president and provost Cheryl Misak, in Canadian Association of University Teachers, "Politicians Attack Toronto Grad Student," *CAUT Bulletin* 58 (2011), https://www.cautbulletin.ca/en_article.asp?ArticleID=3179.

15. Herbert Marcuse, "Repressive Tolerance," in *A Critique of Pure Tolerance* by Robert Paul Wolff, Barrington Moore, and Herbert Marcuse (Boston: Beacon Press, 1969), 90.

16. Marcuse, "Repressive Tolerance," 94.

17. Ben Saifer, "Shalom-Salaam?: Campus Israel Advocacy and the Politics of 'Dialogue,'" *Upping the Anti* 9 (2009), http://uppingtheanti.org/journal/article/09-shalom-salaam/; Nadeau and Sears, "The Palestine Test"; Masri, "A Tale of Two Conferences."

18. Bertall Ollman, *Alienation: Marx's Conception of Man in Capitalist Society* (Cambridge: Cambridge University Press, 1971), 33.

19. Karl Marx, "A Contribution to the Critique of Political Economy," trans. S.W. Ryazanskaya, *Marxists Internet Archive*, accessed February 21, 2012, http://www.marxists.org/archive/marx/works/1859/critique-pol-economy/appx1.htm#205.

20. Nancy C.M. Hartsock, *The Feminist Standpoint Revisited and Other Essays* (Boulder, CO: Westview Press, 1998), 107.

21. Edward W. Said, *Covering Islam: How the Media and the Experts Determine How We See the Rest of the World* (New York: Pantheon, 1981), 154–56.

22. Michel Bakhtin, *Rabelais and His World* (Bloomington: Indiana University Press, 1984).

23. We unpack this statement in relation to Israel and Palestine later in this chapter, but a brief example may be helpful at this point. Consider the US government truth claim that their troops invaded Iraq in 2003 in order to fell a dictator and spread democracy—a claim that arguably abstracts from (to the point of denying) the complex and contradictory experiences that unofficial accounts of the past and present American presence in Iraq can and do reveal.

24. David McNally, *Bodies of Meaning: Studies on Language, Labor, and Liberation* (Albany: State University of New York Press, 2001).

25. Hartsock, *The Feminist Standpoint*, 125.

26. Nigel Harris, *Beliefs in Society: The Problem of Ideology* (London: Watts, 1968).

27. Again, this is not to assert that an account is true *because* it is political, but to argue that the political nature of any particular account does not make it untrue, nor does it mean that all accounts are equally true. Rather, the truth content of an account must be looked for in its relationship to the domain of social, historical human experience.

28. Ilan Pappe, *The Ethnic Cleansing of Palestine* (Oxford: Oneworld Publications, 2006). Similar "monologic" accounts are central to the cultural life of all settler colonial states, including Canada. We focus on Israel here because of its relevance to the controversy surrounding Peto's thesis.

29. Pappe, *Ethnic Cleansing*, xiii; see also, Walid Khalidi, "Why Did the Palestinians Leave, Revisited," *Journal of Palestine Studies* 34 (2005): 42–54; Norman G. Finkelstein, *Image and Reality of the Israel-Palestine Conflict*, 2nd ed. (New York: Verso, 2003).

30. Pappe, *Ethnic Cleansing*, 226.

31. Ibid., 228–29.

32. See Zalman Amit and Daphna Levit, *Israeli Rejectionism: A Hidden Agenda in the Middle East Peace Process* (London: Pluto Press, 2011), 1–13.

33. Antonio Gramsci, *Selections from the Prison Notebooks*, ed. and trans. Q. Hoare and G.N. Smith (New York: International Publishers, 1971), 323.

34. For a discussion of the politics of social theory, see Chapter 7 in Alan Sears and James Cairns, *A Good Book in Theory: Making Sense through Inquiry*, 2nd ed. (Toronto: University of Toronto Press, 2010).

REFERENCES

Abu-Laban, Yasmeen, and Abigail Bakan. "The Racial Contract: Israel/Palestine and Canada." *Social Identities* 14 (2008): 637–60.

Amit, Zalman, and Daphna Levit. *Israeli Rejectionism: A Hidden Agenda in the Middle East Peace Process*. London: Pluto Press, 2011.

Bakan, Abigail, and Yasmeen Abu-Laban. "Israel/Palestine, South Africa and the 'One-State Solution': The Case for an Apartheid Analysis." *Politikon* 37 (2010): 331–51.

Bakhtin, Mikhail. *Rabelais and His World*. Bloomington: Indiana University Press, 1984.

Cairns, James, and Susan Ferguson. "Human Rights Revisionism and the Canadian Parliamentary Coalition to Combat Antisemitism." *Canadian Journal of Communication* 36 (2011): 415–34.

Canadian Association of University Teachers. "Politicians Attack Toronto Grad Student." *CAUT Bulletin* 58 (2011). https://www.cautbulletin.ca/en_article.asp?ArticleID=3179.

Canadian Parliamentary Coalition to Combat Antisemitism. *Report of the Inquiry Panel.*
July 7, 2011. http://www.cpcca.ca/CPCCA_Final_Report_English.pdf.

Chatterley, Catherine. "A Hateful Pedigree: On the Eve of 'Israeli Apartheid Week,'
a Canadian Scholar Traces the Event's Roots to Two Sources: Classic Anti-
Semitism and Stalinist-Era Soviet Propaganda." *National Post*, March 3, 2011.

Cohn, Werner. "The Frauds of OISE." *FringeGroups*, November 8, 2010.
http://www.fringegroups.com/search/label/Peto%20Jennifer.

Cotler, Irwin. "Global Antisemitism: Assault on Human Rights." Submission to the
Canadian Parliamentary Coalition to Combat Antisemitism, November 2, 2010.
http://www.cpcca.ca/Cotler.pdf.

Dale, Daniel. "U of T Slammed Over 'Jewish Racism' Thesis." *Toronto Star*, December 7,
2010. http://www.thestar.com/news/article/902572--u-of-t-slammed-over-jewish-
racism-thesis.

Finkelstein, Norman G. *Image and Reality of the Israel-Palestine Conflict.* 2nd ed. New
York: Verso, 2003.

Gramsci, Antonio. *Selections from The Prison Notebooks.* Edited and translated by Q.
Hoare and G.N. Smith. New York: International Publishers, 1971.

Harris, Nigel. *Beliefs in Society: The Problem of Ideology.* London: Watts, 1968.

Hartsock, Nancy C.M. *The Feminist Standpoint Revisited and Other Essays.* Boulder, CO:
Westview Press, 1998.

Hornick, David P. "U of Toronto Posts Anti-Semitic Tripe." *PJ Media*, November 19,
2010. http://pjmedia.com/blog/u-of-toronto-posts-anti-semitic-tripe/.

Kay, Jonathan. "Jennifer Peto and the New Breed of Self-Hating Jews." *National
Post*, December 9, 2010. http://fullcomment.nationalpost.com/2010/12/08/
jonathan-kay-on-jennifer-peto-and-the-new-breed-of-self-hating-jews/.

———. "Wow—Even Ultra-Politically-Correct Lefties Are Throwing Jennifer
Peto under the Bus." *National Post*, December 9, 2010. http://fullcomment.
nationalpost.com/2010/12/09/wow-%E2%80%94-even-ultra-politically-correct-
lefties-are-throwing-jennifer-peto-under-the-bus/.

Khalidi, Walid. "Why Did the Palestinians Leave, Revisited." *Journal of Palestine Studies*
34 (2005): 42–54.

Marcuse, Herbert. "Repressive Tolerance." In *A Critique of Pure Tolerance*, by Robert
Paul Wolff, Barrington Moore, and Herbert Marcuse, 81–117. Boston: Beacon
Press, 1969.

Marx, Karl. "A Contribution to the Critique of Political Economy." Translated by S.W.
Ryazanskaya. *Marxists Internet Archive.* Accessed February 21, 2012. http://www.
marxists.org/archive/marx/works/1859/critique-pol-economy/appx1.htm#205.

Masri, Mazen. "A Tale of Two Conferences: On Power, Identity, and Academic
Freedom." *Journal of Academic Freedom* 2 (2011): 1–28.

McNally, David. *Bodies of Meaning: Studies on Language, Labor, and Liberation.* Albany: State University of New York Press, 2001.

Nadeau, Mary-Jo, and Alan Sears. "The Palestine Test: Countering the Silencing Campaign." *Studies in Political Economy* 85 (2010): 7–34.

Ollman, Bertall. *Alienation: Marx's Conception of Man in Capitalist Society.* Cambridge: Cambridge University Press, 1971.

Ontario. Legislative Assembly. *Hansard*, December 7, 2010. http://www.ontla.on.ca/house-proceedings/transcripts/files_pdf/07-DEC-2010_L080.pdf.

Pappe, Ilan. *The Ethnic Cleansing of Palestine.* Oxford: Oneworld Publications, 2006.

Peto, Jennifer. "The Victimhood of the Powerful: White Jews, Zionism and the Racism of Hegemonic Holocaust Education." MA thesis, University of Toronto, 2010.

Said, Edward W. *Covering Islam: How the Media and the Experts Determine How We See the Rest of the World.* New York: Pantheon, 1981.

Saifer, Ben. "Shalom-Salaam?: Campus Israel Advocacy and the Politics of 'Dialogue.'" *Upping the Anti* 9 (2009). http://uppingtheanti.org/journal/article/09-shalom-salaam/.

Sears, Alan, and James Cairns. *A Good Book in Theory: Making Sense Through Inquiry.* 2nd ed. Toronto: University of Toronto Press, 2010.

A Hole in the Wall, A Rose at a Checkpoint

SHERENE RAZACK

The Spatiality of Occupied Palestine

SPACE IS ONE WAY to think about the violence of settler states towards the Indigenous populations they have dispossessed. In June of 2007, I was invited to share with Palestinian scholars my research on the spatiality of settler violence against Canada's Aboriginal peoples. The spatiality of power relations has become an important methodological directive for those of us who work on white settler societies. Racial power is anchored spatially, as Rhadika Mohanram succinctly put it, and deconstructing how power operates in and through space (a process I refer to elsewhere as unmapping) is one way of tracking the race and gender arrangements of settler societies.[1]

There is a distinct spatiality to the three most salient features of settler colonialism: the making of the colonizer as modern and the colonized as pre-modern; the eviction of the colonized from the law and thus from civilized space; and the violence that marks the colonial encounter. In my address to the conference, I offered various examples of colonial or racial violence in Canada: Aboriginal men who are driven out of city space by the police, and left to walk back into town in subzero conditions, an eviction many do not survive; Aboriginal women working as prostitutes who often "disappear" and are later found murdered and dumped in spaces outside of civilized life; and alcoholic Aboriginal men who die under mysterious circumstances after being apprehended by the police, often with signs of violence on their bodies (boot prints, handcuff marks, and so on). I suggested that what is discernable in each of these moments of violence is an ongoing colonialism—full of legally authorized evictions to zones where the law does not operate and where violence can take place with impunity. The sequential features of this kind of abandonment are spatial segregation that is legally produced and authorized; a reduction of peoples to a diminished state of existence; violent evictions from settler space, evictions that function as identity-making processes for the colonizer. Law largely forgives the perpetrators of colonial violence. It often does so either by viewing the instances of violence as exceptional and/or considering that the victims brought the violence on themselves—it is they who are dysfunctional, sick, prostituting themselves, posing a security threat, and so on.

The richness of the exchanges that took place at the conference "Palestinian Voices: Feminist Thought As a Tool for Resistance" in Nazareth and Birzeit, and throughout my visit to Israel/Palestine, stimulated a number of additional thoughts on the spatiality of colonial arrangements. Most of all, perhaps because this was my first experience of militarized occupation and with the myriad ways in which daily life is militarized for occupied populations, I came to appreciate in a new way how power is memorialized (to use Achille Mbembe's evocative phrase) on the bodies of the occupied, an awareness gained largely from my experience of the wall being built by Israel to physically separate itself from Palestine. Put another way, I saw parallels between the imprinting of colonial power on Aboriginal peoples in Canada and the same processes in Palestine.

This chapter reflects on the spatial arrangements that memorialize power on the bodies of the colonized in occupied Palestine. These are the reflections of someone whose research is focused on the

Canadian context. I attempt here to have a conversation with those scholars who are more conversant with the Israeli/Palestinian context than I, reading them through the prism of my own extremely brief experience of occupied Palestine, and through my research on violence against Aboriginal peoples in Canada.

At the Level of Skin: The Checkpoint

In her brilliant article on the spatiality of apartheid, South African scholar Lindsay Bremner argues that it wasn't a wall or even the Bantustans that most distinguished apartheid:

> *Instead it was the countless instruments of control and humiliation (racially discriminatory laws, administration boards, commissions of inquiry, town planning schemes, health regulations, pass books, spot fines, location permits, police raids, removal vans, bulldozers) and sites of regulation and surveillance (registration offices, health clinics, post offices, recruitment bureaus, hostels, servants rooms, police spaces, courtrooms, park benches, beer halls) that delineated South African society during the Apartheid years and produced its characteristic landscapes.*[2]

Daily "acts and rituals were transformed into acts of segregation and humiliation that accumulated into an omnipresent violence of everyday life. In this obscene enactment of power, apartheid's walls were nowhere and everywhere," Bremner notes. She concludes, "Apartheid operated as a bio-politics of discrimination and disqualification at the level of the skin. The skin was the site where the categories of violence associated with borders were performed."[3]

Bremner thus invites us to consider that the landscape of apartheid was one of *encounters* as well as separations, and that colonial power is power exercised on bodies. In cities, while each race group had its own residential area and type of housing, there were carefully planned zones of interaction. Bantustans were in fact fragmented and discontinuous. They were not meant to enclose but to force residents into migrant labour. Thus, "Apartheid's characteristic spatial forms were designed to be porous, to regulate the body in motion. They produced a narrative not of closure, but of hundreds of thousands of entries and crossings."[4] It is this porousness that most strikes the first-time visitor about the wall separating Palestinians and Israelis, a porousness that suggests both where and how the bodies of the occupied are imprinted with the power of the occupiers.

Memorializing Power

Power must be inscribed on the bodies of the colonized, a "memorializing," as Mbembe puts it, that is in evidence at moments of contact. Explaining what he terms "graphism" as a principal colonial technology under apartheid, Mbembe describes this process for black miners:

> Graphism consisted foremost in tracing marks on the body and on the territory. But the main site of inscription was the black body itself. It could be searched everyday at the end of the shift in the mines. It could be stripped naked, required to jump over bars. Hair, nose, ears, or rectum could be scrutinized with meticulous care. Floggings with a sjambok (leather whip) or tent rope, or striking with fists were the rule. In order to memorialize themselves, public and private powers traced their signs on the naked flesh of the black body. They belabored it and laid it bare through various techniques: tattooing, excising, carving, sacrifying, mutilating, or encircling.[5]

To memorialize power on the bodies of the colonized requires an apparatus. The apartheid racial state had to organize segregation, jailing, eviction, and "floating spots where 'inhumanity' could be immediately experienced in the body as such. Around them was instituted a field of visibility and surveillance, hierarchies and inspections."[6] One thinks here of the floating checkpoints that are "sprung" on Palestinians anywhere and at anytime.

In contemporary occupied Palestine, the wall with its many checkpoints and openings provides a case in point of graphism. While a great deal has been written on how the wall functions to impoverish and disrupt Palestinian life, less has been said about its effects on individual bodies. In Nadera Shalhoub-Kevorkian's work *Facing the Wall*, one sees how girls and women negotiate their daily crossings.[7] At checkpoints, girls learn that their own communities are limited in their capacity to protect them from all kinds of violence—the violence of the Israeli soldiers but also the patriarchal violence of their own communities as they rush home to avoid curfew. Parents also impose restrictions on girls' activities, fearing that they will be harassed by soldiers. In effect, the wall teaches girls and women in an embodied way that they are under surveillance and condemned to a lesser life. Such effects are clearly gendered in that they do not apply in the same way to boys as to girls. Girls who are forced to climb over hills, ditches, and walls, to take clandestine routes and to risk search and seizure, are denied the bodily integrity of full citizens but also the modesty that under patriarchy would otherwise mark them as the sex to be protected. Palestinian girls are thus evicted from femininity and bear all the attendant, gender-specific risks of such an eviction.

"See How We Jump": A Hole in the Wall at Al-Jeeb

To first-time visitors, the sheer magnitude of the wall (in places where it is a twenty-five-foot concrete barrier) immediately begins to have an impact on the body. One feels small, vulnerable, and hemmed in. The impression of a tremendous power is nowhere more overwhelming than when one stands in the very small space between the wall and the apartment block or building it has simply cut off. Suddenly, someone's bedroom window now looks out on a concrete monstrosity one can almost touch. The wall casts a huge shadow on the buildings it has isolated and it reaches quite literally into daily life, squeezing life's activities into smaller and smaller spaces. Frantz Fanon's description of the world of the colonized as "a world without spaciousness" is particularly relevant here.[8]

The process of inscribing power on bodies is aptly captured in the response of a Palestinian man whose efforts to cross through an opening in the wall were being filmed by a French television crew. "Show them [French viewers] how we jump," he suggested with ill-concealed irony.[9] Openings in the wall, parts somehow left unfinished, or parts of the wall that can be scaled produce Palestinians as pre-modern, animal-like in their movements, clandestine and illegitimate as they navigate the enormous blocks of concrete, the barbed wire, and the electrified fences. At one such opening at Al-Jeeb,[10] I observed a young man jumping perilously from building roof to concrete block to make his way back into Al-Jeeb from Jerusalem. The man seemed small and thin against the massive concrete and his movements brought to mind goats as they scramble up mountain slopes. Others, less agile and perhaps less willing to risk life and limb, made their way to Jerusalem through the opening at a lower level by climbing over the concrete slab that had not yet been placed upright and fixed in its place. One woman carried her computer bag and it swung dangerously as she climbed, aided by some young men.

The lessons for the body are clear: Palestinians do not simply walk or ride to work or school but instead scramble, crawl, and climb. From the roof of a nearby almost empty apartment building, one can see the full extent of the wall and watch the progress of the people climbing through the opening. At one such moment, two military jeeps materialized out of nowhere. The woman carrying the computer, whose black chador was visible from on high as she made her way through open expanse, now stood frozen as a deer caught in headlights. The jeeps came from each direction, cutting off all possibility of escape and making clear that the wall is also an "apparatus of capture."[11] Soldiers regularly tear gas these openings in the wall, making Palestinians "jump" and flee, this time in physical pain.

Asymmetrical Intimacies

Reading online the accounts of young Palestinians at checkpoints, it is clear that the checkpoint, like the opening in the wall, must physically reduce the body to a state of insignificance, and to the status and movements of a trapped animal. The rituals at the checkpoint, Kafkaesque in their absurdity, are nonetheless productive in the same way as the imposed climbing is; they imprint the power arrangements of colonialism on the bodies of the colonized, laying bare for all to see and to know in an embodied way who can have human dignity and who cannot.

The young soldiers who check the papers of Palestinians cannot hope to be making any kind of realistic assessment of who must cross and who must not, precisely because there are many crossings. As under apartheid, when black people from the townships provided the labour for whites in the cities, so too Palestinians must continually journey to Israel for the purpose of work, school, medical care, and family interactions. What, then, is the purpose of checkpoint rituals, if they do not serve any practical purpose? The rituals themselves offer a clue. When boys and girls and young adults describe their experiences of passing through the Qalandiya checkpoint, for instance, they describe the shouting that accompanies the many stages of checkpoint ritual. Twenty-year-old Muhammed Maher comments, "The checking procedure takes some 15-20 minutes. First I put my ID into a small hole, then they shout at me to go to the body checking process." Twelve and thirteen year olds at Ahed secondary school in Al-Ram describe the same shouting as they move from the first set of revolving doors, through the x-ray process and then the checking of ID on children too young to possess it.[12] The checkpoint is an asymmetrical intimate encounter whose asymmetries must be performed. We might think, then, of the structured security encounter as a time and place where occupied and occupier, each comes to know his place in the scheme of things. In short, the identity-making processes at work at the checkpoint come into full focus.

While Palestinians must learn of continuous surveillance and of the febrile texture of the encounter, so too the Israelis must find in these rituals their own sense of entitlement and be able to convince themselves that they have successfully controlled the movements of anyone who encroaches on the settler's claim. Fanon's classic words about "the language of pure force" of colonial police come to mind:

> In the colonial countries, on the contrary [to capitalist countries where force is differently expressed], the policeman and the soldier, by their immediate presence and their frequent and direct action maintain contact with the native and advise him by means of rifle butts and napalm not to budge. It is obvious here that the agents of government speak the language of pure force. The intermediary does not lighten the oppression, nor seek to hide the domination; he shows them up and puts them into practice with the clear conscience of the upholder of the peace; yet he is the bringer of violence into the home and into the mind of the native.[13]

Fanon's point speaks to the wall's overt function and to the language of pure force. However, as many of the contributors to the outstanding collection *Against the Wall* point out, the wall has both overt and covert functions. Ruchama Marton and Dalit Baum observe that the wall is both a defence from bullets and a defence from seeing. With respect to the latter, the wall has the important psychological advantage of enabling those on the Israeli side to imagine that what lies beyond the wall, that is, what they don't see, does not exist. If seeing holds out the possibility of understanding, Marton and Baum wryly comment, then the wall blocks the possibility of "insight" into the conditions of the lives of Palestinians.[14] As in Aldous Huxley's *Brave New World*, the war takes place on far away alien worlds.

If we focus on the covert functions of the wall, as Marton and Baum do, and follow their arguments about what the wall does, we can consider the wall as enabling a fantasy of control and conquest.

For the occupier, the wall serves to keep at bay his terrible anxiety that he is in fact not in control. Marton and Baum characterize the psychic underpinnings of what goes on for the soldier and the state at the checkpoint as an obsessive disorder, a belief that the repetition of certain actions (a cleansing, a checking) will prevent death. They insightfully observe, "Rituals are created with the aim of self-preservation from contamination, diseases and deaths. These rituals are constantly refined in arbitrary ways. The person knows deep down that there is no total control; thus the anxiety is ever present, reinforcing these rituals, which may take over an obsessive person's life, achieving precedence over all aspects of life, requiring an ever-growing investment of resources."[15] Holes in the wall and checkpoints are "zones of friction" in which colonizer and colonized come to know themselves within the hierarchies that sustain and are sustained by them.

For Ariella Azoulay and Adi Ophir, when considering the wall's function, it is important to consider the relation between what they term spectacular violence (which kills instantly) and suspended violence: "The suspended violence is effective without bursting out because it forbids, deters, and delays, complicates simple actions, undermines preferences, undercuts daily schedules, drives people crazy and sometimes even kills. Its impact is more, not less disastrous than that of spectacular violence."[16] The distinction, they write, is sometimes blurred, as when a soldier at a checkpoint (or a settler on a rampage) erupts into spectacular violence. Spectacular violence often "congeals" into suspended violence, as when they produce more troops, more checkpoints, and so on; conversely, suspended violence easily erupts into spectacular violence. Azoulay's and Ophir's understanding that the wall is "a seemingly perfect architectonic-geostrategic machine of suspended violence,"[17] and their insight into the wall as "spatial segregation and reintegration through which conflict management is carried out by the ruling partner," rightly emphasize the importance of gates, openings, and holes in the wall as spaces where performances of power occur. They insist (relying on Tal Arbel's phrase) nonetheless that in such spaces, there is a "measured abandonment," a disciplining of bodies that rarely shows its excess: "Bodies are touched, pushed, detained for hours but not penetrated or butchered, and the soldiers hardly ever shoot and very rarely use sticks."[18]

I am less certain of the neat spatial and psychic separation between measured abandonment and more spectacular moments of violent excess such as torture, killings, and so on. The asymmetrical intimacies performed at the checkpoints and at holes in the wall are performed by dominant subjects whose anxieties about borders and control overwhelm and must be resolved through violence. While they are willing to grant that, on a macro level, the spectacular and the suspended fold into each other, Azoulay and Ophir pay less attention to this melding on an intimate level. The checkpoint and the controls at openings in the wall involve rituals to be sure but they are rituals of violence. People die at checkpoints as they are prevented from seeking medical care. Routinely, they encounter humiliation and degradation. As I have written elsewhere about the rituals of violence evident in lynching, and in the sexualized violence meted out to Arab prisoners at Abu Ghraib, violence transforms racial power into something real. It offers, too, an intimacy that is otherwise forbidden but one that can be immediately repudiated through the act of violence. Through an act of violence, sameness can be disavowed at precisely the moment when it is too present a possibility. Violence, in other words, dispels as nothing else can, any suspicion of a common humanity.[19]

Conclusion: The Rose at the Checkpoint

In the online accounts provided by the Palestinian Grassroots Anti-Apartheid Wall Campaign, Stop the Wall, I encountered the story of the rose at Surda checkpoint. Maher relates the story: "The occupation puts a rose outside the terminal. It is something weird. I don't know what it is supposed to symbolize. You don't know what to do when you see it. I would love to tear it apart. They

put you in this misery and humiliating situation and then they
confront you with this. It is not our hope—it is all that damages our
hope."[20] Ahmed Ayyesh, a twenty-seven-year-old writes, "What
is an even more revolting provocation is the rose they put at the
side of the fortified checkpoint. They treat you as animals and then
they show you roses." Amani Syam, twenty-two, concludes, "It is a
political issue, they also put that rose to make us more angry and
frustrated. They play with our feelings."[21] The reactions of these
young people to the rose, and their analysis of it, brings to mind
the example related by Muneer Ahmed, a lawyer who assisted
prisoners at Guantanamo Bay, including Omar Khadr, the Canadian
teenager detained there for ten years.[22] Ahmed described a new
interrogation site at Guantanamo. The American military have
prepared a room decorated the way they imagine a home in the
Middle East. The room contains a hookah, an "Oriental" carpet, and
pistachio nuts in a bowl. Is the room supposed to remind Khadr
and other Middle Eastern detainees of the home they missed? Is the
orientalized interrogation room meant to play with the prisoners'
feelings, as Syam thought of the rose, or is it also meant to offer
the interrogators a brief excursion into otherness, simulated
though it may be? Whatever its meaning, the rose at the checkpoint
suggests that an encounter is in progress, a play for power full of
ambivalence, obsession, and fantasy.

It is possible to theorize the spaces of occupation and of the wall
in particular in other ways besides those that tell of roses, holes in
the wall, and endless shouting. The story of Al-Jeeb, for instance,
could be told more clinically, with the reports of the Philadelphia
Independent Media Center. For the week of December 1 to 7,
2005, the centre notes, "During the reported period, IOF [Israeli
Occupation Forces] razed areas of Palestinian agricultural land
in al-Khader village, southwest of Bethlehem, and the villages
of Prophet Samuel and al-Jeeb and Dahiat al-Barid area near
Jerusalem, to construct new sections of the wall."[23] House arrests,
demolitions, land seizures, extrajudicial executions, floating

checkpoints, checkpoints arbitrarily closed, and the building of a walled-in bypass road on Al-Jeeb's lands are all detailed, with the time of each action noted with military precision in the twenty-four hour clock. Occupation is above all demanding, requiring the occupiers to expend considerable resources managing the encounter with the occupied. What does it mean to suture this report's clinical account of occupation to the accounts above—the man jumping from roof to roof at the hole in the wall, the woman climbing with her computer, the jeeps racing to intercept her, and the young people outraged by the rose and overwhelmed by the shouting?

In attempting to bring together these accounts, I mean to suggest a reading of colonialism that focuses on its spatiality, on the physical encounter between colonizer and colonized, on the way that spaces express power arrangements that operate on the bodies of the colonized, turning them into small animals scrambling over rocks, or rats prodded and poked to make their way through a maze. Animals, it must be remembered, are driven by instinct and are by virtue of being non-rational, not of the modern. These same spatial arrangements confirm colonizers as rightful owners of the land, convincing them who they are. The shouting, the power to arbitrarily stop and search, these must assist the eighteen-year-old soldier wielding a gun to banish the ghosts on the landscape, the Arab faces, the outlines of buildings, the old Arabic names— anything that suggests that in truth, the land is Arab land.

AUTHOR'S NOTE

I would like to thank Nadera Shalhoub-Kevorkian for her sharing her insight into colonial processes in Palestine. Gada Mahrouse and Leslie Thielen Wilson offered their own uncompromising views of the violence of colonialism and inspire me to name it. This article was first published online in *Journal of Critical Race Inquiry* 1, no. 1 (2012): 90–108.

NOTES

1. Radhika Mohanram, *Black Body: Women, Colonialism, and Space* (Minneapolis: University of Minnesota Press, 1999); Sherene Razack, ed., *Race, Space, and the Law: Unmapping a White Settler Society* (Toronto: Between the Lines, 2002).

2. Lindsay Bremner, "Border/Skin" in *Against the Wall: Israel's Barrier to Peace*, ed. Michael Sorkin (New York: The New Press, 2005), 123.

3. Ibid., 130.

4. Ibid., 131, note omitted.

5. Achille Mbembe, "Aesthetics of Superfluity," *Public Culture* 16, no. 3 (2004): 390.

6. Ibid., 392.

7. Nadera Shalhoub-Kevorkian, *Facing the Wall: Palestinian Children and Adolescents Speak about the Israeli Separation Wall* (Jerusalem: World Vision, 2007).

8. Frantz Fanon, *The Wretched of the Earth* (New York: Grove Press, 1963), 39.

9. *Mur*, directed by by Simone Bitton (France/Israel: Cine-Sud Production, 2004).

10. I observed this moment on my first trip to the wall in June 2007.

11. Mbembe, "Aesthetics of Superfluity," 391.

12. Palestinian Grassroots Anti-Apartheid Wall Campaign, "'They Humiliate Us Like Animals': Tales from the New Checkpoint," January 5, 2006, https://www.stopthewall.org/they-humiliate-us-animals-tales-new-checkpoint.

13. Fanon, *The Wretched*, 38.

14. Ruchama Marton and Dalit Baum, "Transparent Wall, Opaque Gates," in *Against the Wall*, ed. Michael Sorkin (New York: The New Press, 2005), 214.

15. Ibid., 219–20.

16. Ariella Azoulay and Adi Ophir, "The Monster's Tail," in *Against the Wall*, ed. Michael Sorkin (New York: The New Press, 2005), 5.

17. Ibid., 11.

18. Ibid., 25n7 and n8.

19. Sherene Razack, *Casting Out: Race and the Eviction of Muslims from Western Law and Politics* (Toronto: University of Toronto Press, 2008).

20. Palestinian Grassroots Anti-Apartheid Wall Campaign, "'They Humiliate Us Like Animals': Tales from the New Checkpoint," January 5, 2006, https://www.stopthewall.org/they-humiliate-us-animals-tales-new-checkpoint.

21. Ibid.

22. Muneer Ahmed, "No Right to Have Rights: Reflections on Litigation at Guantanamo" (paper presented at the Annual Meeting of Law and Society, Berlin, July 2007).

23. Palestinian Centre for Human Rights, "Weekly Report on Israeli Human Rights Violations in the Occupied Palestinian Territory," December 8, 2005, http://www.pchrgaza.org/portal/en/index.php?option=com_content&view=article&id

=6270:weekly-report-on-israeli-human-rights-violations-in-the-occupied-palestinian-territory&catid=80:weekly-2008&Itemid=305.

REFERENCES

Ahmed, Muneer. "No Right to Have Rights: Reflections on Litigation at Guantanamo." Paper presented at the Annual Meeting of Law and Society, Berlin, July 2007.

Azoulay, Ariella, and Adi Ophir. "The Monster's Tail." In *Against the Wall: Israel's Barrier to Peace*, edited by Michael Sorkin, 2–27. New York: The New Press, 2005.

Bremner, Lindsay. "Border/Skin." In *Against the Wall: Israel's Barrier to Peace*, edited by Michael Sorkin, 122–35. New York: The New Press, 2005.

Fanon, Frantz. *The Wretched of the Earth*. New York: Grove Press, 1963.

Marton, Ruchama, and Dalit Baum. "Transparent Wall, Opaque Gates." In *Against the Wall: Israel's Barrier to Peace*, edited by Michael Sorkin, 212–23. New York: The New Press, 2005.

Mbembe, Achille. "Aesthetics of Superfluity." *Public Culture* 16, no. 3 (2004): 373–405.

Mohanram, Radhika. *Black Body: Women, Colonialism, and Space*. Minneapolis: University of Minnesota Press, 1999.

Mur. Directed by Simone Bitton. France/Israel: Cine-Sud Production, 2004.

Palestinian Centre for Human Rights. "Weekly Report on Israeli Human Rights Violations in the Occupied Palestinian Territory." December 8, 2005. http://www.pchrgaza.org/portal/en/index.php?option=com_content&view=article&id=6270:weekly-report-on-israeli-human-rights-violations-in-the-occupied-palestinian-territory&catid=80:weekly-2008&Itemid=305.

Palestinian Grassroots Anti-Apartheid Wall Campaign. "'They Humiliate Us Like Animals': Tales from the New Checkpoint." January 5, 2006. https://www.stopthewall.org/they-humiliate-us-animals-tales-new-checkpoint.

Razack, Sherene. *Casting Out: The Eviction of Muslims from Western Law and Politics*. Toronto: University of Toronto Press, 2008.

Razack, Sherene, ed. *Race, Space, and the Law: Unmapping a White Settler Society*. Toronto: Between the Lines, 2002.

Said, Edward W. *Culture and Imperialism*. New York: Alfred A. Knopf, 1993.

———. *The Question of Palestine*. New York: Vintage Books, 1992.

Shalhoub-Kevorkian, Nadera. *Facing the Wall. Palestinian Children and Adolescents Speak about the Israeli Separation Wall*. Jerusalem: World Vision, 2007.

EDWARD C. CORRIGAN

13

Israel and Apartheid
A Framework for Legal Analysis

THE COMPARISON of Israeli policies and treatment of the Palestinians to the system of apartheid practiced in racially segregated South Africa immediately draws strong criticism from the supporters of the so-called Jewish State. Critics call the analogy "a foolish and unfair comparison."[1] The apartheid comparison is even frequently called anti-Semitic. Writing in the *Minnesota Daily*, for example, Zach Stern argues,

> *Calling Israel an apartheid state...holds Israel to a standard to which no other country is held, while also influencing anti-Semitic rhetoric in Western and Arabic media. Why is it that when people believe Israel makes one mistake, they attack the Jewish state and immediately scream "apartheid" without knowing what happened, while when other countries commit horrific atrocities, these same people stay silent? Anti-Semites in the Western World use this apartheid claim to create anti-Semitic cartoons and propaganda. Newspapers throughout the US and Europe publish these hateful messages and ignite anti-Semitism.*[2]

David Matas, a highly respected Canadian lawyer who serves as senior general counsel for the B'nai Brith, also argues that "there is no apartheid in Israel," based on the idea that Israel has not "denationalized" Palestinians. He remarks,

> *Basic to apartheid in South Africa was the denationalization of blacks because they were black and allocation of nationality in state created Bantustans or homelands. Blacks assigned to Bantustans were subject to influx controls and pass laws. The objective of apartheid was to denationalize all blacks, to assign every black to one of ten Bantustans. Blacks were forcibly removed from where they lived to their designated Bantustans.*
>
> *Israel has not since its inception taken away vested Israeli citizenship of even one Palestinian for the sole reason that the person is ethnic Palestinian. Israel has not created designated territories within its borders to which it has forcibly removed its own citizens who are ethnic Palestinian.*[3]

There are other supporters of the Zionist state, both Christian[4] and Jewish, who defend its policies toward the Palestinians.[5]

Former US President Jimmy Carter, who was instrumental in negotiating the peace treaty between Egypt and Israel, has criticized Israel's continued occupation of the Palestinian Territories and expansion of "Jewish-only settlements" in the West Bank.[6] In 2006, Carter published *Palestine: Peace Not Apartheid* to help stimulate a debate on the Palestinian issue in the United States, for which he was strongly attacked and even accused of being anti-Semitic.[7] Cecilie Surasky, of the Jewish Voice for Peace and *Muzzle Watch*, characterized the attacks on Carter as "a sad statement." "In fact," writes Surasky, "Carter is one of Israel's few true friends who remains impressively committed to doing whatever he can to bring about some kind of resolution, rather than taking the easy road by giving the self-destructive government more of what it wants—arms and money to occupy more land."[8]

Tom Segev, a prominent Israeli journalist, explained that Carter's book "is outraging 'friends of Israel' in America...[because] it requires them to reformulate their friendship: If they truly want what's good for Israel, they must call on it to rid itself of the territories. People don't like to admit that they've erred; therefore, they're angry at Carter."[9]

Carter also had some supporters in the American Jewish community, including American political scientist Norman Finkelstein, who summarizes the international support for Carter's ideas in a 2006 article in *Counterpunch*. Finkelstein writes,

> If it's "foolish and unfair," "irresponsibly provocative" and "dangerous and anti-Semitic" to make the apartheid comparison, then the roster of commentators who have gone awry is rather puzzling. For example, a major 2002 study of Israeli settlement practices by the respected Israeli human rights organization B'Tselem concluded: "Israel has created in the Occupied Territories a regime of separation based on discrimination, applying two separate systems of law in the same area and basing the rights of individuals on their nationality. This regime is the only one of its kinds in the world, and is reminiscent of distasteful regimes from the past, such as the apartheid regime in South Africa." A more recent B'Tselem publication on the road system Israel has established in the West Bank again concluded that it "bears striking similarities to the racist Apartheid regime," and even "entails a greater degree of arbitrariness than was the case with the regime that existed in South Africa."
>
> Those sharing Carter's iniquitous belief also include the editorial board of Israel's leading newspaper Haaretz, which observed in September 2006 that "the apartheid regime in the territories remains intact; millions of Palestinians are living without rights, freedom of movement or a livelihood, under the yoke of ongoing Israeli occupation," as well as former Israeli Knesset member Shulamit Aloni, former Israeli Ambassador to South Africa Alon Liel, South African Archbishop

and Nobel Laureate for Peace Desmond Tutu and "father" of human rights law in South Africa John Dugard."

Indeed, the list apparently also includes former Israeli prime minister Ariel Sharon. Pointing to his "fixation with Bantustans," Israeli researcher Gershom Gorenberg concluded that it is "no accident" that Sharon's plan for the West Bank "bears a striking resemblance to the 'grand apartheid' promoted by the old South African regime." Sharon himself reportedly stated that "the Bantustan model was the most appropriate solution to the conflict."[10]

Alon Liel, a former Israeli ambassador to South Africa and a former director general of the Israeli Foreign Ministry, has also spoken out on the continued Israeli occupation of the West Bank and endorsed calls for a boycott of goods produced in the Jewish settlements in the West Bank.[11] He too made an analogy to apartheid in South Africa:

Many of us tend to believe that the conflict can be managed forever and Israel no longer has a "Palestinian problem."

However, this is pure self-deception. The continuing settlement expansion threatens to make a two-state solution to the conflict impossible. Israel is sliding into a situation where, short of apartheid or expulsion of the Palestinians, a one-state solution with equal rights for all could become the only possible way out of the conflict. This is the South African model.[12]

Another Israeli Ambassador to South Africa, Ilan Baruch, voiced similar criticisms of Israeli policies toward the Palestinians in 2011. In what was described as a "Foreign Ministry earthquake," the veteran Israeli diplomat says he resigned "because he had a hard time defending the policies of Israel's current government." Baruch sent a personal letter to all Foreign Ministry employees to explain his motives for his action: "Identifying the objection expressed by global public opinion to the occupation policy as anti-Semitic is

simplistic, provincial and artificial," he wrote. "Experience shows
that this global trend won't change until we normalize our relations
with the Palestinians."[13]

There is a growing chorus of voices, including many Jews, Israelis,
and South Africans, that uses the term *apartheid* to describe Israel's
policies toward the Palestinians.[14] The Human Sciences Research
Council of South Africa, for example, released a study in June 2009
indicating that Israel is practicing both colonialism and apartheid
in the Occupied Palestinian Territory.[15]

The question remains: Is the comparison to apartheid valid in
reviewing Israel's policies toward the Palestinians? Is it anti-
Semitic to defend Palestinian human rights?[16] To examine these
questions, and to see if the analogy of apartheid applies to Israel's
occupation of the Palestinian Territories and treatment of the
subject Palestinian population, it is useful to review international
law on discrimination, the prohibition on crimes against humanity—
which includes apartheid—the International Court of Justice (ICJ),
and other international legal instruments. The answer to the second
question should be self-evident as the facts unfold. Charges of anti-
Semitism must be seen as spurious and as attempts to obscure and
deflect discussion from the real issues when the facts reveal that
Palestinians are discriminated against and subjected to cruel and
unusual punishment in defence of their human rights.

The International Convention on the Elimination of All Forms of Racial Discrimination (ICERD)

The United Nations International Convention on the Elimination of
All Forms of Racial Discrimination (ICERD) is a second-generation
human rights instrument that commits all of the members of the
UN to the elimination of racial discrimination and the promotion of
understanding among all races.[17] The convention also requires its
parties to outlaw hate speech and criminalize membership in racist
organizations.[18]

The ICERD was preceded by a United Nations Declaration on the Elimination of All Forms of Racial Discrimination, which was adopted on November 20, 1963.[19] While the declaration was important and symbolic, a convention signed and ratified is binding under international law. The ICERD was adopted and opened for signature by the United Nations General Assembly on December 21, 1965 and entered into force on January 4, 1969.[20] As of January 18, 2013, the convention has 86 signatories and 175 parties. Canada signed the convention on August 24, 1966, and it was ratified into law in Canada on October 14, 1970. Canada has filed no reservations about this convention.[21] The United States signed the convention September 28, 1966 and ratification took place on October 21, 1994. The United States filed a number of reservations on the convention.[22] Great Britain signed the convention on October 11, 1966 and ratified it on March 7, 1969.[23] Israel signed the convention on March 7, 1966 and ratified it on January 3, 1979.[24]

Canada registered an objection to the Democratic Republic of South Yemen's reservation over the convention and the participation of Israel in the convention.[25] Interestingly, part of Canada's objection to Yemen's reservation reads, "the Government of Canada believes that the principle of non-discrimination is generally accepted and recognized in international law and therefore is binding on all states."[26] Accordingly, ICERD is legally binding on Canada, the United States, and Israel. However, Israel has declared a reservation that it is not bound by Article 22 of the convention, which would make it subject to the jurisdiction of the International Court of Justice.[27]

Canada, the United States, and Israel also have not made a declaration under Article 14 that they allow individuals or groups to submit complaints to the United Nations Human Rights Committee for review.[28] This lack of a declaration severely limits the application of the convention and referrals to the UN, but it has spurred governments, including Canada, to adopt legislation to protect against discrimination and to set up enforcement vehicles such as human rights tribunals and commissions and adjudication by the courts.

Article 1 of the ICERD defines *racial discrimination* as "any distinction, exclusion, restriction or preference based on race, colour, descent, or national or ethnic origin which has the purpose or effect of nullifying or impairing the recognition, enjoyment or exercise, on an equal footing, of human rights and fundamental freedoms in the political, economic, social, cultural or any other field of public life."[29] This definition does not differentiate between discrimination based on ethnicity and race. In the British Crown Prosecution Service policy manual, the phrase *racial group* means "any group of people who are defined by reference to their race, colour, nationality (including citizenship) or ethnic or national origin."[30] Distinctions made on the basis of citizenship, between citizens and non-citizens, are specifically excluded from the definition. Affirmative action policies and other measures taken to redress imbalances and promote equality are also excluded.[31] The UN High Commissioner for Human Rights has ruled that discrimination need not be strictly based on race or ethnicity for the convention to apply. Rather, whether a particular policy or action is discriminatory is judged by its impact.[32] To quote the Office of United Nations High Commissioner for Human Rights General Recommendation no. 14: Definition of discrimination (art. 1, para. 2), "In seeking to determine whether an action has an effect contrary to the Convention, it will look to see whether that action has an unjustifiable disparate impact upon a group distinguished by race, colour, descent, or national or ethnic origin."[33] The Committee on the Elimination of Racial Discrimination (CERD) has also considered how to define social groups, and decided that "such identification shall, if no justification exists to the contrary, be based upon self-identification by the individual concerned."[34]

ICERD Articles 2 through 7 deal with the prevention of discrimination, anti-discrimination law, equality before the law, and institutionalized discrimination.[35] These articles are legally binding under international law. Under Article 2, "States Parties condemn racial discrimination and undertake to pursue by all appropriate means and without delay a policy of eliminating racial discrimination in all its forms and promoting understanding among all races."[36] Article 2 details "effective measures" that state parties shall undertake to create or perpetuate racial discrimination. Article 3 specifically condemns racial segregation and apartheid and calls for the prohibition and eradication of such practices.[37] Organizations and propaganda that promote racial superiority are outlawed in Article 4.[38] Article 5 expands upon on the obligations set out in Article 2: "In compliance with the fundamental obligations laid down in Article 2 of this Convention, States Parties undertake to prohibit and to eliminate racial discrimination in all its forms and to guarantee the right of everyone, without distinction as to race, colour, or national or ethnic origin, to equality before the law" in the enjoyment of political, civil, social, cultural, and economic rights.[39] Article 6 requires that the parties provide effective protection and remedies, "through competent national tribunals and other State institutions," against "any acts of racial discrimination" and assure that everyone has the right to seek damages for racial discrimination through such tribunals.[40] Article 7 of ICERD requires that the states parties take effective measures to promote tolerance and the purposes and principles of the United Nations, including those outlined in the Universal Declaration of Human Rights.[41]

Articles 11 through 13 establish a dispute resolution mechanism between parties to the convention. If one party that believes another party is not implementing the convention, it may file a complaint with the Committee on the Elimination of Racial Discrimination. The committee will pass on the complaint to the party, and if the complaint is not resolved between the two parties, the committee may establish an ad hoc Conciliation Commission to investigate and make recommendations on the complaint.[42] This procedure has never been used.[43]

Individual Complaint Mechanism

The convention sets out an individual complaints mechanism in Article 14.[44] This authority makes it legally enforceable against its signatories who have made a declaration that individuals can file complaints to the CERD. This article has led to the development of a limited jurisprudence on the interpretation and implementation of the Convention for the Elimination of Racial Discrimination.[45] However, as noted above, all parties to ICERD have to make a declaration that they agree to be subject to Article 14, which allows individuals and groups to file complaints to the CERD. Canada, Israel, and the United States have not made such a declaration.[46] Accordingly, this mechanism is not available to complainants from those countries. The individual complaints mechanism came into operation in 1982, after it had been accepted by ten states parties.[47] As of 2010, fifty-eight states had recognized the competence of the committee, and fifty-four cases have been dealt with by the committee.[48] Article 22 further allows any dispute over the interpretation or application of the convention to be referred to the International Court of Justice.[49] This clause has been invoked only once, by Georgia against Russia.[50]

The Rome Statute of the International Criminal Court specifically identifies apartheid as a crime against humanity in Article 7(h):[51] "The 'crime of apartheid' means inhumane acts...committed in the context of an institutionalized regime of systematic oppression and domination by one racial group over any other racial group or groups and committed with the intention of maintaining that regime."[52] The International Convention on the Suppression and Punishment of the Crime of Apartheid (also known as the Apartheid Convention) was adopted on November 30, 1973 and entered into force on July 18, 1976. The convention has 31 signatories and 108 parties. Australia, Canada, Great Britain, Israel, New Zealand, and the United States are not signatories to the Apartheid Convention.[53]

The UN General Assembly vote to grant Palestine the status of a state, albeit a non-member state, by a vote of 138 votes in favour, 9 against, and 41 abstentions, has important legal ramifications. Three countries did not take part in the vote. The vote took place on November 29, 2012, the 65th anniversary of the adoption of UN General Assembly non-binding resolution 181, which recommended the partition of Palestine into two states.[54] The UN General Assembly vote clearly recognizes Palestine as a state and conveys legal standing that enables Palestine to take legal action as a state under international conventions, including the ICJ and the Apartheid Convention.[55] Article VIII of Apartheid Convention, for example, states that "any State Party to the present Convention may call upon any competent organ of the United Nations to take such action under the Charter of the United Nations as it considers appropriate for the prevention and suppression of the crime of apartheid."[56]

On December 31, 2014, following the rejection of the UN Security Council resolution calling for an end to the Israel's occupation of the Palestinian territories by 2017, Mahmoud Abbas, president of the State of Palestine, signed the Rome Treaty governing the International Criminal Court and nineteen other international agreements.[57]

It has also been suggested that the 1948 Convention on the Prevention and Punishment of the Crime of Genocide (known also as the Genocide Convention), which arose out of the Nuremberg trials and Nazis extermination campaign against the Jews, should also be applied to the Palestinian issue.[58] The Genocide Convention was approved and proposed for signature and ratification or accession by General Assembly Resolution 260 A (III) on December 9, 1948 and entered into force on January 12, 1951.[59] The 1948 Genocide Convention has 41 signatories and 133 parties. Australia, Canada, Israel, New Zealand, and the United States are all signatories. United Kingdom of Great Britain and Northern Ireland has ratified it by accession.[60]

Raphael Lemkin, a Polish lawyer who immigrated to the United States in 1941, coined the term *genocide* in 1943 in response to the Armenian genocide and the Nazi extermination campaign against the Jews. Facing History and Ourselves, an international educational organization that works to eliminate racism and anti-Semitism, defines genocide as "the deliberate and systematic destruction, in whole or in part, of an ethnic, racial, religious, or national group."[61] This definition has been adopted in Article 2 of the Convention on the Prevention and Punishment of the Crime of Genocide. Persons committing genocide shall be punished, whether they are constitutionally responsible rulers, public officials, or private individuals.[62] In a 2011 online article, I define genocide as "the systematic destruction of a people or culture."[63] There are many ways—fast and slow—to destroy a people or culture.

There is only one important legal case that relates to the Palestinian issue at the International Court of Justice: the advisory opinion on the "Legal Consequences of the Construction of a Wall in the Occupied Palestinian Territory," which was rendered on July 9, 2004.[64] The ICJ court majority decision was fourteen to one. The ICJ found that Israel was an occupying power and that the Fourth Geneva Convention as well as other international conventions and international customary law applied to the Israeli occupation of the Palestinian Territories. Here are some key excerpts from the Summary of the ICJ Advisory Opinion:

> The Court concludes that all these territories (including East Jerusalem) remain occupied territories and that Israel has continued to have the status of occupying Power.

> As to the principle of self-determination of peoples, the Court points out that it has been enshrined in the United Nations Charter and reaffirmed by the General Assembly in resolution 2625 (xxv) cited above, pursuant to which "Every State has the duty to refrain from any forcible action which deprives peoples referred to [in that resolution]...of their right to self-determination." Article 1 common to the International Covenant on Economic, Social and Cultural Rights and the International Covenant on Civil and Political

Rights *reaffirms the right of all peoples to self-determination, and lays upon the States parties the obligation to promote the realization of that right and to respect it, in conformity with the provisions of the* United Nations Charter. *The Court recalls its previous case law, which emphasized that current developments in* "international law in regard to non-self-governing territories, as enshrined in the Charter of the United Nations, made the principle of self-determination applicable to all [such territories]," *and that the right of peoples to self-determination is today a right* erga omnes.

INTERNATIONAL HUMANITARIAN LAW (paras. 89–101)

...Secondly, with regard to the Fourth Geneva Convention, *the Court takes note that differing views have been expressed by the participants in these proceedings. Israel, contrary to the great majority of the participants, disputes the applicability* de jure *of the* Convention to the Occupied Palestinian Territory. *The Court recalls that the* Fourth Geneva Convention *was ratified by Israel on 6 July 1951 and that Israel is a party to that Convention; that Jordan has also been a party thereto since 29 May 1951; and that neither of the two States has made any reservation that would be pertinent to the present proceedings. The Court observes that the Israeli authorities have indicated on a number of occasions that in fact they generally apply the humanitarian provisions of the* Fourth Geneva Convention *within the occupied territories. However, according to Israel's position, that Convention is not applicable de jure within those territories because, under Article 2, paragraph 2, it applies only in the case of occupation of territories falling under the sovereignty of a High Contracting Party involved in an armed conflict. Israel explains that the territories occupied by Israel subsequent to the 1967 conflict had not previously fallen under Jordanian sovereignty.*

The Court notes that, according to the first paragraph of Article 2 of the Fourth Geneva Convention, *when two conditions are fulfilled,* namely that there exists an armed conflict (whether or not a state of war has been recognized), and that the conflict has arisen between two contracting parties, then the Convention applies, in particular, in any territory occupied in the course of the conflict by one of the contracting parties. The object of the second paragraph of Article 2, which refers to "occupation of the territory of a High Contracting Party," is not to restrict the scope of application of the Convention, as defined by the first paragraph, by excluding therefrom territories not falling under the sovereignty of one of the contracting parties, but simply to making it clear that, even if occupation effected during the conflict met no armed resistance, the Convention is still applicable.

This interpretation reflects the intention of the drafters of the Fourth Geneva Convention to protect civilians who find themselves, in whatever way, in the hands of the occupying Power, regardless of the status of the occupied territories, and is confirmed by the Convention's travaux préparatoires. The States parties to the Fourth Geneva Convention, at their Conference on 15 July 1999, approved that interpretation, which has also been adopted by the ICRC, the General Assembly and the Security Council. The Court finally makes mention of a judgment of the Supreme Court of Israel dated 30 May 2004, to a similar effect.

In view of the foregoing, the Court considers that the Fourth Geneva Convention is applicable in the Palestinian territories which before the 1967 conflict lay to the east of the Green Line and which, during that conflict, were occupied by Israel, there being no need for any enquiry into the precise prior status of those territories.

On 3 October 1991 Israel ratified both the International Covenant on Economic, Social and Cultural Rights of 19 December 1966 and the International Covenant on Civil and Political Rights of the same date, as well as the United Nations Convention on the Rights of the Child of 20 November 1989...

After examination of the provision of the two international Covenants, in the light of the relevant travaux préparatoires and of the position of Israel in communications to the Human Rights Committee and the Committee on Economic, Social and Cultural Rights, the Court concludes that those instruments are applicable in respect of acts done by a State in the exercise of its jurisdiction outside its own territory. In the case of the International Covenant on Economic, Social and Cultural Rights, Israel is also under an obligation not to raise any obstacle to the exercise of such rights in those fields where competence has been transferred to Palestinian authorities. The Court further concludes that the Convention on the Rights of the Child is also applicable within the Occupied Palestinian Territory...

IMPACT ON RIGHT OF PALESTINIAN PEOPLE
TO SELF-DETERMINATION (paras. 115–122)

It notes in this regard the contentions of Palestine and other participants that the construction of the wall is "an attempt to annex the territory contrary to international law" and "a violation of the legal principle prohibiting the acquisition of territory by the use of force" and that "the de facto annexation of land interferes with the territorial sovereignty and consequently with the right of the Palestinians to self-determination." It notes also that Israel, for its part, has argued that the wall's sole purpose is to enable it effectively to combat terrorist attacks launched from the West Bank, and that Israel has repeatedly stated that the Barrier is a temporary measure.

The Court recalls that both the General Assembly and the Security Council have referred, with regard to Palestine, to the customary rule of "the inadmissibility of the acquisition of territory by war." As regards the principle of the right of peoples to self-determination, the Court observes that the existence of a "Palestinian people" is no longer in issue, and has been recognized by Israel, along with that people's *"legitimate rights." The Court considers that those rights include the right to self-determination, as the General Assembly has moreover recognized on a number of occasions.*

The Court notes that the route of the wall as fixed by the Israeli Government includes within the "Closed Area" (i.e., the part of the West Bank lying between the Green Line and the wall) some 80 per cent of the settlers living in the Occupied Palestinian Territory, and has been traced in such a way as to include within that area the great majority of the Israeli settlements in the Occupied Palestinian Territory (including East Jerusalem). The information provided to the Court shows that, since 1977, Israel has conducted a policy and developed practices involving the establishment of settlements in the Occupied Palestinian Territory, contrary to the terms of Article 49, paragraph 6, of the Fourth Geneva Convention *which provides: "The Occupying Power shall not deport or transfer parts of its own civilian population into the territory it occupies." The Security Council has taken the view that such policy and practices "have no legal validity" and constitute a "flagrant violation" of the Convention. The Court concludes that the Israeli settlements in the Occupied Palestinian Territory (including East Jerusalem) have been established in breach of international law.*

In sum, the Court is of the opinion that the construction of the wall and its associated régime impede the liberty of movement of the inhabitants of the Occupied Palestinian Territory (with the exception of Israeli citizens and those assimilated thereto) as guaranteed under Article 12, paragraph 1, of the International Covenant on Civil and Political Rights. *They also impede the exercise by the persons concerned of the right to work, to health, to education and to an adequate standard of living as proclaimed in the* International Covenant on Economic, Social and Cultural Rights *and in the* United Nations Convention on the Rights of the Child. *Lastly, the construction of the wall and its associated régime, by contributing*

to the demographic changes mentioned, contravene Article 49,
paragraph 6, of the Fourth Geneva Convention and the pertinent
Security Council resolutions cited earlier...

In sum, the Court finds that, from the material available to it, it is
not convinced that the specific course Israel has chosen for the wall
was necessary to attain its security objectives. The wall, along the
route chosen, and its associated régime gravely infringe a number
of rights of Palestinians residing in the territory occupied by Israel,
and the infringements resulting from that route cannot be justified
by military exigencies or by the requirements of national security or
public order. The construction of such a wall accordingly constitutes
breaches by Israel of various of its obligations under the applicable
international humanitarian law and human rights instruments...

The Court considers that its conclusion that the construction of the
wall by Israel in the Occupied Palestinian Territory is contrary
to international law must be placed in a more general context.
Since 1947, the year when General Assembly resolution 181 (II) was
adopted and the Mandate for Palestine was terminated, there has
been a succession of armed conflicts, acts of indiscriminate violence
and repressive measures on the former mandated territory. The
Court would emphasize that both Israel and Palestine are under
an obligation scrupulously to observe the rules of international
humanitarian law, one of the paramount purposes of which is to
protect civilian life. Illegal actions and unilateral decisions have
been taken on all sides, whereas, in the Court's view, this tragic
situation can be brought to an end only through implementation in
good faith of all relevant Security Council resolutions, in particular
resolutions 242 (1967) and 338 (1973). The "Roadmap" approved by
Security Council resolution 1515 (2003) represents the most recent
of efforts to initiate negotiations to this end. The Court considers
that it has a duty to draw the attention of the General Assembly, to
which the present Opinion is addressed, to the need for these efforts

to be encouraged with a view to achieving as soon as possible, on the basis of international law, a negotiated solution to the outstanding problems and the establishment of a Palestinian State, existing side by side with Israel and its other neighbours, with peace and security for all in the region.[65]

Article 49 of the Fourth Geneva Convention, which was applied in the ICJ advisory opinion on the "Legal Consequences of the Construction of a Wall in the Occupied Palestinian Territory," states,

Individual or mass forcible transfers, as well as deportations of protected persons from occupied territory to the territory of the Occupying Power or to that of any other country, occupied or not, are prohibited, regardless of their motive.

Nevertheless, the Occupying Power may undertake total or partial evacuation of a given area if the security of the population or imperative military reasons so demand...Persons thus evacuated shall be transferred back to their homes as soon as hostilities in the area in question have ceased.

The Occupying Power undertaking such transfers or evacuations shall ensure, to the greatest practicable extent, that proper accommodation is provided to receive the protected persons, that the removals are effected in satisfactory conditions of hygiene, health, safety and nutrition, and that members of the same family are not separated.

The Protecting Power shall be informed of any transfers and evacuations as soon as they have taken place.

The Occupying Power shall not detain protected persons in an area particularly exposed to the dangers of war unless the security of the population or imperative military reasons so demand.

The Occupying Power shall not deport or transfer parts of its own civilian population into the territory it occupies.[66]

Israel's Policies toward Palestinians and the Apartheid Comparison

The following section applies some of the aforementioned laws to Israeli policies in the Occupied Palestinian Territory. This section focuses on the Israeli policies relating to settlements, expulsion, and the treatment of Palestinians, and examines some of the international reports that have dealt with the occupation of Palestinian land and Israel's responsibility to protect the rights of Palestinians.

In an attempt to assert their right to be protected by international law, Palestinians first attempted to join the International Criminal Court (ICC) in April 2012. The chief prosecutor of the ICC at the time, Luis Moreno-Ocampo, "declined the request on the grounds that Palestine was not a state."[67] In a *New York Times* op-ed, George Bisharat, a professor at the University of California's Hastings College of Law, commented on the ICC's findings concerning one of the major Israeli violations of international law—namely, the settlements in the West Bank. Bisharat wrote,

> No doubt, Israel is most worried about the possibility of criminal prosecutions for its settlements policy. Israeli bluster notwithstanding, there is no doubt that Jewish settlements in the West Bank, including East Jerusalem, are illegal. Israeli officials have known this since 1967, when Theodor Meron, then legal counsel to the Israeli Foreign Ministry and later president of the International Criminal Tribunal for the former Yugoslavia, wrote to one of Prime Minister Levi Eshkol's aides: "My conclusion is that civilian settlement in the administered territories contravenes the explicit provisions of the Fourth Geneva Convention."
>
> Under the founding statute of the icc, grave violations of the Geneva Conventions, including civilian settlements in occupied territories, are considered war crimes.[68]

Because Palestine was legally recognized as a state in November 2012, international law now applies to the Occupied Palestinian Territory. The State of Palestine formally became a member of the ICC in April 2015.[69]

The UN Human Rights Council report also affirms that Israel is in violation of Article 49 of the Fourth Geneva Convention, which forbids the transfer of a population into territory that is occupied.[70] The UN fact-finding mission's report on the settlements concludes that

Israeli settlements are constructed for the benefits of Jews only through a system of ethnic segregation and military law, and are in violation of the Fourth Geneva Convention, which forbids the transfer of civilian populations into occupied territory by the occupying force. According to the un report: Israel must, in compliance with Article 49 of the Fourth Geneva Convention, cease all settlement activities without preconditions. It must immediately initiate a process of withdrawal of all settlers from the OPT.

Israel is a signatory to the Fourth Geneva Convention but has concluded that it does not apply to the territories occupied from Jordan and Egypt in 1967, since both countries abandoned any claims to this land. Israel considers the territories "disputed" (a position taken recently by the Levi Commission, which called upon Israel to legalize all outposts built on Palestinian land). However, even the Israeli narrative doesn't explain ethnic segregation in the West Bank, military law and the absence of human or political rights for the non-Jewish civilian population in the West Bank.[71]

After the release of the Human Rights Council report, the Israeli daily newspaper *Haaretz* published an article by a prominent member of the Palestinian parliament, Saeb Erekat, who proclaimed, "The UN report on Israeli settlements should be read by every single Israeli citizen. It is an opportunity for the international community to hold Israel accountable and end a culture of impunity that has all

EDWARD C. CORRIGAN

but destroyed the possibility of a two-state solution. It is time for Israel to relinquish its current state of denial and confront reality."[72]

The Israeli government reacted to the investigation of Jewish settlements in the West Bank by cutting ties with the UN Human Rights Council.[73] By banning the UN probe, "Israel is joining the worst of clubs," read one *Haaretz* headline.[74] After the issuance of the Human Rights Council report on the illegal Jewish settlements, Israel boycotted the UN Human Rights Council, claiming that there was "a unified bias against [Israel] itself."[75]

The government of Israel continues to encourage the transfer of its population into the Occupied Palestinian Territory by expanding settlements. The 2012 declaration of Israeli Prime Minister Netanyahu on the construction in E1, an area of Occupied West Bank, is another example of how Israel does not comply with international law. If completed, E1 would effectively encircle East Jerusalem with a complete ring of Jewish settlements, dividing the city from the rest of the West Bank and its Palestinian population centres. This policy jeopardizes the prospects of a contiguous Palestinian state and violates the right to self-determination of the Palestinian people. The UN secretary-general notes that "the International Court of Justice described the violation by Israel of the Palestinian people's right to self-determination as the violation of an *erga omnes* obligation. Therefore that violation is a matter of concern to all states."[76]

Palestinians currently occupy less than 10 per cent of mandatory Palestine. The rest of the land has been utilized for the sake of the occupiers in contravention to the Fourth Geneva Convention, which states, "the Occupying Power shall not use the occupied land for its benefit and should not deport or transfer parts of its own civilian population into the territory it occupies."[77] In the Occupied West Bank, including East Jerusalem, there are over half a million illegal Jewish settlers occupying land that has been designated for Palestinians.[78]

The Israeli settlements in the Occupied Palestinian Territory are not only illegal under international law but are, according to the Israeli Committee Against House Demolitions (ICAHD), "an obstacle to the enjoyment of human rights by the whole population, without distinction as to national or ethnic origin." Actions that change the demographic composition of the Occupied Palestinian Territory are violations of human rights and international humanitarian law.[79] Amnon Rubinstein, Israeli law scholar and former parliament member, reached a similar conclusion: "In its policy of establishing settlements in the territories, irrespective of the policy's political wisdom or absence thereof, Israel has clearly violated international law: It has violated the prohibitions concerning an occupying power's transferring nationals to the territory it occupies and concerning the expropriation of land for purposes unrelated to the local population's well-being."[80]

Forcibly driving Palestinians out of their homes, which occurs on a daily basis in the West Bank, is considered by many experts a systematic policy based on racial discrimination that is meant to reduce the Palestinian population and achieve a majority Jewish population.[81] Palestinian homeowners are driven out of their homes to allow new Jewish neighbourhoods to arise. Since 1967, the Israeli authorities have demolished some 2,000 houses in East Jerusalem alone. In 2012, a total of 581 homes were demolished, displacing 1,049 men, women, and children.[82] These policies render the lives of Palestinians more and more miserable, pressuring the Arab population into a "voluntary" exodus from the area; one wonders if this is, in fact, the unspoken goal of the Israeli government. As Uri Avnery, a member of Gush Shalom (a peace activism group) and a former member of the Israeli Knesset, writes, "These methods have served the 'redeemers of the soil' (in Zionist terminology) for the last 120 years. The tempo can be increased rapidly. The more hellish the lives of Palestinians become—for security reasons, of course—the more the Israeli leadership hopes that the Arabs will go away 'voluntarily.'"[83] Indeed, there is much evidence to support the notion that the intention of the current political Zionist Jewish leadership of Israel is the drive out the Palestinians.

If so-called voluntary removal does not work, force becomes the alternative.[84] This intention has been clear in Israeli officials' policies and statements. In 1989, at the time of the Tiananmen Square protests in the People's Republic of China, Israeli Prime Minister Benjamin Netanyahu said that "Israel should have taken advantage of the suppression of the demonstrations in China, when the world's attention was focussed on what was happening in that country, to carry out mass expulsions among the Arabs of the Territories." He added, "However, to my regret, they did not support that policy that I proposed, and which I still propose should be implemented."[85] Netanyahu denied making these remarks but the *Jerusalem Post* provided a recording of his speech.[86]

Netanyahu is not alone in his thinking about expelling Palestinians. In *Imperial Israel*, Michael Palumbo explains that there were also threats of expulsion on the eve of the 1987 intifada: "Israeli leaders such as President Chaim Herzog and Defence Minister Rabin warned that if the intifada continued, the Palestinians faced another 'tragedy,' an obvious reference to 1948."[87]

In its report published in March 2012, the UN Committee on the Elimination of Racial Discrimination criticized Israeli policies and called upon its government "to take immediate measures to eradicate apartheid policies or practices which severely affect the Palestinian population in the Occupied Palestinian Territory, and which violate the provisions of the Convention on the prevention of racial segregation and apartheid."[88] The ICAHD reached the same conclusion. This Israeli NGO called upon Israel to consider its policies when it comes to Palestinians' rights, as well as their access to land, resources, and housing. The report also highlighted Israel's protracted non-compliance with obligations stemming from the ICERD, international law, and other human rights instruments.[89]

Discriminatory laws in the Occupied West Bank complicate the lives of Palestinians. In its March 2012 report, the CERD

expressed concerns regarding the existence of two sets of laws—
one "for Palestinians on the one hand and [another for] Jewish
settlers on the other hand who reside in the same territory, namely
the West Bank...[These populations] are not subject to the same
justice system (criminal as well as civil matters)." The CERD was
also concerned about the increase in the detention of Palestinian
children and the undermining of their judicial guarantees, notably
in relation to the competence of military courts to try Palestinian
children, which is inconsistent with international law and the
Geneva Conventions.

Furthermore, there has been a dramatic increase in racist
violence, with Jewish settlers in the Occupied West Bank targeting
Palestinians. The targeting of Christians and Muslims and their
properties was also raised in the CERD report. According to the
report, 90 per cent of Israeli police investigations into settler-
related violence carried out between 2005 and 2010 were closed
without prosecution. The committee was particularly alarmed by
the impact of settler violence on the rights of Palestinian women to
access basic services and education.⁹⁰

The special rapporteur (an independent expert appointed by the
UN Human Rights Council) on the situation of human rights in the
Occupied Palestinian Territory expressed great concern regarding
the situation of Palestinians under occupation. In September 2012,
he stated that "the failure to bring the occupation to an end after
45 years creates an augmented international responsibility to
uphold the human rights of the Palestinian people, who in practice
live without the protection of the rule of law." In this context, the
special rapporteur called on "Member States to apply economic
sanctions against the State of Israel for its unlawful settlement
activities."⁹¹

The Netanyahu government's proposed "Jewish nation-state" bill
is moving Israel even closer to being an apartheid state that discrimin-
ates on the basis of race and religion. As well-known Israeli journalist
Gideon Levy wrote in *Haaretz* on November 27, 2014,

This bill is legal preparation for the right wing's one-state solution, the annexation of the territories and the establishment of the Jewish apartheid state. The bill is the constitutional foundation, and its acceptance is the laying of the cornerstone of the binational segregation state that the right wing is setting up quietly and methodically, unseen and unhindered...Israel is definitely a state ruled by law. Since its establishment, it has based all its injustices on laws. The Jewish nation-state law will one day be the first article in its constitution. Its ramifications at that point will be more serious than they appear: They will not apply only to t̓.̛ Arab minority, the country's citizens, as it seems now they will; they will apply to half the inhabitants of the incipient apartheid state. That is the bill's true purpose.[92]

After this short review of the applicable international law and the International Convention on the Elimination of Racial Discrimination, the Fourth Geneva Convention, the Convention Against Genocide, and the Apartheid Convention, it is clear that many provisions of international law are being violated by Israel in its treatment of the Palestinian people. Israel's mistreatment and violations of Palestinians and Palestinian rights are best described in the words of Moshe Gorali, the legal analyst for *Haaretz*:

Chief Supreme Court Justice Aharon Barak used the phrase "long-term occupation" to justify the Israel government's permanent, massive investments in the territories. To describe a situation where two populations, in this case one Jewish and the other Arab, share the same territory but are governed by two separate legal systems, the international community customarily uses the term "apartheid."[93]

NOTES

1. See, for example, Michael Kinsley, "It's Not Apartheid," *Washington Post*, December 12, 2006, http://www.washingtonpost.com/wp-dyn/content/article/2006/12/11/AR2006121101225.html.

Israel and Apartheid

2.   Zach Stern, "Israel Is Not an Apartheid State," *Minnesota Daily*, November 19, 2012, http://www.mndaily.com/2012/11/19/israel-not-apartheid-state.

3.   David Matas, "Banning Israel Anti-Apartheid Weeks at Universities" (revised remarks prepared for the delivery at the Faculty of Law, University of Manitoba, Manitoba Association of Rights and Liberties Forum, October 21, 2010), http://www.marl.mb.ca/content/hate-speech/banning-israel-anti-apartheid-weeks-universities-david-matas. Also see Howard S. Davidson, "Banning Israel Anti-Apartheid Weeks at Universities: A Reply to David Matas, Senior Legal Counsel, B'nai Brith," *Peace Alliance Winnipeg News*, January 6, 2011, http://www.peacealliancewinnipeg.ca/2011/01/banning-israel-anti-apartheid-weeks-at-universities-a-reply-to-david-matas-senior-legal-counsel-b%E2%80%99nai-brith/.

4.   See, for example, "Inside CUFI's 2011 Washington 'Summit': Our Eyewitness Report on Christians United For Israel's Annual Washington Conference," *JewsOnFirst.org*, July 29, 2011, http://www.jewsonfirst.org/11a/CUFI2011a.aspx; Philip Giraldi "Towards a Christian Zionist Foreign Policy," *Antiwar.com*, February 14, 2013, http://original.antiwar.com/giraldi/2013/02/13/towards-a-christian-zionist-foreign-policy/.

5.   See Sharmini Brookes, "Why Call Israel an Apartheid State?" (blog post), *Engage*, September 23, 2011, http://engageonline.wordpress.com/2011/09/23/why-call-israel-an-apartheid-state-guest-post-by-sharmini-brookes/; Natasha Mozgovaya, "US Jews Battle Apartheid Charges Made against Israel," *Haaretz*, February 16, 2012; http://www.haaretz.com/print-edition/news/u-s-jews-battle-apartheid-charges-made-against-israel-1.413187.

6.   For example, "Jimmy Carter: Israel's 'Apartheid' Policies Worse than South Africa's," *Haaretz*, December 11, 2006, http://www.haaretz.com/news/jimmy-carter-israel-s-apartheid-policies-worse-than-south-africa-s-1.206865.

7.   Jimmy Carter, *Palestine: Peace Not Apartheid* (New York: Simon and Schuster, 2006). For work that attacks Carter's book, see Julie Bosman, "Carter Book Stirs Furor With Its View of Israelis' 'Apartheid," *New York Times*, December 14, 2006, http://www.nytimes.com/2006/12/14/books/14cart.html?fta=y.

8.   Cecilie Surasky, "Jimmy Carter's Apology to the Jewish People," *Muzzle Watch*, December 28, 2009, http://www.muzzlewatch.com/2009/12/28/jimmy-carters-apology-to-the-jewish-people/.

9.   Tom Segev, "Memoir of a Great Friend," *Haaretz*, December 12, 2006.

10. Norman Finkelstein, "The Ludicrous Attacks on Jimmy Carter's Book," *Counterpunch*, December 28, 2006, http://www.counterpunch.org/2006/12/28/the-ludicrous-attacks-on-jimmy-carter-s-book/.

11. Joshua Mitnick, "Ex-Israeli Diplomat: Boycott My Country," *Christian Science Monitor*, July 17, 2012, http://www.csmonitor.com/world/Middle-East/2012/0717/Ex-Israeli-diplomat-Boycott-my-country.

12. Alon Liel, "For Israelis, Palestinian Oppression Is out of Sight and out of Mind," *Guardian*, June 27, 2012, http://www.guardian.co.uk/commentisfree/2012/jun/27/made-in-israel-erasing-green-line. See also Harriet Sherwood, "Former Ambassador Says Settlements Should Be Denied Made in Israel Label," *Guardian*, June 27, 2012, http://www.guardian.co.uk/world/2012/jun/27/former-ambassador-made-in-israel-label.

13. "Diplomat: I Can No Longer Represent Israel," *Yedioth Ahronoth* (*YnetNews*), March 2, 2011, http://www.ynetnews.com/articles/0,7340,L-4036889,00.html.

14. Edward C. Corrigan, "Israel and Apartheid: Is It a Fair Comparison?," *Dissident Voice*, March 1, 2010, http://dissidentvoice.org/2010/03/israel-and-apartheid-is-it-a-fair-comparison/.

15. "SA Academic Study Finds That Israel Is Practicing Apartheid and Colonialism in the Occupied Palestinian Territories," NWO *Observer*, June 5, 2009, https://nwoobserver.wordpress.com/2009/06/05/sa-academic-study-finds-that-israel-is-practicing-apartheid-and-colonialism-in-the-occupied-palestinian-territories/. For the complete report see, Human Sciences Research Council of South Africa, Democracy and Governance Programme, Middle East Project, *Occupation, Colonialism, Apartheid? A Re-assessment of Israel's Practices in the Occupied Palestinian Territories under International Law* (Cape Town: Human Sciences Research Council, May 2009), http://sro.sussex.ac.uk/43295/1/Occupation_Colonialism_Apartheid%2DFullStudy_copy.pdf. For an Israeli view, see Frances H. ReMillard, *Is Israel an Apartheid State?* (Chapel Hill, NC: Israeli Committee Against House Demolitions-USA, March 6, 2010), http://icahdusa.org/multimedia/downloads/2012/12/is-israel-an-apartheid-state-single-page.pdf.

16. Edward C. Corrigan, "Is It Anti-Semitic to Defend Palestinian Human Rights?," *Dissident Voice*, September 1, 2009, http://dissidentvoice.org/2009/09/is-it-anti-semitic-to-defend-palestinian-human-rights/. See also Edward C. Corrigan, "Is Anti-Zionism Anti-Semitic? Jewish Critics Speak," *Middle East Policy* (Winter 2009): 132–45, http://www.mepc.org/journal/middle-east-policy-archives/anti-zionism-anti-semitic.

17. UN General Assembly, UN International Convention on the Elimination of All Forms of Racial Discrimination (ICERD), Article 2.1, January 4, 1969, http://www.ohchr.org/EN/ProfessionalInterest/Pages/CERD.aspx.

18. Ibid., Article 4, http://www.ohchr.org/EN/ProfessionalInterest/Pages/CERD.aspx.

19. UN General Assembly, Resolution 1904 (XVIII), United Nations Declaration on the Elimination of All Forms of Racial Discrimination, November 20, 1963, http://www.un-documents.net/a18r1904.htm.

20. UN General Assembly, Resolution 2106 (XX), ICERD, December 21, 1965, http://www.ohchr.org/EN/ProfessionalInterest/Pages/CERD.aspx.

21. UN General Assembly, ICERD, March 7, 1966, *United Nations Treaty Collection*, http://treaties.un.org/Pages/ViewDetails. aspx?src=TREATY&mtdsg_no=IV-2&chapter=4&lang=en.

22. Ibid. To read the full text of the US reservations about ICERD, see "US Reservations, Declarations, and Understandings," ICERD, 140 Cong. Rec. S7634-02, June 24, 1994, reprinted at University of Minnesota Human Rights Library, http://www1.umn.edu/humanrts/usdocs/racialres.html.

23. UN General Assembly, ICERD, March 7, 1966, *United Nations Treaty Collection*, http://treaties.un.org/Pages/ViewDetails.aspx?src=TREATY&mtdsg_no=IV-2&chapter=4&lang=en.

24. Ibid.

25. Ibid. The full text of Canada's objection, filed on August 10, 1989, and Yemen's reservation can be found at http://www.bayefsky.com/html/yemen_t2_cerd. *Bayesfky.com* is an online archive of UN human rights treaties.

26. Ibid., n8.

27. Article 22 of ICERD states, "Any dispute between two or more States Parties with respect to the interpretation or application of this Convention, which is not settled by negotiation or by the procedures expressly provided for in this Convention, shall, at the request of any of the parties to the dispute, be referred to the International Court of Justice for decision, unless the disputants agree to another mode of settlement" (UN General Assembly, Resolution 2106 (XX), ICERD, http://www.un-documents.net/icerd.htm). In my considered opinion, the application of the law requires that if the parties cannot agree to "another mode of settlement," then the matter must be referred to the International Court of Justice for adjudication.

28. See UN General Assembly, Resolution 2106 (XX), Article 14, ICERD, January 4, 1969, http://www.ohchr.org/EN/ProfessionalInterest/Pages/CERD.aspx.

29. Ibid.

30. Crown Prosecution Service, *Racist and Religious Crime—Crown Prosecution Service Prosecution Policy*, accessed December 9, 2012, http://www.cps.gov.uk/publications/prosecution/rrpbcrbook.html.

31. ICERD, Articles 1.2 and 1.4.

32. See Office of the United Nations High Commissioner for Human Rights (OHCHR), "General Recommendation no. 14: Definition of Discrimination (Art. 1, par. 1): 03/22/1993. General Comments," March 22, 1993, http://www.unhchr.ch/

tbs/doc.nsf/%28Symbol%29/

d7bd5d2bf71258aac12563ee004b639e?Opendocument.

33. Ibid.

34. OHCHR, "General Recommendation no. 08: Identification with a Particular Racial or Ethnic Group (Art.1, par. 1 & 4): 08/22/1990. General Comments," August 22, 1990, http://www.unhchr.ch/tbs/doc.nsf/%28Symbol%29/3ae0a87b5b d69d28c12563ee0049800f?Opendocument.

35. UN General Assembly, Resolution 2106 (XX), ICERD, January 4, 1969, http://www.ohchr.org/EN/ProfessionalInterest/Pages/CERD.aspx.

36. For the full text of articles, see UN General Assembly, Resolution 2106 (XX), ICERD, January 4, 1969, http://www.ohchr.org/EN/ProfessionalInterest/Pages/CERD.aspx.

37. Ibid., Article 3.

38. Ibid., Article 4.

39. Ibid., Article 5. Consult Article 5 for a detailed list of rights.

40. Ibid., Article 6.

41. Ibid., Article 7.

42. Ibid., Articles 12, 13.

43. OHCHR, "Human Rights Bodies—Complaints Procedures," accessed May 20, 2015, http://www.ohchr.org/EN/HRBodies/TBPetitions/Pages/HRTBPetitions. aspx.

44. UN General Assembly, Resolution 2106 (XX), Article 14, ICERD, January 4, 1969, http://www.ohchr.org/EN/ProfessionalInterest/Pages/CERD.aspx.

45. For statistical survey of individual complaints considered jurisprudence, see OHCHR, "FAQ about Treaty Body Complaints Procedures," accessed January 18, 2013, http://www2.ohchr.org/english/bodies/petitions/individual.htm.

46. UN General Assembly, ICERD, March 7, 1966, *United Nations Treaty Collection*, https://treaties.un.org/Pages/ViewDetails.aspx?src=treaty&mtdsg_no=iv-2&chapter=4&lang=en. See also ICERD, Article 14.

47. UN General Assembly, International Convention on the Suppression and Punishment of the Crime of Apartheid, no. 14861, November 30, 1973, https://treaties.un.org/Pages/showDetails.aspx?objid=0800000280035e63.

48. Ibid.

49. UN General Assembly, Resolution 2106 (XX), Article 22, ICERD, January 4, 1969, http://www.ohchr.org/EN/ProfessionalInterest/Pages/CERD.aspx.

50. ICJ, Application of the International Convention on the Elimination of All Forms of Racial Discrimination (Georgia v. Russian Federation), judgment, April 1, 2011, http://www.icj-cij.org/docket/index.php?p1=3&p2=2&case=140&code=GR&p3=5. By ten votes to six, the ICJ found that it has no jurisdiction to entertain the application filed by Georgia on August 12, 2008.

51. For a complete definition of crimes against humanity, see Article 5, "Crimes within the Jurisdiction of the Court," in the Rome Statue of the International Criminal Court, Part II: Jurisdiction, Admissibility and Applicable Law, July 1, 2002, 3, http://www.icc-cpi.int/nr/rdonlyres/ea9aeff7-5752-4f84-be94-0a655eb30e16/0/rome_statute_english.pdf.

52. Rome Statue of the International Criminal Court, Part II: Jurisdiction, Admissibility and Applicable Law, Article 7(h), July 1, 2002, 3, http://www.icc-cpi.int/nr/rdonlyres/ea9aeff7-5752-4f84-be94-0a655eb30e16/0/rome_statute_english.pdf.

53. UN General Assembly, International Convention on the Suppression and Punishment of the Crime of Apartheid, Resolution 3068 (xxviii), November 30, 1973, registered July 18, 1976, http://www.un.org/ga/search/view_doc.asp?symbol=A/res/3068%28XXVIII%29.

54. "At least 17 European nations voted in favor of the Palestinian resolution, including Austria, France, Italy, Norway and Spain. [Mahmoud] Abbas had focused his lobbying efforts on Europe, which supplies much of the aid the Palestinian Authority relies on. Britain, Germany and many others chose to abstain. The traditionally pro-Israel Czech Republic was unique in Europe, joining the United States, Israel, Canada, Panama and the tiny Pacific Island states Nauru, Palau, Marshall Islands and Micronesia in voting against the move." Louis Charbonneau and Michelle Nichols, "Palestinians Win De Facto UN Recognition of Sovereign State," *Reuters*, November 30, 2012, http://www.reuters.com/article/2012/11/30/us-palestinians-statehood-USBRE8AR0EG20121130.

55. Jennifer Parker and Mary Casey, "Palestine Wins De Facto Statehood in UN General Assembly," *Foreign Policy: Middle East Daily*, November 30, 2012, http://mideast.foreignpolicy.com/posts/2012/11/30/palestine_wins_de_facto_statehood_in_un_general_assembly.

56. UN General Assembly, Resolution 3068 (xxviii), International Convention on the Suppression and Punishment of the Crime of Apartheid, November 30, 1973, registered July 18, 1976, http://www.un.org/ga/search/view_doc.asp?symbol=A/res/3068%28XXVIII%29.

57. Peter Beaumont, "Palestinian President Signs up to Join International Criminal Court," *Guardian*, December 31, 2014, http://www.theguardian.com/world/2014/dec/31/palestinian-president-international-criminal-court.

58. Francis A. Boyle, "The United States Promotes Israeli Genocide against the Palestinians," *Global Research*, January 26, 2013, http://www.globalresearch.ca/the-united-states-promotes-israeli-genocide-against-the-palestinians-2/5320559; Francis A. Boyle, *Palestine Palestinians and International Law* (Atlanta: Clarity Press, 2003), 159–60.

59. UN General Assembly, Resolution 260 A (III), Convention on the Prevention and Punishment of the Crime of Genocide, December 9, 1948, entry into force January 12, 1951, http://web.archive.org/web/20080502140534/http://www. unhchr.ch/html/menu3/b/p_genoci.htm.

60. For the US reservations on the 1948 Genocide Convention, see Convention on the Prevention and Punishment of the Crime of Genocide, December 9, 1948, *United Nations Treaty Collection*, https://treaties.un.org/Pages/ViewDetails. aspx?src=TREATY&mtdsg_no=IV-1&chapter=4&lang=e.

61. "Genocide Resource Collection," Facing History and Ourselves, accessed February 18, 2013, https://www.facinghistory.org/for-educators/ educator-resources/resource-collections/genocide-resource-collection.

62. Boyle, "The United States Promotes Israeli Genocide"; Boyle, *Palestine*, 159–60.

63. Edward C. Corrigan, "A Response to the Attempt to ban Dr. Norman Finkelstein from Mohawk College," *rabble.ca*, February 17, 2011, http://rabble.ca/ news/2011/02/response-attempt-ban-dr-norman-finkelstein-mohawk-college.

64. ICJ, "Legal Consequences of the Construction of a Wall in the Occupied Palestinian Territory: Summary of the Advisory Opinion of July 9, 2004," Summary 2004/2, July 9, 2004, http://www.icj-cij.org/docket/files/131/1677.pdf.

65. Ibid.

66. Geneva Convention, Convention (IV) Relative to the Protection of Civilian Persons in Time of War, August 12, 1949, Part III: Status and Treatment of Protected Persons, Section III: Occupied Territories, Article 49, https://www. icrc.org/applic/ihl/ihl.nsf/7c4d08d9b287a421412567390003e636b/6756482d8 6146898c125641e004aa3c5?openDocument. For an Israeli view, see also Israel Committee Against House Demolitions Staff, "UN Human Rights Council: Israeli Settlements Are Illegal in International Law," February 1, 2013, http://www.icahd.org/node/472.

67. George Bisharat, "Why Palestine Should Take Israel to the Court in the Hague," *New York Times*, January 29, 2013, http://www.nytimes.com/2013/01/30/ opinion/why-palestine-should-take-israel-to-court-in-the-hague. html?smid=tw-share&_r=0.

68. Ibid.

69. BBC, "Palestinians Formally Join International Criminal Court," April 1, 2015, http://www.bbc.com/news/world-middle-east-32144186.

70. UN Human Rights Council, *Report of the Independent International Fact-Finding Mission to Investigate the Implications of the Israeli Settlements on the Civil, Political, Economic, Social and Cultural Rights of the Palestinian People throughout the Occupied Palestinian Territory, including East Jerusalem*, January 31, 2013, http:// www.ohchr.org/Documents/HRBodies/HRCouncil/RegularSession/Session19/ FFM/FFMSettlements.pdf.

71. Noam Sheizaf, "UN Human Rights Council: Settlement Issue Could End up in the International Criminal Court," *972 Magazine*, January 31, 2013, http://972mag.com/un-human-rights-council-settlement-issue-could-end-up-in-the-international-criminal-court/65168/.

72. Saeb Erekat, "Enforce the UNHRC Settlements Report to Push Israel out of Its State of Denial," *Haaretz*, February 4, 2013, http://www.haaretz.com/news/diplomacy-defense/enforce-the-unhrc-settlements-report-to-push-israel-out-of-its-state-of-denial.premium-1.501456.

73. Barak Ravid, "Israel Cuts Contact with UN Rights Council, To Protest Settlements Probe." *Haaretz*, March 26, 2012, http://www.haaretz.com/news/diplomacy-defense/israel-cuts-contact-with-un-rights-council-to-protest-settlements-probe-1.420786.

74. Zvi Bar'el, "In Banning a UN Probe, Israel Is Joining the Worst of Clubs," *Haaretz*, March28,2012,http://www.haaretz.com/opinion/in-banning-a-un-probe-israel-is-joining-the-worst-of-clubs-1.421162.

75. Ramona Wadi, "Israel's Boycott of the UN Human Rights Scrutiny Session," *Middle East Monitor*, January 31, 2013, http://www.middleeastmonitor.com/blogs/politics/5135-israels-boycott-of-the-un-human-rights-scrutiny-session.

76. OHCHR, "Compilation of Selected Conclusions and Recommendations from Human Rights Mechanisms," n.d., accessed February 18, 2013, http://www.ohchr.org/Documents/HRBodies/HRCouncil/RegularSession/Session19/FFM/FFMSelectedConclusionsAndRecommendationsHRM.pdf. For the ICJ decision, see ICJ, "Legal Consequences of the Construction of a Wall in the Occupied Palestinian Territory, Summary 2004/2," July 9, 2004, http://www.icj-cij.org/docket/files/131/1677.pdf.

77. Geneva Convention, Convention (IV) Relative to the Protection of Civilian Persons in Time of War, August 12, 1949, Part III: Status and Treatment of Protected Persons, Section III: Occupied Territories, Article 49, https://www.icrc.org/applic/ihl/ihl.nsf/7c4d08d9b287a42141256739003e636b/6756482d861468 98c125641e004aa3c5?openDocument.

78. According to the "Statistics on Settlements and Settler Population" section on B'Tselem's website (modified July 8, 2012), "There are some 501,856 settlers living in the West Bank: 190,425 in neighborhoods in East Jerusalem (according to figures of the Jerusalem Institute for Israel Studies for the end of 2010) and 311,431 in the rest of the West Bank (according to figures of Israel's Central Bureau of Statistics (CBS) for the end of 2010)." This information has been updated since the writing of this chapter. Consult B'Tselem's website at http://www.btselem.org/settlements/statistics. Also see Tovah Lazaroff, "Settler Population Rose 4.9% in 2009," *Jerusalem Post*, March 10, 2010, http://www.jpost.com/Israel/Article.aspx?id=170595.

79. ICAHD, International Convention on Eliminations on All Forms of Israeli Discrimination, accessed February 12, 2013, http://www.icahd.org/node/119.

80. Moshe Gorali, writing in *Haaretz*, cites this quotation from Rubinstein's book *The Constitutional Law of Israel*, 5th ed. (Tel Aviv: Schocken, 1997).

81. For further reading, see Ben White, *Palestinians in Israel: Segregation, Discrimination and Democracy* (London: Pluto Press, 2012).

82. Daud Abdullah, "Ethnic Cleansing Is the Only Way for Israel to Have a 'United' Jerusalem," *Middle East Monitor*, December 29, 2012, http://www.middleeastmonitor.com/resources/commentary-and-analysis/4902-ethnic-cleansing-is-the-only-way-for-israel-to-have-a-qunitedq-jerusalem.

83. Uri Avnery, "Slow Motion Ethnic Cleansing," *Counter Punch*, October 9, 2003, http://www.countercurrents.org/pa-avnery091003.htm.

84. The ethnic cleansing of Palestinians, as well as the massacres, rapes, and illegal confiscation of Palestinian property, is well documented by Israeli historians. These include Simcha Flapan, *The Birth of Israel: Myths and Realities* (New York: Pantheon Books, 1987); Benny Morris, *The Birth of the Palestinian Refugee Problem 1947–1949* (New York: Cambridge University Press, 1987); Nur Masalha, *Expulsion of the Palestinians* (Washington, DC: Institute for Palestine Studies, 1992); Benjamin Beit-Hallahmi, *Original Sins* (New York: Olive Branch Press, 1993); and Ilan Pappe, *The Ethnic Cleansing of Palestine* (Oxford: Oneworld Publications, 2006). There are many more Israeli authorities that confirm the ethnic cleansing of the Palestinians in 1947–1949 and again in 1967. See Akiva Eldar, "A Softer Touch on the Nakba," *Haaretz*, January 24, 2012, http://www.haaretz.com/print-edition/features/a-softer-touch-on-the-nakba-1.408917.

85. Menachem Shalev, "'Use Political Opportunities': Netanyahu Recommends Large-Scale Expulsions," *Jerusalem Post*, November 19, 1989.

86. See Richard Silverstein, "Bibi in 1989 Supported Palestinian Mass Expulsions," *Tikun Olam*, January 13, 2011, http://www.richardsilverstein.com/2011/01/13/bibi-in-1989-supported-expulsion-from-the-territories/; for the original quotation, see Yaakov Lazar, "On the One Hand and On the Other," translated from Hebrew by Mark Marshall, *Hotam supplement of Al Hamishmar*, November 28, 1989, *Palestine: Information with Provenance (PIWP database)*, http://cosmos.ucc.ie/cs1064/jabowen/IPSC/php/art.php?aid=134874.

87. Michael Palumbo, *Imperial Israel* (London: Bloomsbury Publishing, 1992), 301.

88. UN Committee on the Elimination of Racial Discrimination (CERD), Eightieth session, February 13 – March 9, 2012, http://www.ohchr.org/Documents/HRBodies/HRCouncil/RegularSession/Session19FFM/FFMSelectedConclusionsAndRecommendationsHRM.pdf.

89. ICAHD Staff, "UN Human Rights Council: Israeli Settlements Are Illegal in International Law," February 1, 2013, http://www.icahd.org/node/472.

90. CERD, "Consideration of Reports Submitted by States Parties under Article 9 of the Convention: Concluding Observations of the Committee on the Elimination of Racial Discrimination," Eightieth session, February 13–March 9, 2012, http://www2.ohchr.org/english/bodies/cerd/docs/CERD.C.ISR.CO.14-16.pdf.

91. UN General Assembly, "Special Committee to Investigate Israeli Practices Affecting the Human Rights of the Palestinian People and Other Arabs of the Occupied Territories," A/67/375, September 18, 2012, http://unispal.un.org/UNISPAL.NSF/0/D422D9F97DDED69F85257AD90056FA26.

92. Gideon Levy, "And Now Apartheid Is Being Sneaked into Israel's Very Foundations," Haaretz, November 27, 2014, http://www.haaretz.com/opinion/.premium-1.628675.

93. Moshe Gorali, "Legality Is in the Eye of the Beholder," Haaretz, September 26, 2003, http://www.haaretz.com/print-edition/business/legality-is-in-the-eye-of-the-beholder-1.101181.

Contributors

YASMEEN ABU-LABAN is professor in the Department of Political
Science at the University of Alberta. She has published
widely on issues relating to the Canadian and comparative
dimensions of gender and racialization processes, border
and migration policies, and citizenship theory. Her publications include *Surveillance and Control in Israel/Palestine:
Population, Territory, and Power* (co-edited with Elia Zureik and
David Lyon, 2011); *Gendering the Nation-State: Canadian and
Comparative Perspectives* (ed., 2008); *Politics in North America:
Redefining Continental Relations* (co-edited with Radha Jhappan
and François Rocher, 2007); and *Selling Diversity: Immigration,
Multiculturalism, Employment Equity and Globalization*
(co-authored with Christina Gabriel, 2002).

GHADA AGEEL is visiting professor in the Department of Political
Science at the University of Alberta and a columnist for
the *Middle East Eye*, an online news portal based in London,
England. A third-generation Palestinian refugee, Ghada was
born and raised in the Khan Younis Refugee Camp in the Gaza
Strip. She holds a PHD and MA in Middle East politics from

the University of Exeter (Britain) and a BA in education from
the Islamic University/Gaza. Her research interests focus on
rights-based approaches to forced migration, Palestinian refugees, oral history and the Arab–Israeli conflict.

HUWAIDA ARRAF is a Palestinian Amer ican lawyer and human
rights advocate. She is co-founder of the International
Solidarity Movement, which has twice been nominated for
the Nobel Peace Prize, and the former chairwoman of the Free
Gaza Movement. In 2011, Huwaida was one of six Palestinian
"Freedom Riders" to challenge the segregation and overall
injustice of Israel's colonial settlements and infrastructure by
boarding Israeli buses on which Palestinians are not allowed.
In 2012, Huwaida helped conceive of and launch the Witness
Bahrain initiative, an effort to provide human rights observers
on the ground in Bahrain, where an uprising for democracy
is being violently repressed. She was arrested by Bahraini
authorities and deported for her work.

ABIGAIL B. BAKAN is professor and chair of the Department of
Social Justice Education at the Ontario Institute for Studies in
Education (OISE), University of Toronto. She is the co-editor
(with Enakshi Dua) of *Theorizing Anti-Racism: Linkages in
Marxism and Critical Race Theory* (2014). Other publications
include *Negotiating Citizenship: Migrant Women in Canada and
the Global System* (with Daiva K. Stasiulis, 2005) and *Critical
Political Studies: Debates and Dialogues from the Left* (co-edited
with Eleanor MacDonald, 2002). She has also published over
forty scholarly articles and book chapters.

RAMZY BAROUD (PHD) is a consultant at *Middle East Eye*, London.
He is an internationally syndicated columnist, a media consultant, an author, and the founder of *PalestineChronicle.com*. He
has authored several books and contributed to many books,

anthologies, and academic journals. His books include *Searching Jenin, Eyewitness Accounts of the Israeli Invasion*, and *The Second Palestinian Intifada: A Chronicle of a People's Struggle*. His latest book is *My Father Was a Freedom Fighter: Gaza's Untold Story* (Pluto Press, London, 2010). Visit his website at ramzybaroud.net.

SAMAR EL-BEKAI is a second-generation Palestinian refugee. Her father's family are refugees from Birya, Safed, while her mother's family are exiled Palestinians from Salfit and Hebron. Her parents met and married while studying in the former USSR. After completing their studies, they lived for three years in Syria's Yarmouk refugee camp and then settled in a village in Lebanon, where Samar was born. Samar grew up there until, at ten years of age, her family immigrated to Canada. Samar completed a BSC in immunology and infectious diseases at the University of Alberta and also received a diploma in medical laboratory technology from Northern Alberta Institute of Technology. She is currently employed at the Provincial Laboratory of Alberta as a medical laboratory technologist.

JAMES CAIRNS is associate professor of Society, Culture, and Environment at Wilfrid Laurier University, Brantford, Ontario. He is a member of Faculty 4 Palestine, a network organizing to promote Palestinian rights and free expression on university campuses across Canada. He and Susan Ferguson co-published "Human Rights Revisionism and the Canadian Parliamentary Coalition to Combat Antisemitism" in the *Canadian Journal of Communication* (2011). James is the co-author (with Alan Sears) of *The Democratic Imagination: Envisioning Popular Power in the 21st Century* (2012).

EDWARD C. CORRIGAN holds a BA in history and a master's degree in political science from the University of Western Ontario. Ed also has a law degree from the University of

Windsor and was called to the Bar in 1992. In June 2004 the Law Society of Upper Canada certified him as a specialist in citizenship and immigration law and immigration and refugee protection. He also served as the associate editor for *Immigration Law Reporter* (2007–2011) and as the associate editor of *ImmQuest* (2007–2011). Ed has published numerous articles on immigration, refugee law, and the Middle East.

SUSAN FERGUSON is associate professor of journalism and of children and youth studies at Wilfrid Laurier University, Brantford, Ontario. She is a member of Faculty 4 Palestine, a network organizing to promote Palestinian rights and free expression on university campuses across Canada. She has written on nationalism and Canadian public broadcasting, childhood and capitalism and social reproduction feminism. She and James Cairns co-published "Human Rights Revisionism and the Canadian Parliamentary Coalition to Combat Antisemitism" in the *Canadian Journal of Communication* (2011).

KEITH HAMMOND is a philosopher who lectures in the Open Studies Centre of the University of Glasgow. His work is around modernity as a excluding, displacing dynamic that brings about a number of local responses. Palestine is a central focus. He works across several disciplines as a member of the Glasgow Refugee, Asylum and Migration Network. Currently he is co-ordinating a European "Tempus" project on lifelong learning in Palestine. He is a member of British Committee for the Universities of Palestine and chairs the Scottish Committee for Universities of Palestine. Other research interests are Hannah Arendt, Georgio Agamben, and various public intellectuals in the Arab-speaking world.

RELA MAZALI is an author, an independent scholar, and a feminist anti-militarist activist from Israel. Active against Israel's occupation since 1980, Rela is one of the founders of the New Profile movement to demilitarize Israeli state and society (1998) and the Coalition of Women for Peace (2000), a member of the Jury of Conscience of the World Tribunal on Iraq (2005), and co-founder of the disarmament project Gun Free Kitchen Tables (2010). Rela's latest book is *Home Archaeology* (Hebrew, 2011). Her latest pieces include "Changing Consciousness: Autoethnographic Mapping in a Dialog Group" (2013), "A Call for Livable Futures" (2010), "Telltale Maps: Narrated Resistance in a Jewish Palestinian Contact Zone" (2010), and "The Gun on the Kitchen Table: The Sexist Subtext of Private Policing in Israel" (2009).

SHERENE RAZACK is a full professor in the Department of Social Justice Education at the Ontario Institute for Studies in Education of the University of Toronto. Her most recent publications are *Dying from Improvement: Inquests and Inquiries into Indigenous Deaths in Custody* (2015) and *At the Limits of Justice: Women of Colour on Terror* (co-edited with Suvendrini Perera, 2013).

TALI SHAPIRO is an Israeli solidarity activist. She participates in Palestinian demonstrations in the Ramallah area and the villages of Nabi Saleh and Bil'in in the West Bank. She is also part of the Israeli BDS group BOYCOTT! Supporting the Palestinian BDS Call From Within. The group gives voice to the marginalized minority of Israel's citizens who acknowledge the colonization of Palestine by the Zionist project, and takes part in many BDS campaigns, with a particular focus on cultural and academic boycott. She also participates in the Israel Genocide campaign, which raises awareness of the possibility that Israel is committing the crime of genocide against the Palestinian people.

REEM SKEIK is a Palestinian with family roots in Gaza and Jaffa. She immigrated to Canada in the mid-1990s, and currently resides in Edmonton, Alberta. Reem completed her master's degree in molecular biology and genetics at the University of Alberta, and is presently a laboratory instructor at MacEwan University. Reem is a strong believer in the value of education and community service; she actively volunteers within Edmonton's Palestinian community and organizes events with the Palestine Solidarity Network, a campus-based grassroots collective that advocates for Palestinian political and social rights.

RAFEEF ZIADAH is currently a postdoctoral research fellow at the University of London, School of Oriental and African Studies (SOAS), with the Military Mobilities and Mobilising Movements in the Middle East project. Rafeef holds a PHD in Political Science from York University, Canada (2013) where her research focused on the intersection of the political economy of militarization and new forms of privatized warfare in the Middle East, and the impact of these structures on Arab and Palestinian communities in exile, especially in Canada. Rafeef is a secretariat member of the Palestinian Boycott, Divestment and Sanctions National Committee and an established performance poet.

Index

Index

255

Index

Index

Other Titles from The University of Alberta Press

Countering Displacements
The Creativity and Resilience of Indigenous and Refugee-ed Peoples
DANIEL COLEMAN, ERIN GOHEEN GLANVILLE,
WAFAA HASAN & AGNES KRAMER-HAMSTRA, *Editors*
336 pages | 10 B&W photographs, 2 diagrams, 2 maps,
    introduction, notes, bibliography, index
978-0-88864-592-0 | $34.95 paper
978-0-88864-607-1 | $27.99 EPUB
978-0-88864-608-8 | $27.99 Kindle
978-0-88864-756-6 | $27.99 PDF
Cultural Studies | Displaced Peoples | Criticism

Narratives of Citizenship
Indigenous and Diasporic Peoples Unsettle the Nation-State
ALOYS N.M. FLEISCHMANN, NANCY VAN
STYVENDALE & CODY MCCARROLL, *Editors*
408 pages | Introduction, notes, bibliography, index
978-0-88864-518-0 | $39.95 paper
978-0-88864-617-0 | $31.99 EPUB
978-0-88864-667-5 | $31.99 Kindle
978-0-88864-618-7 | $31.99 PDF
Cultural Studies | Literary Criticism | Citizenship

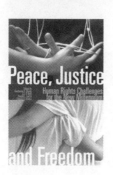

Peace, Justice and Freedom
Human Rights Challenges for the New Millennium
GURCHARAN S. BHATIA, J. S. O'NEILL,
GERALD L. GALL & PATRICK D. BENDIN, *Editors*
448 pages | Notes, appendices
978-0-88864-339-1 | $34.95 paper
Social Policy | Human Rights